Servant and Son

SERVANT and SON

JESUS in PARABLE and GOSPEL

J. RAMSEY MICHAELS

John Knox Press
ATLANTA

Acknowledgments

I would like to thank David Townsley and Russell Bjork for producing the Scripture Index. I would like to thank the Ecumenical Institute for Advanced Theological Research in Jerusalem, and my colleagues there during the fall of 1977, for providing an atmosphere in which to begin writing. And I would like to thank my students in the "Life of Jesus" course at Gordon-Conwell Theological Seminary since 1972 for interacting with me, and by their questions, sending me back again and again to the Gospel texts.

Unless otherwise indicated, translations of biblical and related texts are those of the author from the original languages.

Library of Congress Cataloging in Publication Data

Michaels, J. Ramsey.
  Servant and son.

  Includes bibliographical references.
  1. Jesus Christ—Person and offices. 2. Jesus
Christ—Parables. I. Title.
BT202.M45   232   80–84651
ISBN 0–8042–0409–8   AACR2

CONTENTS

Dedication

To Betty
and our life together

INTRODUCTION

Nowhere is biblical scholarship so polarized as over the question of the historical Jesus. Traditional Christianity sees Jesus of Nazareth as the eternal Son of God, living for a time among us in human flesh, dying for sins, and then returning triumphant to the Father. It carries as its banner the witness of John's Gospel.

The liberalism of the last century used biblical criticism to elevate instead the witness of Mark, Matthew, and Luke, and to proclaim a Jesus dazzlingly human, a religious genius whose experience of God could serve as the supreme model for our own. An appealing theology of love, brotherhood, and human progress took shape, based on the "religion of Jesus," but subsequent scholarship was not kind to it and it began to crumble. And it came to be recognized that Jesus may not have been so much like us as we supposed. His message and ministry now were seen to be dominated by the expectation that the world as he knew it was going to end momentarily. Instead of a religious idealism mirroring its own, one strand of biblical scholarship saw in Jesus a religious fanaticism that only a great deal of special pleading could make relevant to the twentieth century. Alongside this distancing of Jesus from our own world and our own values, a profound skepticism set in about the possibility of knowing *anything* of Jesus' life or teaching.

In a way the two movements were contradictory: one group *knew* that Jesus was an apocalyptic dreamer mistakenly announcing an imminent end to this present world, while the other group decided it could really know nothing (or almost nothing) about him. In another way, however, the two movements complemented and reinforced each other, for in either case the Jesus of nineteenth-century liberalism was lost. Perhaps it was better not to know what he was like than to find out that the real Jesus stood over *against* the lofty ideals of human progress and fellowship as liberalism had understood them.

The quest for the Jesus of history had begun because the traditional Christ of orthodoxy was unacceptable to the liberal mind. The tools and methods of biblical scholarship had been pressed into the service of replacing the orthodox image of Jesus with another, more congenial one. But biblical criticism could not be co-opted, at least not for long. In place of a more acceptable Jesus, the historical-critical method left theologians with a less acceptable Jesus than orthodoxy had known, or with no Jesus at all. The quest was thus suspended for a time, either because it yielded no clear results, or because the results it yielded were unpalatable.

When the quest was resumed in the 1950s it proceeded cautiously, chastened by its past. Its starting point was the *kerygma,* the proclamation of the earliest Christian churches. Points of continuity or parallelism between this proclamation and that of Jesus assumed special importance. The object of the quest was the reconstruction of Jesus' message about the kingdom of God, and behind that message, his "self-understanding." The latter term frequently was used existentially to refer to his sense of being poised between past and future, freed from the one and open to the other, with a commitment to invite us into the same freedom. But this commitment to "authentic existence" entailed no divine or messianic self-consciousness as defined by traditional orthodoxy. Nor was it considered religious experience in the sense in which liberalism had used that term. To speak of the "religion of Jesus" in the midtwentieth century was regarded as presumptuous, as if one were transgressing the historian's bounds by trying to get inside the head of a man who lived almost two thousand years ago. "Psychologizing" or "unwarranted psychologizing" (it amounted to the same thing) was to be avoided at all costs.

Somehow Jesus' self-understanding or "understanding of existence" escaped this stigma, but it was never made clear on what basis these existential categories were abstracted from the broader range of experiences commonly designated religious. If Jesus' self-understanding is crucial, then why not his understanding or experience of God? If his commitment to authentic existence is crucial, then why not his way of perceiving the world around him? Is the one category more inaccessible than the other? If we say as much about Jesus as the new quest was willing to say, then why not a great deal more? Either we limit our horizons to a few externals or we re-open the question of Jesus' "religion." The present volume is an effort to pursue the latter course.

A reassessment of the religious experience of Jesus must begin not with nineteenth-century liberalism, but with the Gospels themselves and with certain New Testament insights preserved to some extent in traditional Christian orthodoxy. The assumption on which this book is based is that what Jesus of Nazareth taught is what he himself first learned by experience. He learned from the observation of everyday life, from his parents, from John the Baptist his predecessor, and above all he was "taught of God" (cf. John 6:46, 7:16). In summarizing Jesus' childhood, Luke remembers that from infancy "the child grew and became strong; he was filled with wisdom, and the grace of God was upon him," and that after the age of twelve he "grew in wisdom and stature, and in favor with God and men" (Luke 2:40, 52NIV). The author of the Epistle to the Hebrews speaks more explicitly of Jesus' religious life: "During the days of Jesus' life on earth, he offered up prayers and petitions with loud cries and tears to the one who could save him from death, and he was heard because of his reverent submission. Although he was a son, he learned obedience from what he suffered and, once made perfect, he became the source of eternal salvation for all who obey him" (Heb. 5:7–9NIV). The phrase "he learned . . . from what he suffered" was an idiom in Greek literature for learning from experience.

Although Jesus' sufferings are conspicuously in view in Hebrews, as in most early reflections on his life, it is valid to assume that he learned from all his experiences, not just from his sufferings. The Gospel of John echoes and re-echoes with the refrain that Jesus speaks only what he has heard from God the Father or seen in the Father's presence. He is undeniably presented in the Gospels as a visionary or seer, even though the Gospel writers show little interest (with one or two exceptions) in the mechanics of his visions and auditions.

Jesus the great Teacher is first of all Jesus the Learner or Disciple. His public words and deeds presuppose an inner life of some kind, a private and personal relationship to God and experience of God—a "religion," if we dare use that word. The deposit of that religion is to be found in the Gospels—the first three Gospels in particular, but to some extent John as well. Nowhere is this more apparent than in the metaphors and images that dominate Jesus' speech. What he says is what he has heard. The pictures he draws for disciples and antagonists alike are pictures that he himself has seen. They are part and parcel of the revelation he comes to make known. A better term, perhaps, than Jesus' religion or religious experience (which have been somewhat romanticized and weakened by overuse) is Jesus' *vision*. Vision is a way of seeing, a way of perceiving reality, whether that reality is a supernatural revelation direct from God, or simply the everyday world in which we live. A visionary may see extraordinary things that no human eye has ever seen or may bring new perspectives to commonplace things that the rest of us have seen all along but taken for granted. Jesus seems to have done both. The stories he told—his parables—and the stories he acted out—his meals with sinners, his words of forgiveness, his miracles of healing—unfold for us his profound and peculiar vision of what is real.

The present volume attempts to bring consistently (perhaps radically) to bear on the entire Gospel tradition the distinctively Johannine insight that what Jesus teaches is what he has first learned from the Father. If Jesus is truly human, as Christianity has traditionally insisted, then in the Gospel drama he is not only actor but also in some sense spectator or observer. He makes things happen, but he also watches things happen. He perceives God at work. In the broadest sense, the Gospels testify to Jesus' experience, and not just to his words and deeds. His message is a message about God even before it is a message about himself. His vision is a theological one. God's kingdom, God's house, God's world—these are his horizons, and his true country.

1.

THE
BAPTIZER

Insofar as the life of Jesus is lived publicly and in the full light of history, it begins with the career of John the Baptist, or Baptizer. Mark begins his story here (Mark 1:2ff.), and (except for its reflections on the eternal Word) John's Gospel follows suit (John 1:6–8, 19ff.). The sermons in the book of Acts portray John the Baptist as an essential preface to the story, if not a part of the story proper (Acts 10:37, 13:24f., 19:4; cf. 1:5). He is therefore the person with whom we must begin.

To many Christians, this will be a surprising decision. We might be expected to begin rather with the birth of Jesus, so that our Lord's life would be seen framed by two great acts of divine intervention: virgin birth and resurrection. By the customary standards of biographical writing, a person's life should begin with ancestry, birth, and childhood—the factors that shape one's adult life and help us understand one's career.

But in the case of Jesus, the accounts of his birth are so extraordinary that they pose their own kinds of historical questions.[1] Only two of the Gospel writers give us any glimpse at all of Jesus before his baptism by John, and only one of them, in one brief passage (Luke 2:40–52), sheds light on the long interval between his infancy and the beginning of his ministry.

It is not clear, from reading their accounts, that Matthew and Luke regarded the birth and childhood of Jesus as factors influencing or helping to explain his subsequent life and ministry. Their interests were more theological. Jesus' miraculous birth is a corroborating witness to what we now know about him because of the resurrection: that he is the Son of God (Luke 1:35) and "God with us" (Matt. 1:23). His wisdom as a child in the temple (Luke 2:41–51) anticipates and further illustrates his adult teaching ministry in the temple (Luke 21:37f.) and elsewhere. But none of these events are public in quite the same sense as the rest of Jesus' ministry, as Luke recognizes in his summary statements that "his mother kept all these things in her heart" (2:19, 51). Rarely in the Gospel tradition is Jesus' virgin birth a conscious presupposition either of his own message or of his hearers' response to him.

And so, we look first at John the Baptist. Whereas Christian tradition remembers him simply as the forerunner of Jesus with little or no independent significance of his own, it is quite different with Josephus. The Jewish historian has more to say about John than he does about Jesus, and what he says is fairly clear and free of controversy:

> But to some of the Jews the destruction of Herod's army seemed to be divine vengeance, and certainly a just vengeance, for his treatment of John, surnamed the Baptist. For Herod had put him to death, though he was a good man and had exhorted the Jews to lead righteous lives, to practice justice towards their fellows and piety towards God, and so doing to join in baptism. In his view this was a necessary preliminary if baptism was to be acceptable to God. They must not use it to gain pardon for whatever sins they committed, but as a consecration of the body implying that the soul was already thoroughly cleansed by right behaviour. When others too joined the crowds about him, because they were aroused to the highest degree by his sermons, Herod became alarmed. Eloquence that had so great an effect on mankind might lead to some form of sedition, for it looked as if they would be guided by John in everything that they did. Herod decided therefore that it would be much better to strike first and be rid of him before his work led to an uprising, than to wait for an upheaval, get involved in a difficult situation and see his mistake.

> Though John, because of Herod's suspicions, was brought in chains to Machaerus, the stronghold that we have previously mentioned, and there put to death, yet the verdict of the Jews was that the destruction visited upon Herod's army was a vindication of John, since God saw fit to inflict such a blow on Herod (*Antiquities* 18: 116–119; trans. L.H. Feldman in Loeb Classical Library, ix, pp. 81–85).

To this account, which supplements in important ways the Markan account of John's death (cf. Mark 6:14–29), we may add the testimony of Jesus himself as found in the so-called Q-material (i.e., sayings believed to be used by both Matthew and Luke):

> When these messengers were leaving, Jesus began to speak to the crowds about John: "What did you go out into the desert to see? A reed shaken by the wind? No, what did you go out to see? A man clothed in soft garments? Those who wear soft garments live in kings' palaces! No, why *did* you go out? To see a prophet? Yes, I tell you, and more than a prophet. He it is of whom it is written, "Behold, I send my messenger ahead of you, who shall prepare your way before you." Truly I say to you, among those born of women there has not arisen anyone greater than John the Baptist, yet he who is least in the kingdom of heaven is greater than he (Matt. 11:7–11; cf. Luke 7: 24–28).

In this remarkable passage, it is as if Jesus steps aside to speak as an outside, almost neutral, observer. For the moment, his role and John's are reversed. He testifies to John's greatness not merely as a forerunner but in his own right, as a prophet beyond all prophets. Though he alludes in a Scripture quotation to "preparing the way," Jesus in no way subordinates John to himself, but only to "the kingdom of heaven." His tribute to John, along totally different lines from that of Josephus, corroborates the latter's claim that John made a powerful impression on all who heard him. Seen purely as a figure in secular history, without reference to an emergent Christian church, John the Baptist might have been a more significant factor in his first century world than Jesus of Nazareth. But it was not to be. Secular and religious aspects of history cannot be separated. The resurrection of

Jesus and the rise of a new community of the Spirit made all the difference.

Obviously the bulk of the New Testament material about the Baptizer is written in the light of these Christian redemptive events and is deeply colored by the awareness that Jesus, and not John, was the one who was to take center stage in the unfolding of the divine plan. The New Testament evidence about this remarkable individual comes from Mark, the "Q" material, Matthew, Luke-Acts, and the Gospel of John. It is necessary to ask, first, how each of these witnesses understood the ministry of John the Baptist, and second, what historical reality best explains the similarities and differences in their testimonies.

MARK

Mark's Gospel confronts us right at the outset with a rather complex biblical quotation of "Isaiah the prophet" based on Malachi 3:1 and Isaiah 40:3. A close reading of the text shows that the quotation goes with what follows rather than what precedes it: "As it is written . . . John came." If we have read the Gospel before, we know that the one being addressed in Mark 1:2 ("before *your* face . . . prepare *your* way") is Jesus. He is the "Lord" whose coming is being prepared. John the Baptist is now introduced both as a fulfillment of the biblical passages just cited (i.e., the "messenger" of vs. 2 and the "voice" of vs. 3), and as the forerunner of someone greater to come. In the latter sense he is an extension of the scriptural testimony. He is doing essentially what the Scripture itself is doing: pointing to Jesus.

In passing, Mark characterizes John as a proclaimer, but what he proclaims is described, rather ambiguously, as "a baptism of repentance for the forgiveness of sins" (vs. 4). No specific content is assigned to his proclamation except that of inviting people to come and be baptized. For the moment, the emphasis falls not on the proclamation as such but on John's baptizing activity (vs. 5) as well as his remarkable physical appearance and habits (vs. 6). The real content of John's preaching is apparently supplied in vss. 7–8: "And he proclaimed:

'The one mightier than I is coming, the thong of whose sandals I am not worthy to untie. I baptize you with water, but he will baptize you with the Holy Spirit.' "

This is all that Mark gives us of John's message. He goes on immediately to tell of the baptism of Jesus. The proclamation of John the Baptist can be described purely and simply as messianic. He announces the coming of one greater than himself, who will baptize in the Holy Spirit and inaugurate the new age. Immediately and dramatically Jesus appears on the scene (vs. 9), making it clear that he is indeed the "mightier one" of John's proclamation. The message of John the Baptist in Mark's Gospel has to do with Jesus and only with Jesus. John has no significance in and of himself. His sole importance is as a witness to the Lord whose way he has come to prepare.

Q

The discourse material common to Matthew and Luke adds another dimension to our understanding of the Baptizer. In Matthew a brief speech is addressed to "many of the Pharisees and Sadducees" (Matt. 3:7), while in Luke it is spoken to "the crowds" who came to be baptized (Luke 3:7). John the Baptist says:

> Brood of vipers! Who tipped you off to flee from the coming wrath? Let's see you produce something worthy of your repentance! And don't think you can plead that Abraham is your father I tell you that God is able to raise up from these stones children for Abraham. The axe is already poised at the root of the trees; every tree that does not bear good fruit is to be cut down and thrown into the fire (Matt. 3:7–10; cf. Luke 3:7–9).

This material is not messianic in the sense that it points to a personal Messiah. It is, of course, eschatological in that it presupposes the imminent end of the present order and the judgment of God on all human works. But its purpose is to call the hearers to repentance in the face of the divine wrath, not simply to inform them about a messianic figure to come. This proclamation stamps John as a prophet in his own right and not merely a herald for someone else. Even though we may agree with the majority of scholars that Mark is the earliest Gospel, we will go seriously astray if we rely exclusively on his record.

In the Q material we find words of warning and challenge that, if we met them in the Jesus tradition, we would take as evidence of Jesus' originality and uniqueness. We would say that they confronted the hearers with an existential decision, calling them away from everything tradition had given them, every privilege of birth or covenant on which they might rely to justify themselves before God. We would read such words as a summons to discard the past and open ourselves to God's future with all its risks and uncertainties. We would say they express a sense of eschatological urgency unprecedented in the prophets or apocalyptic oracles of contemporary Judaism, a radical call to commitment that continues to address us as a word from God today.

But this summarized proclamation does not come from Jesus at all! It is attributed instead to John the Baptist, and we would never have had access to it if we had only the Gospel of Mark. It is hard for us to appreciate the force and the radical nature of the Baptizer's message because we have been schooled to expect such momentous words only from Jesus. Both conservative and liberal Christianity have had such a vested interest in the "uniqueness" or "originality" of Jesus that they have made it difficult to see these qualities anywhere else. We have been told that the words of Jesus most likely to be genuine are the ones paralleled neither in the Judaism out of which he came nor in the theology of the church that confessed his authority.[2] Here, however, we find that the strikingly original and radical announcement of the end times is attributed, not to Jesus, but to his predecessor.

A close comparison of this brief summary with the Gospel tradition of Jesus' words shows further that almost everything said here is paralleled somewhere in sayings attributed to Jesus. For example:

> By their fruit you will know them. Are grapes gathered from thorns, or figs from thistles? Thus every good tree produces good fruits, and a useless tree produces bad fruit. A good tree cannot bear bad fruit,

nor can a useless tree produce good fruit. Every tree that fails to produce good fruit is cut down and thrown into the fire. So then, by their fruit you will know them (Matt. 7:16–20; cf. 12:33). . . . Brood of vipers (Matt. 12:34, 23:33). . . . He trims away every branch in me that bears no fruit, and trims clean every branch that bears fruit, so that it will bear more fruit. . . . If anyone does not remain in me, he is thrown out like a branch to wither; these branches are gathered, thrown into the fire, and burned (John 15:2, 6). . . . I know you are descended from Abraham, but you seek to kill me because my word has no room in your hearts . . . If you were Abraham's children, you would do the works of Abraham, but now you seek to kill me . . . this Abraham did not do (John 8:37, 39f.). . . . Therefore I say to you that the kingdom of God will be taken from you and given to a nation that produces the fruit of it (Matt. 21:43; cf. vs. 34).

Such parallels are quite impressive when we remember what a small body of sayings are attributed to John the Baptist in the Gospel tradition. Three possible explanations come to mind: either the words of Jesus have been projected back on John, or John's words have been projected forward into the Jesus tradition, or Jesus' own teaching was influenced by the Baptist both in substance and in phraseology.

The first alternative is unlikely. It is difficult to conceive of a reason why words of Jesus would be placed in John's mouth. And why just these words and no others?

The second alternative is slightly more plausible. We should not uncritically assume that the ancient church shared totally in the modern concern for Jesus' uniqueness. Repetition may have been highly regarded as a way of reinforcing these words in early Christian communities. But in the face of groups who esteemed John very highly, and perhaps even regarded him as the Messiah,[3] it seems more likely that the dominant tendency would have been to put distance between him and Jesus, stressing his subsidiary role and the provisional character of his teaching.

By far the simplest explanation for the similarities between John's words and those of Jesus is the third one: John the Baptist significantly influenced Jesus. If this was in fact the case, then it affects our understanding of Jesus' own life and ministry to a greater degree than is usually recognized. Even though the Gospel writers were not biographers in the modern sense of the word, the interest of any modern who speaks of Jesus at all is biographical to some degree. As soon as we begin to speak of biography in even a qualified sense, we cannot avoid speaking of formative influences on Jesus, however much we may want to preserve his uniqueness. The evidence suggests that John the Baptist was one such influence, especially with reference to the urgent appeals both men make for repentance and their warnings of imminent eschatological judgment. This influence shows itself most strongly, not in John's messianic preaching as found in Mark (Jesus did not, after all, announce a "greater one" to come), but in the nonmessianic repentance preaching characteristic of the Q material. This material must now be examined in its respective contexts in Matthew and Luke, where it stands side by side with the record of John's distinctly messianic preaching, which was derived, apparently, from Mark.

MATTHEW

If any Gospel writer has a particular interest in emphasizing the similarities between the Baptizer and Jesus, it is surely Matthew. The echoes of John's preaching in the words of Jesus, as listed above, are closer in Matthew than anywhere else. At the very outset (Matt. 3:2) we see that John's proclamation is summarized with exactly the same formula as that of Jesus: "Repent, for the kingdom of heaven is at hand" (Matt. 3:2; cf. 4:17). The two figures are even brought on the scene dramatically with the same introduction: "John came" (Matt. 3:1) . . . "then Jesus came" (Matt. 3:13). Because of this interest of Matthew, scholars have doubted that "Repent, for the kingdom of heaven is at hand" is an authentic saying of John the Baptist. It is natural to surmise that the proclamation of Jesus summarized in Matthew 4:17 has been projected back on John in order to further the parallelistic scheme. As far as I know, no one has reversed the argument by proposing that John alone, and not Jesus, proclaimed the nearness of the kingdom. Not only does Mark 1:15 reinforce the saying as Jesus' own, but the whole subject of the kingdom and its coming is so integral a part of Jesus' teaching that we can scarcely imagine that its programmatic expression has been lifted, deliberately or by accident, from a body of sayings preserved as those of John.

It *is* possible, however, that John the Baptist influenced Jesus at this crucial point. Jesus may have come proclaiming "Repent, for the kingdom of heaven is at hand" at least in part because John had done so before him. If this were the case, it is easy to understand why Mark and Luke might have omitted it to avoid assigning too much importance to John.

The argument can thus cut either way. On the one hand, Matthew may on occasion be accentuating the similarities between John and Jesus. On the other hand, there were very natural reasons for the other Gospel writers to play them down. The larger the memory of John the Baptist loomed in or on the fringes of the church, the more necessary it became to insist on what has been so important ever since —the distinctiveness, or even uniqueness, of Jesus.

No certain answer, therefore, can be given to the question of whether or not Matthew 3:2 represents a phrase uttered by the Baptizer in so many words. In either case it makes no great difference. If Matthew 3:2 was a word of Jesus projected back upon John, it would merely summarize what had already been attributed to John in the Q material (Matt. 3:7–10). For John to proclaim the kingdom is to warn of imminent judgment. Though he also hints at a positive or redemptive dimension in the imagery of gathering wheat into barns in verse 12, this aspect does not loom very large in the overall context. The formula of Matthew 3:2 is peculiar to Matthew but does not represent a major departure from the repentance preaching found already in Q.

When we look closely at the relation between the Markan and Q material found in Matthew, we find that the two blocks of teaching have simply been placed side by side without comment. After describing John's baptismal procedure (Matt. 3:1–6; cf. Mark 1:2–6), Matthew records his proclamation in the form of a rebuke to the Pharisees and Sadducees who have come to be baptized (Matt. 3:7–10; cf. Luke 3:7–9). Then without a break he proceeds to the Baptizer's dramatic contrast between his own activity and that of the Coming One who is greater than he (Matt. 3:11–12; cf. Mark 1:7f.). The impression is given that the message of John is summarized as a continuous whole in Matthew 3:7–12, and that this proclamation includes within itself both the call to repentance and the announcement of John's expected Messiah.

The two sections, one from Q and one from Mark, are linked by the references to "fire" in verses 10, 11, and 12. Mark's baptism "with the Holy Spirit" becomes in Matthew (as in Luke) baptism "with the Holy Spirit *and fire*" (vs. 11), and the mention of fire is picked up by the imagery of judgment in verse 12: "He will burn up the chaff with unquenchable fire." Here, as in verses 7–10, Matthew and Luke agree in what they add to the Markan account, and appear to be following a common source. This strongly suggests that Q (like Matthew and Luke) probably contained *both* the nonmessianic repentance proclamation of John the Baptist *and,* with Mark, a distinctively messianic announcement of a Coming One. Matthew and Luke may in fact be following Q almost exclusively in their account of the preaching of John.

Mark either knows only part of the tradition (i.e., the messianic part), or for reasons of his own has chosen to omit the sections about repentance and judgment. In either case, if we had only Mark we would conclude that John's proclamation focused exclusively on the Messiah; if we had only Matthew, we would see it as including both the repentance preaching and the announcement of the Coming One, without any distinction between the two. The most natural inference from Matthew is that John is calling his hearers to repentance specifically in light of the judgment of Spirit and fire which the Coming One will bring.

LUKE

The basic materials that Luke assembles for his presentation of John the Baptist are, with few exceptions, the same as those of Matthew, but he combines them so as to give a third impression. Luke begins with a very formal introduction of John as a prophet in the Old Testament manner (Luke 3:1ff.), followed by a longer quotation from Isaiah 40 than we find in any other Gospel (Luke 3:3–5). He omits all description of John's physical appearance and lifestyle, but proceeds at once to the Q account of the message of repentance and judgment (Luke 3:7–9).

Luke then goes his own way in supplying some concrete illustrations of how repentance works itself out in practice, i.e. what the fruits of repentance might consist of in specific life situations (Luke 3: 10–14). The material is presented in question-and-answer form. Three groups ask, "What shall we do?"[4] The crowds generally are told to share their food and clothing with the destitute ("The man with two tunics should share with him who has none, and the one who has food should do the same" [Luke 3:11NIV]). The tax collectors are told to collect no more than they are required to. The soldiers are told to renounce extortion and be content with their wages. This section affords some further examples of similarities between John and Jesus. We may compare, for example, Jesus' statement in the Sermon on the Mount:

> And if someone wants to sue you and take your tunic, let him have your cloak as well. . . . Give to the one who asks you, and do not turn away from the one who wants to borrow from you (Matt. 5:40, 42NIV).

or perhaps his mission instructions:

> Take no bag for the journey, or extra tunic, or sandals, or a staff . . . (Matt. 10:10NIV; cf. Luke 9:3).

or his announcement of salvation for Zaccheus who said:

> Here and now I give half of my possessions to the poor, and if I have cheated anybody out of anything, I will pay back four times the amount (Luke 19:8NIV).

or, most memorably, his word to the rich young man:

Go, sell everything you have and give to the poor . . . (Mark
10:21NIV).

Whether Luke 3:10–14 belongs to the repentance preaching preserved in Q or whether it represents Luke's concretization of that
preaching in the light of other material known to him is unimportant.
What is important is that it reinforces the Q picture of John as a
preacher of repentance and to a degree also as a teacher of ethics. It
also adds its support to the notion that John's teaching influenced that
of Jesus.

The question raised in Luke 3:15, one found only in Luke, is
different in character from the three questions in verses 10–14. It is
a question about John himself. Who was he? Was it possible that he
himself might be the Messiah? Up to this point, Luke implies, John's
proclamation had not included heralding the Messiah—if it had, this
last question would hardly have come up. Instead, John had focused
entirely on repentance, judgment, possibly the kingdom of God, and
certainly some of the implied concrete ethical demands. But Luke
indicates that this essentially nonmessianic preaching had had such
a powerful effect on the people that they began to ask whether John
himself might perhaps be the long awaited Deliverer of his people!
Whether the question was actually voiced or whether it only came up
in people's minds, John answers it in Luke 3:16–17 with his announcement of the Coming One and his careful and sharp distinction between the latter's role and his own.

Thus Luke's record of the message of John the Baptist delineates
two stages: a non messianic proclamation of repentance and judgment
(Luke 3:7–14) and a messianic proclamation of a personal Deliverer
and Judge who would become God's agent in bringing the present age
to an end (Luke 3:16–18). The two are separated by the question in
verse 15, and it is possible to infer from what Luke records in the book
of Acts that this shift took place relatively late in the Baptizer's
ministry. Only as John was completing his work did he say, "Who do
you think I am? I am not that one. No, but he is coming after me,

whose sandals I am not worthy to untie" (Acts 13:25NIV). We may even infer that he never would have said it at all except for his concern that his own role was being misunderstood. Although Luke hints that much more could be said about the Baptizer's messianic "gospel" (Luke 3:18),[5] it may be that we are dealing here with a relatively brief sequence near the end of his ministry, or possibly with a single incident in which someone raised the messianic question and John responded.

We would expect the developing tradition to magnify John's role as forerunner and witness to Jesus at the expense of his role as prophet, preacher of repentance, and herald of the kingdom. If this was indeed the tendency, then Luke's Gospel best explains the two other Synoptics at this point, and thus commends itself as representing most fully and faithfully what actually took place. Luke has preserved both the nonmessianic and the messianic aspects of John's preaching, placing them in a rather plausible relationship to one another with the greater emphasis laid on the former. In his own way (especially by means of later reminiscences in Acts 1:5, 13:25, and 19:4), he has underlined the importance of the latter as well, but he has preserved very carefully the distinction between the two.

Matthew removed this distinction even while making use of basically the same sources. The effect of this was to elevate John's messianic preaching to the same level of relative importance as the nonmessianic preaching of repentance and judgment. When the messianic preaching ceased to be a clarification in response to a particular question, placing it at the end of John's preaching material, and just prior to the baptism of Jesus, elevates it to a place of *greater* importance within John's ministry as a whole. And it becomes the central announcement toward which everything else is leading. John the Baptist becomes significant primarily because of what he says about *Jesus.* His stature as a prophet in his own right is subtly diminished.

In Mark the nonmessianic repentance preaching is missing altogether except for the general statement that John proclaimed "a baptism of repentance for the forgiveness of sins" (Mark 1:4NIV). The

Baptizer becomes purely and simply a herald of the coming of Jesus. It appears that our earliest Gospel already stands at the end of a process of editorial reflection about what to include and what to exclude. Luke turns out to be the most useful to us historically, not simply because of a concern for completeness, but because he seems to have given some thought to serious historical reconstruction. The point is not that Luke necessarily gives evidence of being earlier than Mark, but simply that he has put together the materials known to him in a historically plausible way.

JOHN

In the fourth Gospel we come full circle back to the viewpoint represented by Mark—but with a difference. For John the Evangelist, as for Mark, the Baptizer is essentially a witness to Jesus. What distinguishes John from Mark (and from the other Synoptists) is that he has John the Baptist actually point to Jesus in person and say, in effect, "There he is. That's the one I meant" (cf. John 1:29f., 36). At this point the fourth Gospel's credibility has been seriously challenged.

Leaving aside the references in the prologue to the Baptizer (which are not pinned down historically), it appears that the first Johannine reference picks up at the beginning of Luke's *last* stage, namely, with the question of whether John the Baptist is the Messiah. Without attempting to correlate every detail, we see that John 1:19–22 corresponds to Luke 3:15. In one case the people at large, in the other a delegation from the Pharisees, ask John who he is. In the fourth Gospel, the question of whether he is "the Messiah" is expanded to include other messianic figures as well (Elijah, and the Prophet of Deut. 18:15ff.), but the point is the same.

What John's Gospel has done is to provide a close-up of the Lukan last stage, at the time when John was completing his work. In so doing, it provides independent testimony to the fact that this stage was introduced by the raising of questions. John the Baptist's messianic proclamation was not unsolicited, but was given in reply to inquiries

about who this messenger really was. Questions like, "Who are you?"
... "Are you Elijah?" ... "Are you the Prophet?" are not, after all,
asked in a vacuum. They presuppose something that has gone before.
John's Gospel gives us little clue as to what that something was, but
it seems plausible that an urgent proclamation of repentance and
judgment such as we find in Matthew 3:7–10 and Luke 3:7–9 might
help to explain why such possibilities came to people's minds.

The question about John's messiahship in the fourth Gospel is not
only expanded to include three messianic titles (John 1:19–22) but
leads on to other matters. It provides the setting for the quotation of
Isaiah 40:3, found in all the Synoptics, but in John placed on the lips
of the Baptizer himself. He proclaims himself neither Messiah nor
Elijah nor the Prophet, but simply a "voice" in the desert (John 1:23).
His words precipitate one last question: if his claims are so modest,
why does he baptize? (John 1:25).

This final inquiry becomes the immediate context for a messianic
proclamation corresponding to Mark 1:7f., but with an important
structural difference. The saying appears to be built around the contrast, "*I* baptize with water" (John 1:26)... "*He* will baptize you with
the Holy Spirit" (Mark 1:8, cf. Matt. 3:11, Luke 3:16), but the concluding reference to baptizing in the Spirit is deferred to John 1:33.

Moreover, a change of day (and possibly of location) has occurred
in the interval (John 1:28–29). John the Baptist actually begins his
sentence on one day and finishes it on the next! To carry this off, the
Evangelist has to repeat the terminology of "baptizing in water" (John
1:31, 33a), creating an effect of suspense as the reader waits for the
climactic announcement: Jesus will baptize in the Holy Spirit! The
saying now found most concisely in Mark 1:8 serves as a kind of
bracket for a whole block of Johannine material about John the
Baptist. The real reply to the question, "Why do you baptize?" comes
within this intervening material. "I baptize in water. . . . he . . . will
baptize in the Holy Spirit" surely does not answer the question of *why*
John baptizes. The reason (or purpose) is given in rather straightforward fashion in John 1:31: "that he might be made known to Israel,

that is why I came baptizing in water." To the fourth Evangelist, the purpose of the Baptizer's ministry was not simply to preach repentance and judgment (Q), or even to herald the messianic deliverer (Mark), but *to identify Jesus in particular* as that deliverer and to make him known to "Israel." As it turns out, the Israel to whom Jesus is revealed is a *new* Israel, the circle of some who had been John's disciples but who, in response to his witness, put their faith in Jesus (John 1:35–2:11).[6]

It is difficult to know how to assess all this historically. If Mark has accented the messianic aspect in John the Baptist's preaching, the fourth Gospel has taken an additional step. John becomes here not merely a herald of the Messiah, but a herald of *Jesus.* This is a more significant step than may appear on the surface. Though Mark has emphasized (in a sense overemphasized) the messianic element in John's proclamation, there is little reason to doubt that such an element existed. But saying that John the Baptist announced the Messiah and then Jesus came is not identical to saying that John consciously recognized Jesus as the Messiah. What many scholars doubt is not so much the statement, "After me comes a man who has taken precedence over me, because he was before me" (or something to that effect) as the fact that at some point John said, "*This is he* of whom I said, 'After me comes a man . . .' " (John 1:30RSV).

For theological reasons of his own, not least of which may have been the influence of a group that regarded John rather than Jesus as God's final messenger, the fourth Evangelist has turned John the Baptist into a confessing Christian.[7] When questioned about his identity "he confessed, he did not deny but confessed, 'I am not the Christ' " (John 1:20RSV). Like Nathanael, Peter, Martha, Thomas, and others, he confesses his faith in Jesus by the use of messianic or divine titles. Like the intended readers of the Gospel he acknowledges Jesus to be the "Son of God" (John 1:34).[8] And he concludes his last speech with words about Jesus that humble Christian disciples have made their own ever since: "He must increase, but I must decrease" (John 3:30RSV). It seems clear, therefore, that the Baptizer's specific identification of Jesus as the Coming One is not strictly historical, but is a creation of the fourth Evangelist.

Or is it? Just when historical criticism appears to have slammed the door on a traditional opinion, its own inquisitive tendencies have a way of reopening the door a crack, and sometimes more. Two Synoptic passages add their witness to that of John's Gospel that the Baptizer did at some point recognize Jesus as the Messiah. The first and more explicit of these may not give us pause. The second does. In Matthew 3:14, when Jesus comes to John for baptism, John says "I need to be baptized by you, and do you come to me?" Jesus assures him that this is the proper way to "fulfil all righteousness" (Matt. 3:15), but implicit in John's hesitancy is the idea that John recognizes Jesus as the baptizer in the Holy Spirit mentioned in verse 11. Matthew seems to be saying to the reader, "Even though it may look as though Jesus is inferior to John by virtue of submitting to his baptism, John himself knew that this was not the case." At this point, Matthew becomes suspect for the same reason that the fourth Gospel does: he makes John sound too much like a confessing Christian. This verse must be discussed further in connection with Jesus' baptism and temptation, but in the present argument its witness adds little to that of John's Gospel.

The other passage is more significant. It is the question sent to Jesus from the imprisoned Baptizer not long before the latter's death: "Are you one who was to come, or should we expect someone else?" (Matt. 11:3, Luke 7:19NIV). This is part of the Q passage that continues with Jesus' tribute to John the Baptist and some crucial statements about the kingdom of God. Its authenticity has generally been taken seriously. Jesus responds to the question not with outright messianic claims but with signs of the presence of the kingdom.

Against the background of traditional orthodoxy, John's question from prison has often been regarded as a problem passage. It suggests that John entertained doubts as to whether Jesus was the Messiah. Unlike the bold witness who in the fourth Gospel announces, "Behold the Lamb of God," John the Baptist is seen here as uncertain and confused. For this reason, perhaps, critics who reject Matthew 3:14f. and the Johannine tradition tend to be more positive about the authenticity of the question from prison. But the logic of the passage cuts two ways. On the one hand, it clearly indicates that John had doubts about whether Jesus was the one whose coming he had announced. On the other, the doubts make no sense unless we assume that John had at some point entertained seriously the notion that Jesus *was* the Coming One. In an indirect way this "problem passage" in Q supports the witness of the fourth Gospel, at least in part.

The impression is not that John here for the first time conceives of the possibility that Jesus may be the Messiah, but rather that he begins to think, "What if he is *not?*" From this passage, there is no way of telling whether John's previous intimation of Jesus as the Coming One was merely a private opinion or whether it found its way into his public proclamation. The important thing is that at *some* time in his life he did make the identification. Whether the identification was as clear and unmistakable as the fourth Gospel suggests is more difficult to say. But at least the judgment that the Gospel of John is unhistorical at this point must be seriously questioned. The Q passage suggests instead that the fourth Gospel may have depicted as public and explicit something that was originally private, perhaps implicit and tentative, but nonetheless real.

The other noteworthy feature of the fourth Gospel's witness to John the Baptist is that the ministries of Jesus and John overlap. In the Synoptics, Jesus' ministry does not begin until John's has come to an end. It is only when the Baptizer has been imprisoned that Jesus comes into Galilee to proclaim the kingdom of God (Mark 1:14, Matt. 4:12; cf. Luke 3:19f.). Jesus comes *after* John in a temporal sense (Mark 1:7, Matt. 3:11, and most explicitly Acts 13:25). It is different in the fourth Gospel, where as late as John 3:24 we are reminded that "John had not yet been sent to prison." By that time Jesus had already called his first disciples, performed his first miracle, cleansed the temple, and told Nicodemus about the new birth!

In the immediate context, Jesus and his disciples are carrying on a baptizing ministry in Judea simultaneously with John (John 3:22f.; cf. 4:1f.). Clearly, Jesus is well into his ministry, at least as the fourth Evangelist defines it. Already in chapter 1, some kind of continuing relationship between the Baptizer and Jesus subsequent to Jesus' baptism is presupposed, for in John 1:32ff. the Baptizer is looking back to the baptism of Jesus from a later vantage point. It is from this later perspective (and continuing acquaintance) that he is able to make his identification of Jesus as the Coming One. He has seen the Spirit not only come but remain on Jesus (John 1:32f.). Unlike Matthew, who has the Baptizer suspecting Jesus' uniqueness before he even baptizes him (Matt. 3:14f.), John's Gospel makes the baptism itself the beginning (though only the beginning) of this realization. Jesus has indeed been "with" John beyond the Jordan (John 3:26).

A continuing relationship of this kind after Jesus' baptism is exactly what we would expect historically. That John had disciples is amply attested throughout the Gospel tradition. Whether or not everyone baptized by him became his disciple, his disciples were presumably drawn from among those whom he had baptized.

A possibility exists that in submitting to John's baptism, Jesus became John's disciple. As several scholars have pointed out, the phrase "he who comes after me" *could* be understood in a nontemporal way: "he who is my disciple."[9] The same preposition is used that we find used of discipleship to Jesus in Mark 8:34: "If anyone would *come after me,* he must deny himself and take up his cross and follow me." The fourth Gospel emphasizes the point, not that Jesus "comes after" John temporally, but rather that he *preceded* John (John 1:15, 30). Their ministries overlap, as we have seen, so that the phrase "he who comes after me" may well refer to discipleship instead of temporal succession.

If Jesus was for a time a disciple of the Baptizer, it is easy to understand why this fact might have been omitted from the tradition. If there were in the first century, as there seem to have been in later periods, groups that regarded John as the Messiah, it would have been an embarrassment to Christians to admit that their Christ was once

John's disciple. It was difficult enough to admit that he had submitted to John's baptism! The Synoptics therefore pass over in silence the period of Jesus' association with the Baptizer, except for the single incident of Jesus' baptism by John in the Jordan River.

This was important to the Synoptic writers because of the tradition of the voice from heaven inaugurating Jesus' ministry. However, to deal more extensively with the period of Jesus' association with John would have raised more questions than it answered. Yet the Synoptics, as we have seen, record a number of Jesus' words that appear to have been strongly influenced by the words of John the Baptist, especially the latter's proclamation of repentance and judgment. Such parallels would be appropriately explained by the theory that Jesus learned from John over a period of time. To the Synoptists, this period of association and possible discipleship does not count as part of Jesus' public ministry, which they are careful to date from John's imprisonment. Luke, in fact, goes so far as to narrate John's imprisonment early, so as formally to dissociate John even from the baptism of Jesus (Luke 3:19–20)!

The fourth Evangelist broke the conspiracy of silence and opened to the view of his readers the early period during which the activity of the Baptizer and Jesus overlapped. This he seems to have done in the face of people he knew who regarded John the Baptist and not Jesus as the decisive messenger of God.[10] How else can we explain his insistence that John "was not the light, but came to bear witness about the light" (John 1:8)? Or the elaborate disclaimer of the Baptizer when he "confessed, he did not deny, but confessed. . . . 'I am not the Christ' " (John 1:20)? Or John's testimony to Jesus as the "Lamb of God" and "Son of God"? Or his concern to point his own disciples to Jesus, virtually delivering them over to him? Or his characterization of himself as only the "friend of the bridegroom" who is joyful and content simply to hear the bridegroom's voice? Or his parting words, "He must increase but I must decrease" (John 3:30)?

The fourth Gospel, it appears, has done two things simultaneously. It has deliberately set out to shed light on that early period of contact between Jesus and John the Baptist, but in such a way as to make unmistakably clear that Jesus is already the Messiah, acting independently of John. And it suggests that John himself recognized and confessed that this was the case. Instead of passing over in silence this "embarrassing" stage in the ministry of Jesus, the fourth Evangelist has met the issue head on. He argues that though Jesus may actually have been for a time John's disciple ("he who comes after me"), he was even then the "designated Messiah," awaiting the time when he would take precedence (John 1:15, 30) over the one who had set the stage for his manifestation to the new Israel (John 1:31). The Gospel of John thus supplements decisively the picture of Jesus that we have in the Synoptics. Yet it must be admitted that its own portrayal of Jesus during this early stage of his ministry is strongly colored by its distinctive theological and polemical concerns.

As early as Eusebius, the fourth-century church historian, scholars have tried to relate the fourth Gospel to the Synoptics on the basis of an "early Judean ministry."[11] Even though this theory has at times been made the basis of a forced and unwarranted harmonization, in some form it seems inescapable. If Jesus had no particular association with John at all except in the incident of the baptism, why would the fourth Evangelist have created such an association? Surely to do so would have left many unanswered questions, especially in view of the writer's apparent sensitivity to those who wanted to put the Baptizer first.

It is well to speak cautiously about Jesus' having been John the Baptist's disciple. The mere fact of Jesus' baptism creates a presumption in this direction, however, and there is also evidence (John 3:22ff., 4:1ff.) that Jesus and John worked concurrently (though *not* together) for a time in the Judean desert, doing much the same kind of thing: baptizing and making disciples. The fourth Evangelist's parenthetical remark that Jesus did not personally baptize, but left that to his disciples, suggests that we have here a piece of early tradition which the Gospel writer is laboring to assimilate, not a product of his own literary ingenuity. He passes it on because it has a bearing on the period on which he wants to shed light, but he seems uncertain as to what to make of it. All of this suggests that this early Judean ministry was not a static period but a changing one.

Jesus may have begun as John's disciple or coworker and later undertaken a baptizing ministry of his own. We know little of this period, and what we do know has been the subject of considerable theological interpretation. Yet these are not "silent years" in the sense in which Jesus' childhood and youth are silent years. We have seen that Jesus' contact with John shaped his own teaching ministry; it may have shaped his actions as well. Jesus' hard line on the subject of divorce (e.g., Mark 10:2–12) corresponds closely to the position taken by the Baptizer with regard to Herod and the wife of his brother Philip (Mark 6:17ff.). And it is quite possible that Jesus saw John's death at the hands of the authorities as an anticipation of his own (Matt. 17:12ff., and somewhat less clearly, Mark 9:12ff.).

CONCLUSION

After we have assessed the testimony of all four Gospels about John the Baptist, we are still left with the question, "Who was he?" His origins are shrouded in mystery. There is general agreement that he carried on a baptizing ministry in and near the Jordan river,[12] that he called for repentance and warned of judgment, that he baptized Jesus, that he was executed by Herod for political or personal reasons or both, and that people seriously entertained the notion that he was the Messiah. But where did he come from? Luke's Gospel gives the circumstances of his birth, and here, as in his ministry, his life is closely intertwined with that of Jesus. They were in fact cousins, but we cannot be sure whether they even knew each other personally before the moment when Jesus came to be baptized. Matthew's "I need to be baptized by you" (which may imply previous knowledge) has to be weighed against the Baptizer's insistence in John 1:30 that "I . . . did not know him" (cf. John 1:33) (until the sign at the baptism). If there are silent years in the life of Jesus, there is also such a period in the life of John; he was in the desert until the time of his public appearance to Israel (Luke 1:80; the public appearance comes in Luke 3:1ff.).

In the case of Jesus, pious legend has filled in the silent years.[13] In the case of John, scholarly speculation (especially since the Qumran discoveries) has fulfilled much the same function.[14] The plausibility is obviously much greater in this instance, yet when all has been said we have to admit that we simply do not know who John was. The location of John's silent years (i.e. the desert) as well as of his active ministry corresponds to the location of the Qumran community. His reason for being in the desert (according to a Scripture cited by all the Gospel writers) is the same as that of the Qumran covenanters—at least formally. He is there to prepare the way of the Lord and make his paths straight (Isa. 40:3). But the Qumran sectarians prepared a way for the Lord by faithful study of, and obedience to, the Torah (1 QS viii. 13–16), while John did so by means of his eschatological preaching of repentance and his (apparently) once-for-all requirement of baptism. The differences are as striking as the similarities. John the Baptist was a public, not a monastic, figure. He carried out a mission, and assumed a responsibility to the whole nation, not to a separate group who already considered themselves the elect. To all, from the religious leaders to the despised tax collectors and the very soldiers occupying his land he extended the possibility of forgiveness. At the same time he insisted that all *needed* the forgiveness that his baptism represented. The most religious "son of Abraham" was reduced to the level of a mere outsider submitting to a ritual of initiation into Israel. All these things differentiate John the Baptist from Qumran.

Most likely, John's flight to the desert and the flight of the Qumran community were called forth by similar ways of reading the ancient Scriptures and similar disillusionment with the spiritual condition of the Jewish nation and of its religious institutions. But the parallels are limited by the fact that the Dead Sea sectarians were a community, while John was a prophetic or charismatically-endowed individual. He established his own community on the basis of his own baptism and teaching. It is possible that his movement is an offshoot of Qumran, even as it is possible that, as the child of aged parents from a priestly family (Luke 1) he was brought up by Essenes in the vicinity of the Dead Sea, and that this is the historical reality behind Luke 1:80. But there is no way to be certain, or even to come close to certainty. An orphan from a priestly family *might* have been brought up in a sectarian priestly community, and from this base have launched a priestly ministry of reconciliation with messianic overtones. It makes a story just as fascinating, though not as fantastic, as the apocryphal legends about the childhood and youth of Jesus. But for John, no less than for Jesus, the "silent years" remain silent. From the New Testament (and somewhat from Josephus), we can trace the profile of his ministry and message. We have the Lukan testimony to his parentage and birth. But who he was, and exactly what elements in his world helped to shape him, we do not know.

2.
THE BAPTISM
OF JESUS

There is no doubt, even among skeptics, that Jesus was baptized by John in the Jordan River. John's baptism is clearly said to be "for the forgiveness of sins" (Mark 1:4; Luke 3:3) and, as they were being baptized, people confessed their sins (Mark 1:5; Matt. 3:6). It is unthinkable that the early church would have invented an incident that seemed to depict Jesus as a sinner in need of forgiveness. The Baptizer's protest in Matthew 3:14, "I need to be baptized by you, and do you come to me?" indicates that the church sensed a problem. Far from being a fabrication, John's baptism of Jesus was a firm tradition from the start, and something with which the church had to come to terms. After the time of the New Testament, it seems to have become even more of a problem. In the apocryphal *Gospel of the Hebrews,* as cited by Jerome, the hesitation is shifted to Jesus himself: his mother and brothers say to him, "John the Baptist is baptizing for the forgiveness of sins; let us go and be baptized by him," and in response Jesus says, "What sin have I committed, that I should go and be baptized by him? Unless this very thing which I just said is a sin of ignorance."[1]

The canonical Gospels record no such hesitation on Jesus' part. Even in the apologetically-oriented Matthean passage he insists on the need to "fulfill all righteousness" (Matt. 3:15). To this day, theologians find it necessary to explain *why* Jesus was baptized. It is usually said that right at the outset of his ministry he wanted to express publicly the solidarity that he felt with his people. The theme of the cross (Christ in our place) already finds expression at the baptism. But it is all too easy to conceive of this identification in an artificial and unreal way. There is no hint in the text that we have here simply a divine Being, conscious of his own perfection, deciding to stand beside others in a ritual for which he felt no real personal need, simply to identify with them, or to put his endorsement on John's ministry.

The Christian church has rightly guarded the doctrine of Jesus' sinlessness (Jesus' baptism was, after all, an occasion of divine approval!). He took on himself the guilt of his people. Yet the distinction between corporate and individual guilt is probably more significant to the modern theologian than it was to Jesus of Nazareth. Formally, the usual explanation is correct; Jesus *does* come to John as an expression of his solidarity with sinners. But the solidarity is real; he is not simply pretending to be human. In becoming flesh he has assumed the full human condition, with all the feelings of need that go with it.[2] There is no reason to think that his reaction to the message of John, or his motives for seeking baptism, were different psychologically from those of the people who preceded or followed him into the water. He was touched by the word of God, and because he actually *felt* the weight of his people's guilt, he came to the Jordan much as anyone else would come.

Jesus' baptism was extraordinary not in what led up to it, nor in its actual procedures (for the text does not dwell on these), but rather in certain supernatural events beyond the control of baptizer and baptized alike, witnessed by all the Gospels. As soon as we speak of these, the descent of the Spirit and the voice from heaven, we move from the ground of acknowledged historicity to something often dismissed out of hand as myth or legend. Historical research has no categories, we are told, for dealing with voices out of the sky or dove-like spirits. To defend the historicity of the baptism itself poses no difficulty; to do so for the heavenly voice and dove is another matter. If we wish to defend what is said in the text, is it even historicity that we should defend, or is it simply the reality of what happened? And if we wish to deny what the text affirms, where does this leave us as far as the significance of Jesus' baptism is concerned? Can we still speak of it as the beginning of his ministry, and if so in what sense? All these questions demand answers, but the best starting point has to be simply the determination of what the texts intend to say. Only when we have decided that can we make a judgment about their reliability.

The question that the modern reader most naturally raises was of little or no importance to the Gospel writers themselves. Yet it is one which we cannot avoid. Who, if anyone, actually saw the Spirit descend and heard the voice of God? Granted that the baptism of Jesus was a public event, was it public even in its miraculous aspect, or are we dealing here with a private religious experience that belonged to Jesus alone? Or is the whole scene a legend created by the church? The Gospel writers would have rejected the third of these alternatives. But it is not so clear what they would have said about the first two. Their common purpose was above all to testify to the fact that Jesus was truly the Son of God and thus to underline, right at the start of their narratives, his supreme authority. There is no evidence that the question of whether this truth was made known at the baptism only to Jesus or to the public at large was of any concern to them at all.

MARK

With his characteristic economy with words, Mark indicates that in due course the Mightier One who was to come came—all the way from Nazareth in Galilee—and was baptized by John in the Jordan River (Mark 1:9; cf. v. 7). Nothing remarkable is said about the baptismal act itself. But after he had been baptized and as he came out of the water, Jesus "saw the sky torn open and the Spirit descending on him like a dove" (Mark 1:10). Then there came a voice out of the sky with the words "You are my beloved Son; with you I am well pleased" (Mark 1:11). There is no indication here that anyone but Jesus saw the dove or heard the voice. The verb "saw" has Jesus alone as its subject, and the words from above are addressed to him in the second person: "*You are* my beloved Son." One may infer other hearers and onlookers, but the focus of the text is on a very personal experience of Jesus himself, most naturally described as a visionary experience.

Visions and auditions had, of course, been a familiar feature of Old Testament and late Jewish stories about patriarchs, prophets, and other charismatic leaders (e.g., Jacob, Moses, Isaiah, Ezekiel, Daniel), and there is no reason to regard this experience of Jesus any differently. The reality of visions in the biblical world had nothing to do with how many people saw them, and the reality of the voice of God had nothing to do with how many people heard it. The very purpose of prophecy was, in fact, to make known to a wider audience what *one* person had seen and heard from the Lord. On occasion we find in the Bible efforts to make clear exactly who heard or saw something "objectively" (e.g., John 12:28ff.; Acts 9:7; 22:9), but the purpose of these explanations is not so much to stress the objectivity as to make the point that *only* one person actually grasped what was happening. The crowd in John 12 mistakenly thought they heard thunder or the voice of an angel, while Paul's companions in Acts merely heard a sound or saw a light. To the biblical writers, a vision or audition to one person was just as objective as if it came to a whole multitude.

The modern distinction between subjective and objective, and especially the equating of the latter with "real" and the former with "unreal," has tended to prejudice our reading of such Gospel incidents as the baptism of Jesus. Conservatives who want to hold on to the reality of what happened often feel the need to objectify it by insisting that everyone saw what Jesus saw, and heard what he heard. Sometimes this goes to the point of supposing that if a camera and tape recorder had been available at the scene, the whole thing could have been preserved for the benefit of pilgrims and worshipers ever since. On the other hand, those who wish to deny that anything exceptional happened may begin by stressing the absurdity of such an objective public display, and speak of a "merely" subjective experience inaccessible to historical investigation. The experience thus becomes, for all practical purposes, unreal in that it is given no place in any historical reconstruction. The consciousness of Jesus, whether in general or on this particular occasion, is regarded as holy ground on which the historian is not allowed to set foot.

But Mark does not regard it in that way. He tells in rather straightforward fashion what Jesus saw, not just what it really was (i.e., the Holy Spirit), but what it *looked like* to him (a dove). And he lets us hear, with Jesus, the words "You are my beloved Son; with you I am well pleased." To Mark and his original readers it was something objective. If we were to explain to him our confusing—and sometimes confused—modern categories, he would doubtless reply, "All right. If you are using words that way, then in *your* terms it is subjective." But the difference would only be a difference of language. The important thing to the narrator is that the experience was real.

MATTHEW

It is often said that Matthew has objectified the Markan account of the baptism. The main reason is that the form of the heavenly pronouncement has been changed from the second to the third person: not "*You are* are my beloved Son . . ." but "*This is* my beloved Son, in whom I am well pleased." Besides this, the word "Behold" or "Look" has been added both in connection with the vision ("Behold the sky was opened," Matt. 3:16) and the audition ("And behold a voice out of the sky," Matt. 3:17).

It is wise, however, not to form conclusions prematurely concerning Matthew's text. Matthew has retained Mark's singular verb "he saw" (Matt. 3:16); it is still Jesus, and presumably he alone, who witnesses the descent of the dove. The close connection between the opening of the skies and the appearance of the dove suggests further that the word "behold" in verse 16 introduces what *Jesus* saw (and what the reader is to visualize), not something Matthew thought was visible to the bystanders. Neither Mark nor Matthew, in fact, even mention bystanders in their accounts of Jesus' baptism.

As for the third-person form of the voice from heaven, it is more likely that this is more a testimony to the reader of the Gospel than to someone thought to have been at the scene. Unlike Mark, Matthew has conformed the voice at the baptism to the voice at Jesus' transfiguration (Matt. 17:5), where the context demands the third person. At the transfiguration we know exactly who the bystanders were (Peter, James and John), and that the voice from the cloud is intended for them is shown by the additional phrase, "Hear him" in Matt. 17:5b. The voice in this instance is a directive to the disciples to listen to Jesus as God's appointed prophet promised by Moses (cf. Deut. 18:15ff.). At the baptism it is different. There is no directive to anyone, and no one's reaction to the divine voice is recorded.

Matthew appears to have made the formulas parallel because he wants them to form a sequence for the reader: God proclaims Jesus as his Son at the beginning of his ministry, and once again just at the decisive turning point after Peter's confession at Caesarea Philippi. It is more likely that theological (or literary) motives of this kind lie behind Matthew's small changes in Mark than that he wants to correct Mark in the direction of a more objective account of Jesus' experience at the baptism.

LUKE

In Luke's Gospel the evidence for deliberate objectification of the baptismal voice and vision seems stronger. First, the text does not say that Jesus *saw* the sky opening and the dove descending, but simply that these things happened. Second, Luke adds that the dove came down "in bodily form" (Luke 3:22). It is natural to conclude that Luke wants to remove the incident from the category of vision and classify it as a tangible and public reality. Unlike Mark and Matthew, Luke also notes that these things happened "while all the people were being baptized" (Luke 3:21), thus leaving open the distinct possibility that bystanders witnessed the dove's descent in bodily form and the voice from God.

Even here, however, caution is required. Luke never says in so many words that anyone except Jesus saw or heard anything exceptional. And, unlike Matthew, he preserves the Markan form of the voice from heaven: *"You are* my beloved Son; in you I am well pleased."* Clearly he wants to describe the scene in such a way as to emphasize its reality. He differs from Mark only in wanting to underscore that reality by avoiding any possible implication of a mere appearance or deceptive vision. Luke has no intention of denying that Jesus *saw* and *heard* things, even though he has dropped the actual words. In fact, the phrase "in bodily form" unmistakably points to something which is *seen* (presumably by Jesus). If we look closely at Mark's wording, we notice a certain ambiguity. Does Jesus actually see something that *looks like* a dove, or does he "see" the Spirit (in whatever form we may imagine) descending in the manner in which a dove descends? In other words, does the phrase "as a dove" describe "Spirit" or the act of descending?

Luke has clarified Mark by his use of the phrase "in bodily form." He wants his readers to understand that Jesus actually saw what looked like a dove. The omission of "he saw" and the addition of "in bodily form" are not unrelated. The latter takes the place of the former. Luke objectifies the vision only in the sense of insisting that Jesus saw something recognizable. The Spirit became visible to him in the form of a dove. Though Luke may thereby create for the reader an impression of greater objectivity, he is careful not to violate the limits set for him by his tradition. He has no evidence that anyone but Jesus experienced anything unusual, and he is careful not to assert that they did. The phrase "in bodily form" objectifies the vision *only as vision.* The differences between Luke and the other two Synoptics should therefore not be exaggerated.

It is true that Luke wants to underscore what Mark simply assumes from the start, i.e., that Jesus not only heard a voice telling him that he was the Son of God, but that he actually was (cf. Mark 1:1). Matthew had done this by changing the words of the baptismal voice to *"This is* my beloved Son . . ."* and by his use of the title "Son of

God" in the temptation narrative that followed (Matt. 4:3, 6). Luke does the same thing even more explicitly.

Immediately after mentioning the voice from the sky, he inserts his genealogy of Jesus (Luke 3:23–38), which he introduces with a statement that has been notoriously difficult for translators (vs. 23). Literally the text says, "And he was Jesus, beginning at about thirty years, being son (as was supposed) of Joseph, of Eli . . . of Adam, of God" (Luke 3:23, 38b). Either the pronoun "he" picks up the immediately preceding announcement, "You are my beloved Son in whom I am well pleased," or else the statement summarizes the whole of Luke's narrative up to this point. In the former case, the point is that after the voice of God, "You are my beloved Son . . .," Luke adds in effect: "And that is exactly what Jesus was, beginning his ministry at the age of thirty; he was the son (supposedly) of Joseph, who was the son of Eli . . . who was the son of Adam, who was the son of God."

The genealogy thus comes back full circle to the affirmation of the voice from heaven. Then, as in Matthew, "Son of God" becomes the reference point for the temptation narrative that follows (Luke 4:3, 9).

The alternative is to take Luke 3:23 as a summary of 1:1—3:22 in its entirety. After the narratives of the births of John and Jesus, and the account of Jesus' baptism, Luke pauses to say: "This, then, was Jesus, beginning his ministry at the age of thirty . . ." In this case the reference in Luke 3:23 is not to the baptismal voice in particular, but to *everything* that has gone before. Jesus has, after all, already been declared "Son of God" in Luke 1:35, and it seems natural for the author to pick up the thread of Jesus' life at the age of thirty after previous glimpses of him "on the eighth day" (Luke 2:21–38) and at "twelve years" (Luke 2:41–52).

It is difficult—and perhaps unnecessary—to decide between these two alternatives. They are nuances at best. It is likely that Luke 3:23 does function, first of all, as a kind of summary. Luke has put the genealogy at the end of his introduction instead of at the beginning, as does Matthew. Having introduced Jesus as infant, child, and adult, Luke supplies his lineage and will proceed to tell his story. Yet at the same time he has placed the summary where it will reinforce the reality of Jesus' divine sonship revealed to him by voice and vision at his baptism. Luke's objectification thus takes place in his own terms and for his own purposes, not in terms dictated by later apologetics.

JOHN

Strictly speaking, the fourth Gospel should not come into a discussion of the baptism of Jesus at all, for it never states in so many words that Jesus was baptized. By reading between the lines (automatically and almost unconsciously), readers assume that the baptism of Jesus is in view in John 1:32-34. It is a fair assumption in light of what we know from the Synoptics. Yet the Evangelist's interest is in John the Baptizer's testimony about what he saw, not in the baptism itself. The most remarkable difference between the Synoptics and the fourth Gospel is that the latter asserts unmistakably that *John the Baptist* saw "the Spirit descending as a dove," while omitting any mention of Jesus' own vision! Yet it would be imprecise to say that the fourth Evangelist objectifies the experience in the sense of transforming it into a public miracle. Rather, he simply makes John, rather than Jesus, the visionary. There is no voice from above; instead the decisive testimony to Jesus comes from the Baptizer himself: "And I have seen and I testify that this is the Son of God" (John 1:34).

Still another difference is that emphasis is laid on the Spirit not only descending but *remaining* on Jesus. This occurs both in God's promise to John of a sign (vs. 33) and in the description of what John saw (vs. 32).

Once again, the discrepancies between the fourth Gospel and the Synoptics raise the historical question in acute form. If we take these accounts of a visionary experience seriously, we have to ask who actually saw the vision—Jesus, John the Baptist, or both? Posed that way, the relatively unified witness of the Synoptic Gospels is clearly to be preferred. If John the Baptist actually had received such an unmistakable personal revelation, it would likely be reflected in the Gospel tradition more than it is. The Baptizer's own ministry would

surely have been decisively changed by such an experience. There is
no evidence of such a change, either in the fourth Gospel or in the
Synoptics. It is doubtful that John the Baptist himself would have
been regarded as a messianic figure if he had pointed so unmistakably
to another. Even in the fourth Gospel, which makes the Baptizer a
confessing Christian, John continues to carry on a baptizing ministry
simultaneously with Jesus, and only in reponse to a dispute does he
stand aside for the "heir apparent" (John 3:23–30).

We must not, however, overlook the more immediate question:
What exactly does John the Evangelist *intend* to assert in 1:32–34?
Our attention is drawn particularly to the references about the Spirit
remaining on Jesus in verses 32 and 33. Are we to imagine that the
Baptizer stared for a long time at a dove that would not go away? Or
does the term "remaining" have a more theological significance,
namely, that the Spirit is with Jesus always, becoming from that time
on his continuing possession? Something of this kind may be indicated
in John 3:34 ("He whom God sent speaks the words of God, for [God]
does not give the Spirit by measure"), and, with regard to the disciples, in John 14:16 ("He will give you another Counsellor, to be with
you forever"). But if the term "remaining" is theological in significance and not a literal description of what John saw, then a question
must be raised about the literal intent of John 1:32–34 as a whole.
Does the Evangelist intend to describe an actual vision *at all,* or is this
a highly theological account of something the Baptizer at some point
realized to be true and to which he now bears his testimony?

The best analogy perhaps is another "vision" at the end of this
same chapter of John's Gospel, the promise to Nathanael: "Truly,
truly I say to you, you shall see heaven opened and the angels of God
ascending and descending to the Son of Man" (John 1:51). All efforts
to connect this promise to some particular incident, whether historically or in the literary intention of the Evangelist, have been unsuccessful. There is fairly wide agreement among commentators that the
passage is drawing on Jacob's specific vision at Bethel (Gen. 28:12)
as a way of characterizing Jesus' intimate relationship to the Father

throughout his earthly ministry. In similar fashion, it appears that John 1:32–34 is drawing on Jesus' specific experience at his baptism (known from the tradition) in order to characterize the *whole* of his ministry as the life of the Son of God lived in the Spirit. As Nathanael is drawn into Jacob's vision so as to become an imaginary participant in it, so John the Baptist is made to participate in the vision of Jesus. But in neither case are we dealing with a strictly historical assertion that allows us to ask, *"When* exactly did Nathanael see all this?" or *"When* did John the Baptist witness the descent of the dove?" In the case of Nathanael, it is possible that the Evangelist intends the display of Jesus' glory at the Cana wedding (John 2:11) as a provisional fulfillment,[3] but if so, it is no more than provisional. The Gospel seems more intent on affirming the reality of the relationship set forth in John 1:51 than in pinpointing the circumstances by which Nathanael and the rest of the disciples would become *aware* of that reality.

At first glance it seems to be different in John 1:32–34, which specifically mentions not only the divine promise of a sign (vs. 33), but the realization of that promise (vss. 32, 34). Someone who has read the Synoptics might assume that the realization comes in connection with a specific historical incident, the baptism of Jesus. The Evangelist has no qualms about leaving that impression because this is in fact the incident he has chosen as his dramatic framework for the testimony, much as Jacob's Bethel vision served as the dramatic framework for the promise to Nathanael. In the case of Nathanael we run no risk of confusing the literal and the dramatic because we know it was impossible for Nathanael to become Jacob's contemporary and literally enter into what Jacob experienced. In the case of John the Baptist no such impossibility exists; John actually *was* present at Jesus' baptism. Therefore the risk of confusion stands. But the same is true here as in John 1:51: the Evangelist is more concerned with the *reality* of the Spirit's "abiding" on Jesus than with the process by which John the Baptist becomes aware of that reality. What matters is that John testifies to Jesus as the bearer of the Spirit. The historical witness of the Baptizer on a particular occasion in his ministry, and the continuing witness of his life to the Christian community in the author's day, merge into one in the fourth Gospel. He has already been introduced to the readers not only as a past historical figure (John 1:6ff., 19ff.), but in a very real sense as their contemporary (John 1:15f.). Again in chapter 3, a testimony of John elicited by a specific incident in the past (vss. 23–26) shifts almost immediately into the time framework of the Gospel's readers (vss. 27–30 and especially vss. 31–36). So too, in John 1:32–34 the Baptizer's vision and testimony cannot be limited to a particular occasion, but represent rather a continuing realization and a continuing testimony, extending even to the time of the author of the fourth Gospel and his readers. It is therefore precarious to use this passage, which does not, after all, claim to be a baptismal account, as conclusive evidence that John the Baptist saw the sign of the dove and confessed faith in Jesus at his baptism.

CONCLUSION

Nothing in the Gospels of Matthew, Luke or John compels us to reject the impression we gain from Mark: Jesus and Jesus alone saw the Spirit in the form of a dove at his baptism, and only Jesus heard the voice of God saying, "You are my beloved Son; with you I am well pleased." This conclusion stands despite the fact that there arose very early in the church rationalizing and harmonizing tendencies that have affected the way students of the Bible have pictured this event ever since. One thoroughgoing, and rather amusing, example of such tendencies can be found in the ancient Jewish Christian Gospel of the Ebionites, as cited by Epiphanius:

> When the people were baptized, Jesus also came and was baptized by John. And as he came out of the water, the heavens were opened and he saw the Holy Spirit in the form of a dove coming down and approaching him. And there was a voice out of heaven saying, "You are my beloved Son; in you I am well pleased." And again, "Today I have begotten you." And immediately a great light illumined the place. John, when he saw it, said, "Who are you, Lord?" And again a voice out of heaven came *to him*: "*This is* my beloved Son, in whom I am well pleased." And then John, falling before him, said, "I pray

you, Lord, baptize me." But he prevented him, saying, "Let it be; for thus it is fitting that all things should be fulfilled." *Heresies* 30, 13, 7–8.[4]

Patchworks of this kind miss the intentions of all the Gospel writers. Yet when the latter are allowed to speak for themselves in their individuality, their testimonies do exhibit surprising similarities alongside the inevitable differences. It is precisely these points of agreement that call into question the preconceptions that both theologians and historical scholars often bring to the texts.

The Synoptics agree that Jesus submitted to John's baptism, and the fourth Gospel does not contradict it. That he was baptized is historically certain. Nor is there reason to doubt that this rite was connected in both men's minds with the forgiveness of sins. The Synoptics also agree that Jesus' baptism was accompanied by a vision and audition; the fourth Gospel, in indirect fashion, supports this as well. An estimate of the historical reliability of this aspect of the baptism obviously hinges on an estimate of visions and auditions generally. Most historians of religion have little hesitancy in acknowledging the occurrence of such experiences within a rather wide spectrum of religious settings. Any hesitancy in the case of Jesus may be traceable more to a stubborn expectation that Jesus must be unique than to a sober assessment of the evidence. Some would rather believe that the church attributed this experience to him falsely, than run the risk of placing him in such a problematic category as that of visionary or seer. And yet if we are simply describing the phenomenon, a visionary is exactly what Jesus was.

As to the *validity* of his experience, i.e. whether the dove was truly the Holy Spirit and whether the voice was truly the voice of God, that question is outside the competence of the contemporary historian and can only be answered confessionally. But the experience itself is as much a datum of history as any other sense experience. If Jesus saw something and heard something at his baptism, such an occurrence must have powerfully shaped his subsequent words and actions.

Alongside the question of validity is the question of meaning. What does it mean for Jesus to hear the words, "You are my beloved Son, in whom I am well pleased"? This is the same as asking òut of what *context* these words come. It is easy for us to put them into our own ready-made context of Christian theology: Jesus is the eternal Son of God, and now he is either hearing this for the first time, or he is being reminded of what he has known from all eternity. This is one kind of answer. To accept it in just this way is to forego all further questions and to leave the matter to the realm of faith. But it is also possible to accept this answer as being true so far as it goes, while still continuing to press the question of context. When Jesus hears the words "You are my beloved Son," what *previous* understanding of the phrase "beloved Son" is he bringing to the experience? With whom or what does he hear himself being identified? Unless we regard Jesus as already a trinitarian theologian long before the Council of Nicea, we cannot avoid this question.

The answer most commonly given is that Jesus' ready-made context for hearing the pronouncement is Old Testament Scripture. In some way Jesus is being told that his existence (and presumably the task that awaits him) fulfills Scripture: "The 'beloved Son' (of biblical prophecy) is *you,* Jesus of Nazareth!" But what passage is in view? The first part of the sentence parallels Psalm 2:7: "You are my Son; today I have begotten you," and one textual tradition in Luke has made the baptismal voice an exact quote from this passage. But the assimilation only serves to highlight the differences between Psalm 2 and Mark, Matthew, and most of the Lukan manuscripts. Neither the adjective "beloved" nor the entire last half of the pronouncement bear any particular resemblance to the Psalm.

Some commentators have suggested Isaiah 42:1 as the appropriate background:

> Behold my servant whom I have chosen. My beloved in whom my soul delights. I have filled him with my spirit, and he will bring justice to every nation.

Here the similarities are considerable. "Servant" corresponds in function at least to "son," the ideas of election and divine favor are conspicuous in both passages, and the reference to the spirit in the Isaiah passage fits in well with the descent of the dove at the baptism. But even a free quotation is out of the question. Matthew, for one, knows how to quote Isaiah 42:1ff. when it fits his purpose (Matt. 12:18–21), and he has not done so in 3:17. The most that can be claimed is a similarity in thought between these Old Testament passages and what Jesus hears at his baptism. Perhaps by this experience Jesus finds his identity in certain texts which speak of one loved by God and chosen uniquely to be his servant. Jesus' messianic consciousness might then be understood as a particular self-understanding brought about by a combination of visionary experiences of this kind and a messianic reading of certain texts of Scripture.

Another possibility is that the Old Testament point of reference was not a directly prophetic passage at all, but rather a piece of narrative, such as Genesis 22:1–14. Perhaps Jesus, either before or after the baptismal experience, read and found himself drawn into the story as a participant, and by a process of audience identification began to think of himself as an only son (cf. Genesis 22:2, 12) set apart to God for a particular task or purpose. Just as Isaac was Abraham's "only" or "beloved" son, so Jesus was God's only Son. It has become customary to regard such a development as taking place *after* Jesus' death on the cross, but it is almost universal in human experience that those who hear or read a story find themselves engaged by it so as to identify with one or another of its characters.

"How would it feel," we ask, "to be in that situation? What if that happened to me?" A possible context, then, for the voice at Jesus' baptism might be a narrative which he had read or heard, and for which the heavenly voice supplied the key, in the form of a decisive self-identification.

In a somewhat different vein, we may compare the story which Nathan told to David in 2 Samuel 12:1–4, with David's consequent anger at the injustice of what happened in the story, and Nathan's prophetic word of identification that drew David into the story and condemned him: "You are that man" (2 Sam. 12:7).

There is no reason why a story might not function positively as well as negatively. By hearing or reading stories we experience self-revelation, and the revelation may be either of something bad and devastating, as in the case of David, or momentous for good, as in the case of Jesus. But if a story of some kind was the context for Jesus' self-understanding at his baptism, what story was it? Can we suggest Genesis 22:1–14 and let it go at that? Surely it is no more likely to have been that passage by itself than Psalm 2:7 or Isaiah 42:1ff. by themselves. Though we may have opened some possibilities, we are no closer to certainty than before.

The analogy (a reverse analogy to be sure) between Jesus' experience and that of David with the prophet Nathan, suggests that perhaps the true context for the revelation to Jesus at his baptism is not Scripture (or at least not Scripture alone) but a parable, or several parables. The story that Nathan told David comes very close to the parabolic form as we find it in the Gospels. The dominant feature of Jesus' teaching as recorded in the Synoptics is the fact that he taught in parables.

Where did he learn this parabolic method? Recent scholarship has come closer and closer to agreement that Jesus' parables offer us the key to his deepest and most basic understanding of both himself and his world. Where did these deceptively simple and tantalizing little stories and images come from? Did he invent them with the rhetorical and dramatic skill of a born storyteller, a kind of artistic genius? Did they arise out of careful observation of the everyday world around him?[5] Or did he hear them from someone? And if so, from whom? From the rabbis, or his parents, or John the Baptist? Or did he hear them from God?

These questions must be kept in mind as we go on to consider other elements in Jesus' religious experience, and especially his parabolic teaching itself. When we read the words of the baptismal voice,

"You are my beloved Son; in you I am well pleased," we cannot help but remember how often the figure of a son appears in the parables of Jesus. We think especially of the "beloved son" sent to the evil vineyard keepers in Mark 12:6. Is it possible that the voice of God at Jesus' baptism has a *parabolic* context, that what it expresses is in fact the interpretation of a parable? Before answering that question it is necessary to look at the sequel to Jesus' baptism (and itself a visionary experience)—his temptation in the Judean desert.

3.

IN THE DESERT
—AND BEYOND

In all three Synoptic Gospels the baptism of Jesus is followed immediately by his temptation in the desert. Continuity between the two incidents is maintained by a reference to the Spirit at the beginning of the temptation story. When Mark says "immediately the Spirit cast him out into the desert" (Mark 1:12), the "Spirit" can only be the Spirit that came on Jesus as a dove at his baptism (Mark 1:10). The same is true in the Matthean (3:16, 4:1) and the Lukan (3:22, 4:1) accounts. In Luke and Matthew continuity is also provided by the term "Son of God" (Matt. 4:3, 6; Luke 4:3, 9), which picks up the christology of the baptismal voice. The association of the Spirit with sonship is reminiscent of the experience of early Christians as expressed in the letters of Paul (e.g., Rom. 8:15f.; Gal. 4:6). Interpreters of the baptism and temptation narratives need to keep in mind the question of what relates to Jesus uniquely and what is intended to portray the experience of his followers as well. Without doubt the pattern of a momentous crisis experience followed by a time of hardship and severe testing is as old as the Exodus, Sinai, and the desert wanderings of the people of God on their way to the Promised Land.

In studying the Gospel accounts of Jesus' temptation it is important to let each Gospel writer speak in his own integrity. Familiarity with the general outlines of the story can lead the interpreter to read

Mark too much in the light of the other Synoptics, and to forget that much that has become a part of the common Christian memory of the temptation of Jesus is not to be found in Mark at all. The procedure of letting Mark speak before hearing from the others becomes, in this case, a definite advantage.

MARK

If we had only Mark's account of the temptation of Jesus, it is not certain that we would ever have entitled it "the temptation" at all. The theme of these two brief verses (Mark 1:12–13) might more aptly be summarized as "Jesus in the desert." Though Mark includes a reference to Jesus being "tempted by Satan," this comes in a subordinate clause. The basic assertion is that Jesus was "in the desert for forty days," and in connection with this several circumstances of his life are mentioned: he was "tempted by Satan," he was "with the beasts" and "angels were ministering to him."

Jesus "temptation" is only one detail along with others. Much has been written concerning what Mark may have had in mind with the statement, "he was with the beasts." One suspects that if we did not have Matthew and Luke, a similar degree of scholarly effort would have been expended on the question of what it meant for Jesus to be "tempted by Satan." Few of us give much thought to that question in Mark because even the most critical among us, consciously or unconsciously, supply the answer for ourselves from Matthew and Luke: he was tempted by three questions from the Adversary, and he successfully withstood these challenges so as to vindicate his sonship.

All of this *may* be implied in Mark, but none of it is actually mentioned. There is no series of three questions; no precise content is given to the temptation. There is no mention of a forty-day fast, only that Jesus was "in the desert" for forty days. The reference to the angels' ministering to him *may* involve supplying him with food to end a fast, as some have thought; but it need not do so, nor is there any hint in Mark that they ministered to him only when the forty days were over. The imperfect tense of the verb suggests in fact that their ministry extended throughout the forty-day period. Finally, the "temptation" has no explicit outcome. It has been argued[1] that Jesus' victory over Satan is implied by the exorcisms recorded later in Mark's Gospel and by the saying in 3:27 about the binding of the strong man. This may be so, but no victory is formally declared in Mark's "temptation" account itself. Except for the forty-day limit mentioned at the outset, there is not even a mention of when or how the temptation came to an end (contrast Matt. 4:11, Luke 4:13).

The theme of "Jesus in the desert," however, is integrated quite well into Mark's introduction to his Gospel (Mark 1:1–15), which is structured according to a chiastic (a, b, c, c, b, a) pattern:

a. the *gospel* of Jesus Christ (vs. 1);

b. John the Baptist *in the desert*, in fulfillment of Scripture (vss. 2–4);

c. John *baptizing in the Jordan* (vss. 5–8);

c. Jesus *is baptized in the Jordan* (vss. 9–11);

b. Jesus *in the desert* (vss. 12–13);

a. the *gospel* of God (vss. 14–15).

"Jesus in the desert" in verses 12–13 thus corresponds in a way to "John in the desert" in verses 2–4. The theme serves as part of the Markan preparation for the gospel which Jesus begins to proclaim when he comes into Galilee.

The desert carries a rich set of connotations from the Old Testament and late Judaism. From the time of Israel's forty-year wandering in the Sinai, the desert had represented a place of hardship, suffering, and hazard—as well as hope. John, like the Qumran community before him, had gone into the desert to prepare a way for the Lord, and Jesus' sojourn there also seems to anticipate decisive events to come. It is attractive to draw parallels between the corporate experience of Israel in the Exodus and the individual experience of Jesus— the crossing of the Red Sea (paralleling Jesus' baptism) is followed by the desert wanderings (paralleling Jesus' temptation). Thus the forty days of Jesus' experience would correspond in a way to Israel's forty years in the desert.[2] The reference to Jesus' being "with the beasts" would then be simply an implication of his being "in the desert." The presence of snakes and scorpions is emphasized in Moses' reminder to the people of their desert wanderings in Deuteronomy 8:15. The fact that this is the same general context from which the Scripture quotations in the Matthean and Lukan temptation narratives are taken makes this an especially plausible theory.

At the same time, there is another biblical context that provides an exact parallel to the phrase "with the beasts." In the book of Daniel, King Nebuchadnezzar is told in a dream that he will be expelled from human society and made to live "with the beasts" and for seven years "eat grass like an ox" (Dan. 4:25, 32). When the dream, as interpreted by Daniel, comes true, Nebuchadnezzar learns his lesson: "that the Most High controls all human kingdoms and that he gives them to whomever he chooses" (Dan 4:25b). When the seven years are over, he testifies that God "will rule forever, and his kingdom will last for all time" (Dan. 4:34). The connection between Nebuchadnezzar's experience and the recognition of the rule of God is striking in view of Jesus' proclamation in Mark of the kingdom of God just after the temptation in the desert (Mark 1:14f.).

A Jesus-Nebuchadnezzar parallel seems far-fetched indeed in light of the Babylonian king's identity and character. Yet the possibility cannot be excluded that Jesus may have read even such a story as this and found his own point of reference in one who needed to learn a lesson of kingship. The experience of Nebuchadnezzar is formally not unlike that of David in the parable told him by Nathan in 2 Samuel 12. Like David, Nebuchadnezzar is told "You are that man," though in the context of dream-visions rather than parables. In Daniel 2, he is told "You are the head of gold" (Dan. 2:38) with reference to his dream of the giant image (Dan. 2:31–35). In chapter 4 Daniel tells him, "You are the tree, tall and strong" (Dan. 4:22) with reference to his vision of a tree that reached the sky and gave shelter to birds and animals, and fruit enough for the whole world—only to be cut down (Dan. 4:10–15).

It cannot be argued conclusively, on the basis of the terse language of the Markan temptation account, that Jesus found his point of self-identification in Daniel's stories about Nebuchadnezzar, still less that the early church depicted him in these terms. Yet the image of the tree cut to the ground recurs in the preaching of both John the Baptist and Jesus, while the picture of the tree reaching toward the sky and sheltering birds in its branches is similar to Jesus' parable of the mustard seed. Jesus' familiarity with the book of Daniel is undeniable in view of his use of the terms "Son of man" and "kingdom of God" (or heaven); and the possibility of a Danielic background to the Markan portrayal of Jesus "with the beasts" in the desert cannot be excluded.

In the final analysis, no one set of Old Testament motifs—neither the Exodus, nor the Nebuchadnezzar story, nor any other— fully explains the short and puzzling temptation account in Mark. We are only given a momentary glimpse, a brief vignette of "Jesus in the desert," as part of a series of Markan cameos bringing the reader as quickly as possible to the opening of Jesus' Galilean ministry.

MATTHEW

The temptation, as the Christian church customarily remembers it, rests on Q material. The profile of this Q source, which showed up plainly in the section on John the Baptist but then went into eclipse in the account of Jesus' baptism, now emerges again. The probable reason for the eclipse is that the Q account of the baptism, like the Q account of John's messianic preaching, was virtually identical with Mark's. But in the temptation narrative, Matthew and Luke agree together on a dialogue between Jesus and the devil of which Mark knows nothing. For these two Evangelists, the dialogue spells out the full implications of the cryptic Markan phrase, "tempted by Satan." There are three questions and answers, the same three in Luke as in Matthew. Only their order differs. Both Matthew and Luke add to Mark the important detail that Jesus fasted during the forty days. His hunger thus becomes in both Gospels the immediate occasion for the first of the three temptations. After the first temptation, Matthew and Luke exhibit small but significant differences, so it is well to look at them separately from the beginning.

According to Matthew, the devil says: *"If you are the Son of God,* tell these stones to become bread" (Matt. 4:2NIV). This appears at first to be a simple appeal to hunger. But the devil does not offer Jesus food. He only shows him the stones of the desert and invites *him* to transform them into something he can eat. This is not a temptation that any of us could ever regard as real for ourselves. It assumes the existence of a power we neither possess nor claim. It is Jesus' temptation, not ours, for it rests on the premise that he is the Son of God. In its literary setting it presupposes the baptism and the baptismal voice. It is a direct challenge to Jesus' divine sonship.

The same is true of the second Matthean temptation. The devil takes Jesus to "the holy city" and the "pinnacle of the temple," and challenges him once more: *"If you are the Son of God,* cast yourself down," adding a quotation from Psalm 91:11f. Again a situation is portrayed with which we do not identify. A human being would not find the prospect of jumping to his or her death a "tempting" one! The challenge makes sense only on the premise with which it begins—that he *is* in fact a divine being—or claims to be. To put it in the categories of later Christian theology, Jesus is being challenged here at the point of his deity, not of his humanity, and therefore the temptation is his alone.

In both of the first two temptations, however, Jesus' *response* to the challenge arises from his humanity, not his deity. In the first instance he says, "People shall not live by bread alone, but by every word that proceeds from the mouth of God." (Matt. 4:4, cf. Deut. 8:3). His own point of self-identification in the Scripture text is "people." He applies it to himself. *He* shall not live by bread alone but by the words which God has to teach him. There is therefore no reason why he should do as the devil commands him. Though bread is as important to him as to any other human being, it is less important than obeying the word of God. In the second instance, Jesus replies, "You shall not put the Lord your God to the test" (Matt. 4:7, cf. Deut. 6:16). Again, as any other Israelite would have done, he takes the verse as being addressed to himself. He does not appeal to distinctly messianic texts in order to reinforce the idea that he is "Son of God."

Instead he draws on the vast store of Old Testament passages that call
the pious Jew to a life of obedience to the divine will. His application
of the passage from Deuteronomy is not that "You, Satan, must not
put me—the Lord your God—to the test." It is rather that "I, Jesus,
must not put the Lord *my* God to the test" as he would be doing if
he were to yield to the devil's challenge and jump from the high corner
of the temple wall. Once again, his point of self-identification is not
with the God who speaks in the biblical text but with the human
reader who is being warned. In both of the first two temptations, Jesus
is tested or challenged as God, but responds to the challenge as a
human being, using as his only weapon something available to every
human being who submits to its authority—the word of God, as it
finds expression in the Jewish Scriptures.

The third temptation in Matthew represents an abrupt shift in the
devil's strategy. The introductory clause, "if you are the Son of God,"
disappears, and Jesus is now approached, not as a divine being whose
power is being tested, but as a human being without power who stands
to gain everything from what the devil has to offer him. It is as if the
Tempter has taken to heart the two previous responses of Jesus as
man, and deliberately chosen to approach him on human terms. Thus,
the third temptation, unlike the first two, is one with which we can
identify, however strange or remote its dramatic setting may seem to
us. Essentially it is the Faustian temptation to sell one's soul to the
devil in order to gain the whole world.[3] It is not at all subtle, but very
direct and blatant. If the first two temptations were directed to Jesus
in his deity, the third is unmistakably aimed at his humanity, and at
the greed and ambition that characterize human nature.

In his response, however, Jesus does not shift his ground. Again
he answers with a text from Deuteronomy, and again he applies the
text to himself as a human being called to obedience: "You shall
worship the Lord your God, and him only you shall serve" (Matt.
4:13RSV; cf. Deut. 6:13). It is much the same here as in the second
temptation. The point is not that "You, Satan, must worship me—the
Lord your God, but that "I, Jesus, must worship the Lord my God

and serve Him alone"—not Satan, even to gain the glory of all the world's kingdoms. Here, for the third time, Jesus' point of self-identification is with the pious Israelite who hears God's word addressing him in the words of Moses in Deuteronomy. Before he can go out to proclaim a new word of repentance and the kingdom of God to his generation, Jesus must first stand where we stand—under the word of God, as one who listens to what God has said, bows to its authority, and uses it to overcome the Evil One. This appears to be the general thrust of the Matthean account of the temptation of Jesus.

Other aspects of the narrative, however, should not be overlooked. Strictly speaking, Matthew has no forty-day temptation but a forty-day fast preparatory to the three temptations. Matthew has divided Mark's theme of "Jesus in the desert" into three phases: (a) the fast (unmentioned by Mark), which he equates with Mark's forty-day period; (b) the temptation proper, which comes only at the end of that period and consists of the three questions and answers; and (c) the ministry of angels, which does not begin until after the devil leaves. These three divisions are represented by Matthew 4:2, 3–11a, and 11b respectively. They are marked off by the approach of the Tempter in verse 3, and of angels in verse 11b. Elements that in Mark characterize the whole time in the desert are thus placed by Matthew in a dramatic sequence. Matthew moves his characters on and off the set like a stage director: Enter the devil (Matt. 4:3) . . . Exit the devil (Matt. 4:11a) . . . Enter the angels (Matt. 4:11b).

Matthew follows Mark, however, in making the desert the place of the temptations and not merely the place of fasting. The first verse of his account states that Jesus was led by the Spirit into the desert specifically "to be tempted by the devil." Thus the desert should be understood as the true location of all that happens in Matthew 4:1–11, despite the references to Jesus being transported "to the holy city" (Matt. 4:5) and "to an extremely high mountain" (Matt. 4:8). If the first and second temptations have in common the introductory clause about Jesus' divine sonship (Matt. 4:3, 6), the second and third have in common the statement that the devil takes him away (Matt. 4:5,

8) to a specified place where a temptation ensues. These are not to be taken as serious geographical assertions but as descriptions of what Jesus experienced. We are not to think that Jesus' time in the desert was interrupted by actual excursions first to Jerusalem and then to an extremely high mountain of undefined location which seemed to overlook the whole world. As far as we can tell from the text, Jesus is still in the desert when the devil leaves him, now receiving, like Elijah before him, the help of angels.[4] But if the whole sequence of events takes place in the desert, then the changes of scene mentioned in verses 5 and 8 must, like the dove and the voice at Jesus' baptism, be understood as visions. Jesus' journeys to the Holy City and to the high mountain belong in the same category as the journeys of Ezekiel in the Old Testament or of Enoch and others in Jewish apocalyptic literature.

The one remaining feature of Matthew's narrative that deserves attention is the cryptic notice in verse 11a, "Then the devil let him be." The word "then," which has punctuated the passage from the start (Matt. 4:1, 5, 11) so as to emphasize decisive stages in the unfolding drama, here terminates the conflict and signals victory. The brief statement is remarkable in its Matthean context because it parallels almost exactly the notice that Matthew had used to terminate the exchange between Jesus and John the Baptist just before the baptism in Matthew 3:14f. After John's protest that Jesus should be doing the baptizing, Jesus had said "Let it be so now, for in this way it is appropriate for us to fulfill all righteousness." The encounter concludes with the same words used in Matthew 4:11: "Then he let him be," (Matt. 3:15). Though the similarity is easily obscured in translation, it can hardly be missed when the two passages are read together.

The parallel suggests that the encounter in Matthew 3:14f. is also, in its own way, a kind of temptation, even though the Tempter is not the Enemy but a well-meaning ally and friend. The Baptizer's suggestion that Jesus himself assume the baptizing role (whether in water or fire!) has the effect of placing before Jesus an option not unlike that of changing stones to bread, or jumping from the temple wall, or ruling the kingdoms of the world. It calls Jesus away from his determination to stand where we stand: under the word of God and under the judgment and forgiveness of God, represented by the waters of John's baptism. As such it is in effect the first temptation for Matthew. Even though Jesus' rebuke to John (if it is a rebuke at all) is a very gentle one, the situation in Matthew 3:14f. is analogous to that in Matthew 16:22f. where an equally well-meaning Peter tries to rule out for Jesus the possibility of a violent death and draws the stinging reply: "Get back in line, Satan" (Matt. 16:23; cf. 4:10). Temptation comes to Jesus from his friends no less than from his enemies. Matthew's repetition of the same words in 3:15 and 4:11 thus serves as a third element (along with sonship, and the Spirit) binding together Jesus' baptism and temptation. Together, these events strike a keynote for the whole of Jesus' ministry that is to follow: Christ in our place, under the word of God.

LUKE

The most obvious difference between Luke and Matthew in their temptation accounts is that Luke has reversed the order of the last two temptations. Such, at least, is the impression we receive when we come to Luke fresh from a close study of Matthew's text and with a tacit assumption of Matthew's priority. But the question of who has reversed whom is a difficult one to answer. Matthew's order has a certain appropriateness theologically, but with a little imagination an equally good rationale can be given for the Lukan order. If the focus of the Matthean temptations is christological, that of the Lukan temptations can be regarded as homiletical. That is, the order of the temptations in Luke is the order of *our* temptations. The appeal is first to the satisfaction of immediate needs (i.e., hunger); then to the realization of our long range goals (i.e., power and material possessions); and finally to the noblest aspiration of all—the religious motive of total and unqualified trust in God.

This means that in each instance Jesus is being tempted as a human being. His temptations are something with which we can identify, and in connection with them he becomes our example. Thus, the emphasis in the first temptation is on the satisfaction of hunger, not on the challenge to work a miracle; similarly in the last temptation the emphasis is more on the spiritual danger of putting God to the test than on the question of a miraculous deliverance as such. The offer of the kingdoms of the world, which even in Matthew is directed at Jesus in his humanity, is placed in Luke between the other two so as subtly to shape their character as well. It separates the two temptations that are introduced by "If you are the Son of God," so as to lessen somewhat their cumulative force. Though Luke preserves this formula from the Q tradition and even prepares for it in his baptismal account and genealogy (Luke 3:22, 38), it is less important for his understanding of the temptation narrative than are Jesus' scriptural responses to the devil from the book of Deuteronomy (Luke 4:4, 8, 12). These sayings, no less applicable to Jesus' followers than to Jesus himself, have become determinative for understanding the incident as a whole. A plausible theological rationale can thus be given for the Lukan order of the three temptations.

The actual reasons for Luke's distinctive arrangement, however, appear to be not only theological but, at least in equal measure, geographical. Whereas Mark and Matthew locate Jesus' temptation in its entirety in the desert, Luke places it in the context of a journey from the Jordan River through the desert to Jerusalem, and from there back to Galilee.

As we have seen, Mark's temptation narrative is actually a brief report about a forty-day sojourn of Jesus in the desert, characterized by three memorable features: temptation at the hands of Satan, the presence of wild animals, and the ministry of angels. Matthew has attempted to clarify Mark by creating a sequence: first he defines the forty-day sojourn specifically as a fast; when the forty days are up he begins the temptation proper (now interpreted as three specific questions and answers); he ignores completely the Markan reference to wild animals and introduces the ministering angels only *after* the three temptations have run their course. But the whole sequence still fits appropriately under the rubric, "Jesus in the desert."

In Luke it is different. Temptation begins in the desert but runs its course as Jesus makes his ascent from the Jordan valley to Jerusalem, ending at "the pinnacle of the temple." Luke intends this itinerary to be taken seriously in a geographical sense. It serves as a miniature of the journey to Jerusalem that dominates the latter two-thirds of his Gospel. Jesus' movements are framed by two uses of the verb "return" and carried forward by three occurrences of the verb "lead." Jesus is said to have *returned* from the Jordan, full of the Holy Spirit (Luke 4:1a) and to have *returned* in the power of the Spirit to Galilee, presumably from Jerusalem (Luke 4:14). He is *led* by the Spirit in the desert for forty days (Luke 4:1b). Afterward the devil *leads him up* to show him the kingdoms of the world (Luke 4:5), and finally *leads* him to Jerusalem for the third and final test. Anyone who has traveled from the Jordan valley or the Dead Sea to Jerusalem knows that this Lukan itinerary, brief as it is, is geographically realistic. The journey is a steep climb; and so the verb "to lead up" in verse 5 is entirely appropriate. From many points along the way one could look back on a panorama of sea, desert, and mountains, as well as fertile fields around Jericho and lavish Herodian streets and buildings. There is no one "extremely high mountain," as in Matthew, from which Jesus views the world's glory.[5] Jerusalem with its temple mount overlooking the valleys of Kidron and Gehenna is a natural terminus for such a pilgrimage.

The literary method of *both* Matthew and Luke is to join two accounts: the Markan temptation in the desert, and a story of three "temptations" that are not necessarily localized in a desert at all (the Q account). As we have seen, Matthew has integrated the two by placing the latter, understood as visionary experiences, within the framework of the former. Luke has simply left the two side by side; it is more apparent in Luke than in Matthew where the one leaves off and the other begins. Luke 4:1–2a closely parallels the Markan narrative (minus the enigmatic references to beasts and angels). Mark's twofold statement that the Spirit drove Jesus *into* the desert, and that he was *in* the desert for forty days being tempted by Satan, is telescoped in these opening verses of Luke: ". . . and he was being led by the Spirit *in* the desert for forty days, being tempted by the devil."

The phrase "tempted by the devil" remains unexplained just as its equivalent does in Mark. The content of this desert temptation is not given in Luke 4:3–12, which take up instead three *subsequent* temptations on the way to Jerusalem. Whereas for Matthew the forty days did not involve temptation but rather a preparatory fast, Luke presents *both* a forty-day period of unspecified testing, and a formal series of three "temptations" afterward in the course of a journey. He links the two by his own mention of a fast (vs. 2b), and by his assumption of the devil's continuing presence from verse 2 on through verses 3–12. The devil does not make his "approach" as Tempter when the forty days are over, as in Matthew 4:3, but simply begins to speak (Luke 4:3), having been present all along. The appeal to hunger in the first of the devil's challenges serves in Luke, as in Matthew, to bind the two scenes into one continuous narrative. Despite their differences in order and literary method, both Evangelists thus found it necessary to place the first exchange first.

When Luke comes to the end of his account, his reference to "every temptation" (Luke 4:13) must be understood as encompassing two stages: not only forty days of testing in the desert, but also a threefold test in dialogue form that brings Jesus to the same place in which Luke had allowed the reader a glimpse of him in infancy and in childhood—to Jerusalem and the temple (cf. Luke 2:22–38, 41–52). It was there, apparently, that the devil made his departure "for a time" (Luke 4:13), and from there that Jesus "returned in the power of the Spirit to Galilee" (Luke 4:14). No angels minister to him because he is no longer in the desert, and has no immediate need of their help.

CONCLUSIONS: THEOLOGICAL AND HISTORICAL

Our study suggests that there are in the gospel tradition two temptation stories; the one cannot be regarded merely as an elaboration or expansion of the other. The distinction between them has to be maintained in the face of Matthew's efforts to integrate them into one. Luke has also joined them very closely, but has at the same time allowed the distinct profiles of each to remain visible. The Markan story is only marginally a temptation narrative; the theme of temptation is subsumed under that of "Jesus in the desert." The Q account of the three questions and answers, on the other hand, is not intrinsically a desert experience. Matthew seems to have made it a series of visions in which the geographical setting does not matter. Luke shows a keen awareness of geography, but in terms of a journey to Jerusalem rather than the desert as such.

Such diversity suggests that the temptation should not necessarily be confined to a single incident in the life of Jesus, but may represent a recurring experience in his ministry. Jesus' confrontation with Satan will be seen most clearly in his ministry of exorcism, but it comes to expression in other ways as well. He is often put to the test in disputes with his adversaries not unlike in his dialogue with the devil in Matthew and Luke (e.g., Mark 8:11ff., 10:2, 12:15). He claims to have seen "Satan fallen as lightning from heaven" (Luke 10:18). He teaches his disciples to pray, "Lead us not into temptation," and invites their participation with him in his final struggles to obey God in the face of testing in the garden of Gethsemane. When they themselves are occasions of testing to him, he can address them as "Satan" (Mark 8:33), yet he speaks of them as having stood by him all along in his "temptations" (Luke 22:28), and he battles Satan for their very souls (Luke 22:31f.). In his conflict he experiences in some traditions the help of angels (Luke 22:43). In John the ministry of angels becomes the image used to characterize his whole life (John 1:51). This ongoing awareness of personal supernatural adversaries, as well as personal and supernatural allies, means that the Synoptic accounts of *the* temptation are wholly congruent with what we know of Jesus' consciousness of temptation in his ministry generally.

The three-part dialogue in Matthew and Luke can be regarded as a mirror image of Jesus' ministry in its entirety. The first of the three exchanges fixes Jesus' priorities. Before he speaks, he listens; before he commands, he obeys. When he announces the kingdom of God, when he commands demons to leave their victims or a storm to subside, his pronouncements are made against a background of prayer and of hearing "every word that comes from the mouth of God." Aspects of this first temptation are echoed in Jesus' teaching to his disciples about prayer in Matthew 7:9f. and Luke 11:11f. No father will give his son a stone when he asks for bread, or a snake when he asks for a fish, or a scorpion when he asks for an egg. If Jesus is God's Son, as the devil's question assumes, he too can depend on his Father to supply his need, whether for bread, or for revelation from God (Matt. 4:4) or for the power of God's Spirit (cf. Luke 11:13). Yet victory in testing is not gained through the intimacy of the Father-Son relationship that found expression in the voice at the baptism.

The Scriptures with which Jesus responds to the devil's challenges have no more to do with God's fatherhood than with the sonship or messiahship of Jesus. They refer to Jesus' Father simply as "God" or as "the Lord your God," placing Jesus on exactly the same footing as any other Jew who undertook to live by the words of God revealed through Moses, or any sinner who had come to John for baptism. Jesus in the desert or on the way to Jerusalem stands in no privileged position before his God. The only visions granted him are the work of his Adversary. Ironically, the face (and voice) of his Father is hidden from him, even as his sonship is put to the test. He stands wholly and without qualification in our place. His sonship is defined practically as servanthood, and his first responsibility as the hearing of the word of God.

If the first temptation is a foil for the subsequent gospel portrait of Jesus as proclaimer of the word, the second temptation in Luke (third in Matthew) is the mirror image of what he is about to proclaim: the kingdom of God. This exchange determines that the kingdom he announces will be God's kingdom, not the kingdoms of the world, and not a kingdom over which the devil exercises control or authority (Luke 4:6). The Scripture that serves as his response to the challenge drives home the God-centered character of this kingdom: "You shall worship the Lord your God and him only shall you serve." To a reader familiar with the gospel story in its entirety, the devil's

promises come through as a feeble parody of Jesus' own later declara-
tions: "All things have been given me by my Father, and no one knows
who the Son is except the Father, or who the Father is except the Son
and anyone to whom the Son reveals it" (Luke 10:22; cf. Matt. 11:27).
"All authority in heaven and on earth has been given to me; go then
and make disciples of all the Gentiles, baptizing them in the name of
the Father and of the Son and of the Holy Spirit" (Matt. 28:19). By
illustrating the nature of the kingdom that Jesus refuses, this temptation throws into sharper focus the nature of the kingdom that he
accepts and proclaims. Again, and more directly than in Mark, we see
the parallel with Nebuchadnezzar. Jesus demonstrates the lesson that
the Babylonian king had to learn in his time, "that the Most High
rules the kingdom of men, and gives it to whom he will" (Dan. 4:25)
and that "the God of heaven will set up a kingdom that shall never
be destroyed, nor shall its sovereignty be left to another people. It shall
break in pieces all those kingdoms and bring them to an end, and it
shall stand forever" (Dan. 2:44).

The third Lukan temptation (second in Matthew), places before
Jesus the ever-present possibility of death, and specifically death in
Jerusalem. The devil's challenge carries the implication that Jesus is
somehow exempt from the rule that prophets die in Jerusalem (cf.
Luke 9:51, 13:33ff.). But Jesus refuses to put his God to the test. In
due time he *will* face death in Jerusalem, but he will do so in the
unfolding of a genuinely historical drama of cause and effect, not in
a situation contrived by his Adversary to test his sonship and his God.

Thus the temptation narratives, especially in Matthew and Luke,
serve the Gospel writers as a kind of microcosm of the whole story
of Jesus. Their theme, like the theme of Jesus' baptism, is "Christ in
our place," and their function for the reader is preparatory. In the
overall structure of the Synoptic Gospels, the baptism and temptation
of Jesus are best viewed together as the negatives for a set of photo-
graphs representing all that is to follow. Jesus must hear God's voice
and obey God's word *before* he can declare it to others. He must
distinguish God's kingdom from the kingdoms of the world *before* he

can announce its coming. He must stand in the waters of baptism with those forgiven *before* he can extend God's forgiveness to the sinners and outcasts of Israel. Like any other prophet, he must wait for the circumstances of history to run their course *before* he dies in Jerusalem, even though it must take place "for the sins of many." The mystery of the Christian gospel emerges already in these two programmatic episodes: God is *with us;* he has chosen to come over on our side, to see and hear and feel with us, to live our life and die our death.

The question remains: Was the temptation a historical event? Did it actually happen, or did the church invent it in order to have a concise mirror image of the gospel story as customarily told? Obviously, the conclusion that the temptation accounts are congruent with what we know generally of Jesus' life and reflect the major concerns of his ministry, is one that could be pressed either for or against historicity.

In answering the historical question, we must keep in mind the distinction between the Markan desert *temptation* and the Matthean and Lukan set of three *temptations.* There is little reason to doubt the historicity of the former. If Jesus was baptized by John in the Jordan River, it is not so strange that he might afterward have spent some time alone in the nearby Judean desert thinking about the implications of what had happened. As we have seen, the temptation in Mark is only one aspect of the desert sojourn. Its nature is not specified in any way, and Mark draws from it no theological conclusions. He even neglects to make the point that Jesus withstood Satan's challenge. Only the detail of angels ministering to Jesus provides a touch of the miraculous. Mark's apparent point is that they sustained Jesus through his time of trial by providing him with food, as they did for Elijah in the Negev and the Sinai (1 Kings 19:4ff.).

But Mark is content to record even this without comment or theological interpretation. If Jesus was a visionary, as our study of his baptism suggests, it is not so incredible that the cryptic notices found in Mark 1:12–13 were based on his own testimony to his disciples. The most likely reason Mark added nothing to them was that he had nothing to add! He simply allowed the incident to speak for itself, knowing that the only implications he could draw from it were ones that would in any case emerge more clearly from later episodes in his Gospel.

It is more difficult to settle the question of historicity with respect to the threefold temptation in Matthew, and Luke, or even to define clearly what historicity means in their case. We have seen that the connection between these dialogues and Mark's generalized account of the temptation in the desert is most likely secondary, the two stories being linked together by the mention of a fast. The purpose both of Luke and Matthew was apparently to group their temptation traditions into a single continuous narrative placed strategically near the beginning of their Gospels, and thus to flesh out Mark's terse and mysterious allusion to forty days in the desert.

If we look at the Q account apart from this desert setting, we have little basis for locating it chronologically in Jesus' ministry, and only slightly more evidence for locating it geographically. Not even the order of the temptations can be fixed with certainty. It should not be forgotten that, like virtually all the Q traditions, this material consists primarily of sayings rather than narrative. The difference from the rest of Q is that here we have not a discourse of Jesus to his disciples, nor a controversy with human opponents, but a story of a supernatural controversy between Jesus and the devil. There is no exact analogy with anything else in Q. The appeals to specific passages in Old Testament Scripture, for example, are unique. The closest equivalents in Q are perhaps the patterns of challenge and response found in the story of John the Baptist's question from prison (Matt. 11:1–6; Luke 7:18–23) and in the so-called Beelzebub controversy (Matt. 12:22–30; Luke 11:14–23).

If we look at the three sayings with which Jesus responds to the devil's challenge simply as sayings of Jesus—without forgetting that they are at the same time biblical citations—we may establish a basis for assessing their historicity. There is certainly nothing improbable

in the notion that Jesus quoted Scripture to his disciples, as any
teacher would. The critical dictum that no saying can be assigned to
Jesus if there is evidence that it had been said before or that he took
it from somewhere[6] is absurd when applied to the matter of Scripture
citation. It effectively removes Jesus from the historical sequence of
cause and effect, and makes of him a grotesque kind of Melchizedek
"without father, mother, or genealogy" (Heb. 7:3), with no significant
predecessors or true successors in the history of thought.

On the contrary, as we have seen, the words of John the Baptist
had a profound influence on him, as did the revelatory words and
visions that he was conscious of receiving from God. We have suggested that Jesus, being thoroughly familiar with Scripture, may have
found a point of reference in certain Old Testament narratives, such
as those of Abraham and Isaac, or Nebuchadnezzar and his dreams.
If this is possible, then it is even more likely that Jesus, like any other
pious Jew of his time, found himself also drawn into the story of the
Exodus and the desert wanderings of the people of God. He would,
as a matter of course, read Deuteronomy as a word addressed directly
to himself and his followers. When he quoted it, he would in effect
adopt its words as his own. Though the three responses to the devil
are obviously Scripture citations, they are presented by Q no less as
sayings of Jesus. Like other sayings found in miracle stories and
controversy stories throughout the Synoptic tradition, they have been
given a narrative setting. The impression left is that the story has been
preserved for the sake of the sayings.

The temptation narrative may thus be regarded as a kind of "pronouncement story"[7]—but with a difference. If the temptations actually took place, the church's knowledge of them must have come from
Jesus himself, for there are no observers in the picture. If the temptations are cast in the form of a pronouncement story, the most natural
assumption is that Jesus himself has supplied the narrative setting for
the pronouncements. He has three things which he wants to say to his
disciples: "People shall not live by bread alone" "You shall worship

the Lord your God and him only shall you serve," and "You shall not put the Lord your God to the test."

The framework he supplies for these sayings is a personal, very private experience of his own. The effect of this technique is to identify Jesus very closely with his disciples as one who *listens with them* to the word of God. (This is perhaps why Matthew cannot resist the very apt addition to the first response: ". . . but by every word that proceeds from the mouth of God"). The clear implication is that *they* must remember not to try to live on bread alone, that they (like Jesus) must worship and serve the Lord their God and him alone, that they must never put him to the test. But instead of telling them these things as their authoritative teacher, Jesus in this instance hears the words of Scripture as they address Teacher and disciple together.

The sentiments expressed in these three sayings are fully in accord with what we know of Jesus' teaching generally. Elsewhere he reminds his disciples that they have no need to worry about bread or other material things because God will supply all their needs, as any good father does for his children (Matt. 6:25–34, 7:7–11). Concern for God's kingdom and his righteousness must come first (Matt. 6:33). The second part of the Lord's Prayer adds to the petition for daily bread a petition for forgiveness and one for deliverance from temptation and the Evil One. It may be more than coincidence that the concern about forgiveness matches the theme of the baptism to which Jesus himself had submitted, while the concern about temptation matches his encounter with Satan in the desert, and beyond.

The command to worship and serve "the Lord your God" and him alone is strongly reminiscent of another passage from Deuteronomy that has been taken up into the Gospel tradition so as to function and be remembered in the church as primarily a word of Jesus: "You shall love the Lord your God with all your heart and all your soul and all your mind and all your strength" (Deut. 6:5; Mark 12:30). The strongly God-centered quality of both sayings is characteristic of one major strand of what are usually recognized as authentic sayings of

Jesus. The later church has imposed no post-resurrection high christology here. Jesus speaks as a Jew, and points his hearers to the radical
demands of obedience that their radical monotheism places upon
them. God alone must be the focus of their love and worship. Again,
we may think of Jesus' reminder to a rich questioner that "no one is
good except one, God" (Mark 10:18; Luke 18:19), as he calls him to
poverty and discipleship. Like these sayings, the rebuke to the devil
in Matthew 4:10 and Luke 4:8 is perfectly credible on the lips of Jesus.

Exact parallels in the Gospel tradition for the warning not to "test
the Lord your God" are more difficult to find. It is arguable that the
prayer for deliverance from temptation in the Lord's Prayer and in
Gethsemane includes the concern not to put God to the test as well
as the concern to pass safely through our own times of testing. At least
the two are brought into close relation to one another in Paul's
warnings to the Corinthians in 1 Corinthians 10. After cautioning his
readers not to "put the Lord to the test" as the Israelites did in their
desert wanderings (1 Cor. 10:9), Paul concludes that "no temptation
has overtaken you except what is common to humanity, and God is
faithful, for he will not allow you to be tested beyond your endurance
. . ." (1 Cor. 10:13). Thus the command to Christians not to put God
to the test finds a place in the early church's ethical instruction even
if it cannot be paralleled exactly in words ascribed to Jesus. In any
event, the command stated here is a rather logical corollary of the
preceding injunction to worship and serve God alone.

Though its primary source is the Old Testament desert wandering
tradition, its prominence in the New Testament is more readily understood if it was taken up and repeated by Jesus. Surely the sentiments
expressed are those that lie behind Jesus' warnings to his contemporaries against seeking signs from heaven. Like Satan in the desert, the
Pharisees tempted Jesus (Mark 8:11) by trying to induce him to put
his God to the test. This seems to have been a temptation that Jesus
was conscious of facing on many occasions, and one against which he
often warned his disciples. The conjunction in Deuteronomy 6 of such
commands as "Hear, O Israel" (vs. 4; cf. Jesus' characteristic refrain,

"He who has ears, let him hear"), "Love the Lord your God with all your heart . . ." (vs. 5), "Worship and serve the Lord your God" (vs. 13), "Do not put the Lord your God to the test" (vs. 16), and "Keep the commandments of the Lord your God" (vs. 17; cf. John 14:15, 21, 15:10) suggests that this portion of Scripture powerfully informed the teaching of Jesus at many points.

Without minimizing the christological importance of the story of the three temptations in its present form, we may legitimately propose that it took shape in the tradition as a kind of triple pronouncement story, designed to give an effective dramatic setting for some words of the Scripture *and* of Jesus that the church needed to hear. But who provided this dramatic setting, Jesus or the church? This is the question on which the issue of historicity rests. Has the church simply used this opportunity to express in a mythological way its faith in Jesus the Son of God, now victorious by the resurrection? Or has the earthly Jesus himself undergirded his scriptural admonitions to his disciples by revealing to them exactly how these admonitions are grounded in his own personal experience? The assumption of much recent scholarship has been that mythological elements in the Gospels must be secondary and post-resurrection, but it is difficult to understand why this must be so. There is nothing strange in the notion that one who pictured the coming of the kingdom and the driving out of demons as a consequence of the binding of the strong man (Mark 3:27), or who claimed to have seen "Satan fallen as lightning from heaven" (Luke 10:18) would have described his conflict with the Adversary in this way.

The historian has no way of determining whether or not these temptations occurred all at one time under the circumstances set forth in Matthew and Luke. It is idle to speculate about whether the devil really appeared to Jesus, or what a camera on the scene would have recorded. The differences between the accounts in Matthew and Luke as to whether Jesus traveled to a high mountain and to the Jerusalem temple in a visionary experience, or by means of an actual climb from the Jordan to Jerusalem through the Kidron Valley or the Wadi Qilt, are in themselves sufficient to rule out this kind of historical certainty. What is plausible, however, is the notion that the Q account of the three temptations, no less than the desert scene in Mark, is based on Jesus' own testimony to his disciples. It is Jesus' story, not the church's story, and serves as a framework for his teaching. Whether it is a literal account of what happened on one particular occasion in the desert, or whether it is the distillation of a conflict Jesus experienced again and again throughout his ministry, is neither possible nor necessary for the reader to decide with certainty. In either case we are dealing with something rooted in Jesus' actual experience, not with something invented later by the church to enhance his messianic authority.

If the Gospel writers have followed a correct impulse in placing the temptations in close conjunction with the baptism, it is natural to locate the reality of both events in the personal (and at first private) religious experience of Jesus himself. They are expressions of the faith of Jesus, not of the church's faith in Jesus. Whether the temptations are best described as a visionary or auditory experience comparable to the baptism, or whether they simply represent Jesus' interpretation of his many encounters with hostile Pharisees or his own uncomprehending disciples, is uncertain. The fact that Mark, who omits these temptations, nevertheless represents Jesus as addressing *Peter* with the words "Get back, Satan" (Mark 8:33) suggests that the latter possibility cannot be ruled out. In any event, it is fair to say that Jesus was deeply conscious of being addressed and challenged by Satan again and again during his ministry, and of addressing and rebuking the Adversary in return. The Markan witness suggests that *one* such occasion was in the Judean desert, shortly after the baptism.

Those who deal with the historical question in connection with apparently supernatural events such as the baptism and temptation of Jesus cannot avoid facing the question of the religion of Jesus (which historical scholarship has studiously avoided for a century). If history cannot make pronouncements about what really happened when voices and doves came out of heaven or when Satan appeared and carried on a scriptural debate with a Jewish teacher, it must address itself to the next most pertinent question: What was the Jewish teacher conscious of perceiving? What did he experience, and how did it affect what he said and did? This issue of the religious faith of Jesus himself must be kept in view as we go on to examine more closely his teaching about the kingdom of God, his parables, his works of healing and forgiveness, and his call to discipleship.[8]

4.

THE ANNOUNCEMENT
OF A KINGDOM

In all three Synoptic Gospels Jesus' return to Galilee after his baptism and temptation in Judea marks the beginning of his public ministry. Although there is disagreement about much in his ministry, scholarship agrees that the message he began proclaiming was the message of the kingdom of God. We move here from the realm of Jesus' private religious experience, about which we know relatively little, to the realm of his public teaching and activity, about which we know a great deal more.

Mark and Matthew connect this transition with the imprisonment of John the Baptist. Jesus' ministry officially begins as John's comes to an end. Mark's language is terse and vague: "After John was imprisoned, Jesus came into Galilee . . ." (Mark 1:14). He neither asserts a causal link between the two events nor indicates how long it was after John's imprisonment that Jesus made his move. Matthew suggests, but does not state explicitly, that the move occurred as soon as John was imprisoned and that the two events were related. He does this by referring to a message that somehow reached Jesus in the lonely Judean desert: "*When he heard* that John had been delivered up, he withdrew into Galilee . . ." (Matt. 4:12). Luke, whose account places John in prison almost a chapter earlier (Luke 3:20), chooses simply to continue the itinerary that had led Jesus "in the Spirit" from the Jordan through the desert to Jerusalem. Jesus now "returned in the power of the Spirit to Galilee . . ." (Luke 4:14), where his home had been earlier (Luke 2:50). Even the fourth Gospel, which actually begins the public ministry much earlier and never records the Baptizer's imprisonment, has Jesus going to Galilee (John 4:1–3) immediately after John's last appearance in the narrative and his "farewell speech" (John 3:27–36).

It is fair to conclude from this information that the removal of John the Baptist from the scene probably did mark a major turning point in the life of Jesus. Whether Jesus was John's disciple or simply one who acknowledged John's formative influence on his thinking, the imprisonment could only reinforce the question the baptismal voice and vision must have placed before him: "Where do I go from here? What is my role to be?" Whatever we say about the historical intent of the Matthean and Lukan accounts of the three temptations, there is, as we have seen, no reason to doubt the actuality of Jesus' forty-day exile in the desert according to Mark, and his being "tempted by Satan" in unspecified ways.

Whether this desert stay was occasioned by the baptismal experience alone, or whether John had already been imprisoned and Jesus was reflecting in the desert on the implications for him of that imprisonment, it is impossible to say. Luke allows for the latter possibility though Mark, and especially Matthew, seem to imply the former. If not the desert temptation, at least the journey to Galilee is closely intertwined in Mark and Matthew with the imprisonment of John. This is the more significant when we notice that the message Jesus begins to proclaim in Galilee closely resembles the Baptizer's message of repentance in the Judean desert and the Jordan valley.

This fact supports a thesis none of the Gospel writers seem interested in advancing, yet which explains much of what they record: that Jesus comes into Galilee specifically to take up where John the Baptist had left off. Such a thesis cannot be argued in a simplistic or extreme way. Obviously, Jesus' ministry is not a mere extension of John's. The elements of continuity and discontinuity between the two must be carefully explored. But first, we should not forget that the dominant tendency of the later church would naturally be to play down the continuity in the interests of Jesus' uniqueness and, second, that comparisons are difficult because we have so much less of the teaching of John than of Jesus. In any discussion of the kingdom of God in Jesus' teaching, especially with respect to its eschatological nearness, it is important not to overlook the proclamation of the one we call the forerunner.

Of the three Synoptists, it is *Mark* who comes most quickly to a summary of Jesus' Galilean proclamation. Almost in one breath, Mark covers the whole transition: "And after John was imprisoned, Jesus came into Galilee, proclaiming the gospel of God, and saying, 'The time is fulfilled, and the kingdom of God is at hand; repent and believe in the good news.'" (Mark 1:14–15).

Matthew's account moves more slowly but reaches a similar goal. When Jesus hears of John's imprisonment, he withdraws to Galilee (Matt. 4:12), but before summarizing Jesus' message, Matthew pinpoints a specific base for his operations in Galilee—the town of Capernaum. He explains that Jesus left Nazareth, where he had been raised (Matt. 2:23), and settled at Capernaum, in agreement with a prophecy of Isaiah (Matt. 4:13–16). This interest in sacred places in terms of biblical prophecy represents an extension of one of Matthew's major concerns in his birth narrative. Here he uses it to give a ceremonious setting to his shortened version of the Markan summary: "From that time on, Jesus began to preach and to say 'Repent, for the kingdom of heaven is at hand'" (Matt. 4:17). As we have seen, the formula matches word for word the summary of the Baptizer's proclamation in Matthew 3:2. Matthew's economy of words, and the associations that his words have with the earlier context in 3:2, tend to place his initial emphasis on repentance, and particularly repentance in view of impending judgment.

Luke differs from the other two Synoptic writers in that he omits any programmatic formula announcing the kingdom's nearness.

Though elsewhere he shows a strong interest in repentance as one of Jesus' major themes, he also omits the Markan and Matthean call to repentance at the outset of the ministry. Like Matthew, however, and unlike Mark, he begins to trace for Jesus a simple itinerary within Galilee before attempting to summarize his message. This itinerary is vague and general at first (". . . and he was teaching in their synagogues, being glorified by all,"(Luke 4:15), but attention quickly settles on Nazareth (Luke 4:16) and Capernaum (Luke 4:31), just as it does in Matthew. The difference is that Matthew mentions Nazareth only to speak of Jesus leaving it (Matt. 4:13), whereas Luke devotes a major section to Jesus' synagogue teaching and proclamation there on a Sabbath day (Luke 4:16–30).

This first encounter with the hostility of his contemporaries appears to be a more detailed version of an incident recorded somewhat later in the narratives of Mark and Matthew (Mark 6:1–6a; Matt. 13:53–58). Luke has placed it in this strategic position at the beginning of Jesus' Galilean ministry for at least two reasons. First, it anticipates the passion, showing how Jesus' rejection at the hands of his countrymen began with rejection in his home town. The rejection ends in a threat to his life that, like the crucifixion, takes place "outside the city" (Luke 4:29). Second, this incident serves as a kind of extension of the three temptations related in Luke 4:1–13. Not only does Luke's itinerary here represent a continuation of the itinerary from the Jordan up to Jerusalem (cf. Luke 4:1, 14), but Jesus senses now, as before, a challenge to prove himself by working miracles (Luke 4:23). The end of the story is that the crowd "led him to the brow of the hill on which their city was built, that they might throw him headlong. But passing through the midst of them he went away" (Luke 4:29f.RSV). We are reminded of the devil leading Jesus up through the desert toward Jerusalem (Luke 4:5), and then to the peak of the temple (Luke 4:9) with the challenge to throw himself down. In Nazareth as in Jerusalem, Jesus comes face to face with death and turns his back on it. If John were the evangelist telling either of these stories, he would likely have concluded them with his characteristic refrain: "For his hour had not yet come" (John 7:30, 8:20; cf. 8:59, 10:39).

It is in the course of this encounter with unbelief at Nazareth that Luke provides his version of Jesus' "kingdom" proclamation (Luke 4:18ff.). As in the three temptations, Jesus takes the words of Scripture and makes them his own (Isa. 61:1f.). But no longer does he focus on general words of admonition to the pious Israelite about one's responsibility to "the Lord your God." Instead, his point of identification is with biblical prophecy, and specifically with an unnamed prophetic messenger mentioned in the latter part of Isaiah. In a very narrow and specific sense, he is a *messianic* figure for he is "anointed" (Hebrew: *mashiach*) to bring his message of "good news" to the poor, to captives, to the blind, and to the oppressed. The description of this announcement as "good news" (or "gospel") parallels the Markan term for Jesus' kingdom proclamation, "the gospel of God," or simply "the gospel."

When Luke finally pauses to look back in summary fashion on Jesus' itinerary, after bringing him from Nazareth to Capernaum, he pictures Jesus saying: "I must proclaim the *good news of the kingdom of God* to these other cities as well, for that is why I was sent" (Luke 4:43). Later in his Gospel, Luke can represent Jesus as teaching his disciples the same formula for announcing the kingdom that we have found to be basic for Mark and Matthew: "The kingdom of God is at hand" (Luke 10:9, 11). For Luke this is simply a more concise way of saying what Jesus had said programmatically at Nazareth in Luke 4:18ff. The words from Isaiah 61 in the latter passage serve as Luke's equivalent to Mark 1:15. In a way, the Lukan statement that "today this Scripture is fulfilled in your hearing" corresponds to Mark's phrase, "the time is fulfilled and the kingdom of God is at hand."

Mark's opening summary of the message Jesus brought to Galilee combines three elements: "good news," "fulfilled," and "kingdom of God." Luke embodies the first two of these in the Nazareth incident, reserving the third for subsequent development, beginning at Luke

4:43. Matthew preserves Mark's emphasis on the kingdom and on fulfillment (i.e., in terms of eschatological nearness), but postpones the term "good news" until after the call of the first disciples. Sooner or later, all three Markan elements come to full expression in Matthew and Luke as well: Jesus' message is "good news" as well as judgment, it has to do with a "kingdom," and the kingdom's time is now *fulfilled,* or "at hand."

The question has been asked again and again: What did Jesus mean by the phrase "kingdom of God"? And if John the Baptist used it before Jesus, what did *he* mean by it? The most striking thing about this expression is its God-centeredness. The image of a kingdom demands careful study, but this kingdom's most crucial characteristic is that it is the kingdom *of God.* It is generally agreed that in Matthew's phrase, "kingdom of heaven" (or "the heavens"), "heaven" is simply a customary Jewish circumlocution to avoid a direct mention of the sacred name of God. Mark refers to the proclamation as "the gospel of God" (Mark 1:14; cf. 1 Thess. 2:2,8). In Matthew and Luke it follows close on the heels of the three Deuteronomic responses of Jesus to the devil's challenges, centering on "the Lord your God." Jesus' proclamation has to do not with himself, but with the God of Israel.[1] Only Luke 4:18ff. puts the focus of the message on Jesus himself, ("the Spirit of the Lord is on *me,* for he has anointed *me* . . ."), but even here the attention is on Jesus only as the proclaimer. What he proclaims is, unmistakably, the "acceptable year of the Lord."

The God-centered quality of Jesus' announcement of the kingdom is, ironically, a factor that has made this topic a difficult one for Christian theology and theologians. In view of Jesus' resurrection, Christianity has come to think of Jesus as king. The Gospel accounts of his passion are tinged with the heavy irony of the crown of thorns, Pilate's discussion with Jesus about kingship and his sarcastic words to the crowd, "Behold your king," and the inscription "King of the Jews" placed over Jesus' cross. Christians have traditionally read between these lines their belief that Jesus was and is truly the King, though still unrecognized by the world at large. The kingdom of God that he proclaimed is customarily identified with the messianic age, or age to come, predicted in considerable detail by the various Old Testament prophets. A messianic age is inconceivable to Christians without a Messiah. If the messianic age is pictured as a kingdom, Jesus must be its King. But then, why is Jesus' proclamation of the kingdom not at the same time an unambiguous declaration of himself as King? Christian preachers after the resurrection were quick to make the connection between the kingdom of God and the things concerning Jesus Christ (cf. Acts 28:23, 31).

Mark suggests the necessary link by the way he develops his introduction from the "gospel of Jesus Christ" in 1:1 to the "gospel of God" in 1:14f. Matthew and Luke place Jesus' kingdom proclamation in the context of an understanding of Jesus as a messianic king by beginning their Gospels with accounts of his royal birth (cf. Matt. 2:2; Luke 1:31f.). It is more difficult, however, to show that Jesus himself, when he proclaimed the kingdom of God, was consciously proclaiming himself as its king.

Jesus' self-understanding is a subject that can be approached only in light of a careful study of virtually all his recorded sayings. There is a great deal about him that we may finally conclude is *implicit* in his words, but we have to begin with what is explicit. On the face of it, there appears to be no real difference between Jesus announcing that "the kingdom of God is at hand" and John the Baptist (or any other prophet or teacher) making the same declaration. Paul can exclaim "The Lord is near" (Phil. 4:5NIV) or "The night is far gone, the day is at hand" (Rom. 13:12RSV); James can say "The coming of the Lord is at hand" (James 5:8RSV); Peter can warn his readers that "The end of all things is at hand" (I Pet. 4:7). Probably all of these sayings derive from Jesus' initial proclamation, even as Jesus' own proclamation derives from that of John.

It appears that Paul and James have made an adjustment in the light of the resurrection, focusing on Jesus the *Lord* as the specific object of their hope. The burden of proof is to show that their sense of the nearness of what is coming is any different from Jesus' own sense of nearness. There is no evidence that Jesus' terminology contains hidden depths of meaning absent from John the Baptist or these New Testament writers. Despite volumes that have been written on what Jesus could have meant by "near" or "at hand," it appears unlikely from these other uses that it can mean either that the kingdom has already come, or that its coming is a long way off in the future. If words mean anything, Jesus is speaking of chronological nearness: the kingdom is to come very soon; the time is fulfilled and God has everything ready.[2] Therefore the hearers must get busy right away and make the appropriate response. Jesus' announcement is news—good news, to be sure, but *urgent* news first of all, a blessed emergency. Like the message of John the Baptist, this news comes as a call to action, except that this time Galilee instead of Judea is the first to hear.

What is this urgent news? What is the kingdom of God, or kingdom of heaven, that is about to come? What are we to make of the fact that Jesus never defines what he means by this phrase? Two alternatives present themselves: either Jesus assumes that his hearers share with him a common understanding of what "kingdom of God" means (presumably from the Old Testament), or he is deliberately enigmatic in order to build in his hearers' mind a meaning for the term by the contexts in which he uses it, and especially by the parables he tells in connection with it. The alternatives are not mutually exclusive. Jesus unquestionably draws on Hebrew thought and language about a kingdom belonging to God, but he develops and enriches this imagery by placing it within a thought-and-picture world of his own.

It is widely acknowledged that the Greek and Hebrew words commonly translated "kingdom" in English have both a concrete and an abstract meaning. They can refer to a realm or territory that is ruled, or to the act or state of rule exercised by a king or queen.[3] This is important to keep in mind, because the English word "kingdom" does not have the same flexibility. Normally when we use the word "kingdom," we speak of *a* kingdom, meaning a territory that is ruled.

When we want to convey a more abstract meaning, we customarily turn to other words, such as "kingship," "rule," "reign," or "sovereignty."

When the Old Testament uses its word for "kingdom" (i.e., the Hebrew *malkuth*) in relation to God, the abstract meaning predominates. The Psalmist, for example, says to God: "Thy *malkuth* is an everlasting *malkuth,* and thy dominion endures throughout all generations" (Ps. 145:13RSV). In the same vein, the Chronicler writes : "For all that is in the heavens and the earth is thine; thine is the *malkuth,* O Lord, and thou art exalted as head over all" (1 Chron. 29:11RSV). The Psalmist proclaims: "The Lord has established his throne in the heavens, and his *malkuth* rules over all" (Ps. 103:19RSV). In passages of this kind, it makes no sense to debate the time reference of the statements about the "kingdom." God's *malkuth* is past, present, and future. It is not so different from what Protestant Reformed theology, centuries later, was to call the sovereignty of God.

If the sovereignty or rule of God is eternal in this sense, how can it be said to "come" or to "draw near"? We can hardly imagine a Calvinist, with a staunch belief in the sovereignty of God, announcing that this sovereignty was now *at hand* or praying for it to *come.* If God has been king over his creation from the beginning of time, and will continue to rule forever, how can the proclamation of his sovereignty be regarded as *news,* good or otherwise? Something more is involved in the message of Jesus than simply a reiteration of biblical passages about God's eternal dominion. The abstract understanding of the Hebrew *malkuth* or its Greek equivalent *basileia* is insufficient in itself.

The dilemma some students of the Gospels place before us when discussing Jesus and the kingdom—rule or realm—is a false dilemma. It is senseless to speak of the rule of God (or of anyone else!) without reference to some realm or territory in which that rule is (or was, or could be) exercised. The realm may be a geographical or political entity (England or ancient Israel), a cosmic one (heaven or earth), a metaphorical one (the human heart), or even a fictitious one (Oz or

Narnia), but at least within the framework of the story we are relating and the language we are using, there must be such a realm. Even the Old Testament passages that speak of God's rule in an abstract way presuppose such a territory, universal and undifferentiated though it may be (e.g., "heaven," "the heavens and the earth," "all").

In the case of Jesus, it is fair to assume from his use of terms such as "draw near" or "come" that the realm in which God's rule is to be exercised is *here* (even as the time is *now*), in our world and in our history. It is interesting to note that in the "Lord's Prayer," the reference to the kingdom added later by the church ("For thine is the kingdom . . .") corresponds exactly to the Old Testament usage described above, while the reference belonging to the original prayer of Jesus ("Thy kingdom *come* . . .") corresponds rather to the temporal and historical way in which Jesus usually speaks of the kingdom in the Gospel tradition. Jesus prays for what he proclaims: a decisive and specific expression or exercise of the rule of God here and now, in this world and in history.

No one English word quite does justice to all that is involved in the *malkuth* or *basileia* of which Jesus speaks. "Kingship," "rule," and "sovereignty" are too abstract, while "kingdom" suffers under several limitations as well. Not only does it appear archaic or medieval to some in the twentieth century, but it suggests a geographical particularity that the Gospels do not intend. The kingdom of God is not a territory comparable to the kingdom of Rome or the kingdom of Spain. Kingdom is, moreover, a sexist term in a way in which its Hebrew and Greek equivalents are not. We all know that a kingdom may be ruled by a queen, but the English derivation of the word tends subtly to set aside this possibility. Yet for all its drawbacks, *kingdom* is still the best English word to express Jesus' meaning. It has a long tradition of common as well as scholarly usage in its favor, but beyond this it has the decisive virtue of concreteness. Its very archaism gives it a story-like quality that works to its advantage. Jesus' words, "the kingdom of God is at hand," in our English Bibles carry something of the excitement we gain from an imaginative tale of the clash of kings and kingdoms, of royal announcements and celebrations of victory. They raise our expectations, as the opening lines of any good story should do. Here is a kingdom that is not static but dynamic, one which *draws near* and *comes* and *touches* us, one which even sweeps over us *violently* (e.g., Matt. 12:28, 11:12).

Before we trace the profile of this "kingdom" in the teaching of Jesus, however, we have more to learn from the Old Testament. What are the biblical roots for a story about a kingdom that does not simply exist unchanged through all generations, but comes to concrete realization in history? For the most part, this kingdom is seen as the kingdom of *Israel*, based on the God of Israel's promise to King David. The prophet Nathan says to David:

> Moreover the Lord declares to you that the Lord will make you a house: When your days are fulfilled and you lie down with your fathers, I will raise up your offspring after you, who shall come forth from your body, and I will establish his kingdom. He shall build a house for my name, and I will establish the throne of his kingdom forever. I will be his father and he will be my son. . . . And your house and your kingdom shall be made sure forever before me; your throne shall be established (2 Sam. 7:11–17 RSV).

Initially, this is the kingdom of Solomon, but it comes to be seen as the kingdom of the Davidic line, and finally of the greater David to come, the Messiah descended from that line. The Psalmist pictures God swearing an oath to "David my servant": "I will establish your descendants forever, and build your throne for all generations" (Ps. 89:4, cf. 89:29, 132:11).

The Pharisaic Psalms of Solomon from the first century B.C. apply these promises unmistakably to a coming king who will liberate his people from their political captivity to the Gentile nations. They also furnish a link between this kingdom of David, and the "kingdom of God":

> O Lord, you are our King forever and ever, for in you, O God, does our soul glory. . . . For the might of our God is forever with mercy, and the kingdom of our God is forever over the nations in judgment.

> You, O Lord, chose David to be king over Israel, and swore to him regarding his descendants that never should his kingdom fail before you. . . . Behold, O Lord, and raise up to them their king, the son of David, at the time in which you see, O God, that he may reign over Israel your servant. And gird him with strength, that he may shatter unrighteous rulers, and that he may purge Jerusalem from nations that trample her down to destruction. . . . And he shall be a righteous king, taught of God, over them, and there shall be no unrighteousness in his days in their midst, for all shall be holy and their king the anointed, the Lord. For he shall not put his trust in horse and rider and bow, nor shall he multiply for himself gold and silver for war. . . . The Lord himself is his king, the hope of him who is mighty through his hope in God (Ps. of Sol. 17:1–15, 23–25, 35–38).

This memorable chapter ends with the words, "The Lord himself is our king forever and ever" (Ps. Sol. 17:51). Here the kingdom of Israel, or of David, is seen always and first of all as the kingdom of *God.*

How are we to assess the relationship between the divine and the human, between the universal and the national-political, elements in the teaching of Jesus? There are New Testament passages that simply attach Jesus without any qualification to the Jewish national hopes centering on the line of David. The angel's promise to Mary in Luke 1:32f. could have come right out of the Old Testament: "He will be great, and will be called the Son of the Most High; and the Lord God will give to him the throne of his father David, and he will reign over the house of Jacob forever; and of his kingdom there will be no end." Between his resurrection and ascension, when he is asked "Lord, will you at this time restore the kingdom to Israel?", Jesus makes no attempt to correct the premises on which the question is based, but merely refuses to speculate about "times or seasons that the Father has fixed by his own authority"(Acts 1:6ff.). Yet the stubborn fact remains that "kingdom of Israel" and "kingdom of David" are not the terms Jesus chose to express his message. Even when he introduced the particularistic language of Jewish expectation into his teaching, he did so only with the addition of some shocking twists:

" I tell you, many will come from east and west and sit at table with Abraham, Isaac, and Jacob in the kingdom of heaven, while the sons of the kingdom will be thrown into the outer darkness, where there is weeping and gnashing of teeth" (Matt. 8:11 RSV); "Therefore I tell you, the kingdom of God will be taken away from you and given to a nation producing the fruits of it" (Matt. 21:43 RSV); "As my Father appointed a kingdom for me, so do I appoint for you that you may eat and drink at my table in my kingdom, and sit on thrones judging the twelve tribes of Israel" (Luke 22:30).

One does not have to read far into the parables of Jesus to discover how characteristic is the theme of a shocking reversal of what the hearers would have been expecting. There is every evidence that Jesus was aware of the Jewish messianic hopes and that these formed part of the background for his announcement of the kingdom of God. But there is no evidence that either his message or his ministry can be fitted into the pattern of these expectations in any simple or obvious fashion. There was no way his hearers could have drawn the conclusion that the heir apparent to the Davidic throne was now on the scene, and for that reason the long-promised messianic kingdom of Israel was about to begin. Instead, Jesus resorted to a vaguer, more elemental and universal language, "the kingdom *of God* is at hand," separating out what the Psalms of Solomon had integrated so well with Israel's national hopes, and perhaps raising more questions in the minds of the hearers than he answered.

One more set of Old Testament passages helps us better understand how Jesus could proclaim a kingdom with so little direct reference to the long-expected messianic reign so close to the hearts of many of his hearers. If there is some question as to whether Jesus in his temptations thought of himself in any kind of analogy with Nebuchadnezzar, the pagan king, who had to learn a lesson about kingship,[4] there is no doubt that Daniel's interpretation of this king's dream sheds light on Jesus' kingdom proclamation. Daniel reminds Nebuchadnezzar that God "removes kings and sets up kings" (Dan. 2:21 RSV), that Nebuchadnezzar himself is the "king of kings, to whom the God of heaven has given the kingdom, the power, and the might, and the glory" (Dan. 2:37RSV). After describing four of the kingdoms (starting with that of Nebuchadnezzar) that God will establish for the kings of the world, Daniel concludes: "And in the days of those kings shall the God of heaven set up a kingdom that shall never be destroyed, nor shall its sovereignty be left to another people; but it shall break in pieces and consume all these kingdoms, and it shall stand forever" (Dan. 2:44).

Later, Daniel has a dream of his own, in which

". . . behold, with the clouds of heaven
   there came one like a son of man,
and he came to the Ancient of Days
   and was presented before him.
And to him was given dominion
   and glory and kingdom,
that all peoples, nations, and languages
   should serve him;
his dominion is an everlasting dominion,
   which shall not pass away,
and his kingdom one
   that shall not be destroyed" (Dan. 7:13, 14RSV).

The interpretation is that "the saints of the Most High shall receive the kingdom, and possess the kingdom for ever, for ever and ever" (Dan. 7:18 RSV). The connection here between the imagery of the Son of man and that of the kingdom provides a remarkably close parallel with the ministry of Jesus, in which the one who proclaims the nearness of the kingdom consistently speaks of himself as the Son of man.

Admittedly, the kingdom in Daniel is still the kingdom of Israel, just as it is in the passages about the Davidic Messiah. The "saints of the Most High" (Dan. 7:18) are clearly the Jewish people, or a remnant of them, and the author is careful to say that sovereignty shall not "be left to another people" (Dan. 2:44).

Yet there is an emphasis here that brings these passages in Daniel closer to the thought world of Jesus and John the Baptist. Major stress is laid on the fact that this kingdom belongs to God alone, that he gives the authority to rule to whomever he chooses, and that in the last days, by his own sovereign authority, he will bring his kingdom to realization on earth. When it comes, it will bring violently to an end all the kingdoms of the world. The stone that strikes the feet of the image in Nebuchadnezzar's dream shatters it in tiny pieces and becomes a great mountain, filling the whole earth (Dan. 2:35). Though still Jewish, this kingdom is universal in scope. Though grounded in the eternal rule of God, it finds concrete expression in the world. Though transcendant and spiritual, it is also political in that its path toward realization lies on a collision course with all human rule or authority. These characteristics of the kingdom of God in the book of Daniel make it the single most important Old Testament source for parallels to the kingdom that Jesus proclaimed.

Perhaps the most conspicuous feature of the kingdom depicted in the teaching of Jesus, in Daniel, and to a certain extent in the Psalms of Solomon, is the element of conflict. The kingdom of God is set over against other kingdoms in a kind of mortal combat, containing within itself the promise of their destruction. God's kingdom is not a static, peaceful realm, but a dynamic power at work against an evil foe. John the Baptist speaks of the kingdom in this way when he says, "The axe is laid to the root of the trees; every tree that does not bear good fruit will be cut down and thrown into the fire" (Matt. 3:10, Luke 3:9; cf. Jesus in Matt. 7:19). John's words recall the imagery used to describe the kingdom's violent coming in another Danielic passage, in which Nebuchadnezzar sees a mighty tree (representing himself) cut down, its leaves stripped off and its fruit scattered, leaving only a stump (Dan. 4:14, 23–25).

In the teaching of Jesus, the adversary is characteristically singular rather than plural. The kingdom of God threatens and encroaches upon another kingdom, that of Satan, or Beelzebub. We are familiar with the formula used to introduce Jesus' parables ("The kingdom of God is like . . .") but we tend to forget the very first saying in Mark that is actually referred to as a parable: "If a *kingdom* is divided against itself, how can that kingdom stand? And if a *house* is divided against itself, that house is unable to stand" (Mark 3:24f.). Jesus is here responding to the charge that he drives out demons by the power of Beelzebub, the ruler of the demons and is himself demon-possessed (Mark 3:22, 30). He uses parables (Mark 3:23) to show that the charge is self-contradictory and absurd. First he poses the rhetorical question, "How can Satan drive out Satan?" (Mark clearly equates Beelzebub with Satan); then he uses the twin images of a kingdom (Mark 3:24) and a household (Mark 3:25) to make the point that no institution can survive very long divided against itself.

The two "if" clauses are phrased in much the same way. "Kingdom" and "household" are images used to dramatize the absurdity of the charges leveled against Jesus. Quickly, Jesus brings them to bear again on the point with which he began in verse 23: "So if Satan has really risen against himself and is divided, he cannot stand, but has come to an end" (Mark 3:26). Notice that "kingdom" in this passage is not a *concept* that needs to be illustrated by the figurative language of a parable, but is itself part of a *parable.* We speak of Jesus' "parables of the kingdom," by which we mean parables illustrating certain truths *about* the kingdom of God. But ironically, this first Markan parable could be entitled "The Parable of the Kingdom," even as its twin could be entitled "The Parable of the Household." "Kingdom" is not a concept illustrated by a parable, but an image used parabolically to illustrate something else. Ironically, it becomes clear that in Mark 3:26 what "kingdom" and "household" are both being used to illustrate is "Satan." Like a kingdom or like a household, Satan cannot be at odds with himself and survive.

This *reductio ad absurdum* represents the first part of Jesus' reply to the charge that he is demon-possessed and in league with Beelzebub (Mark 3:22). It is a purely *ad hominem* argument, designed to trap his opponents in their own self-contradictory charges. The second, more serious and direct, stage of his answer comes in Mark 3:27, which may be translated, "Yes, and what's more, no one can enter the house of the strong man and carry off his goods unless he first binds the strong man, and then he shall rob his household." This final parable is Jesus' real answer to the charges being made against him. Far from indicating an alliance with Satan, his exorcisms prove that the strong man is already bound, so that those he has taken captive can now be set free. The image of the household is carried over from the ironic twin parables of verses 24ff. to the more serious parabolic response in verse 27. In this story, a strong man's household is under attack from the outside, not divided against itself. It is impervious to such encroachments *unless* the attacker is able somehow to bind the strong man. Then the plundering of the household presents no difficulty. Jesus gives no interpretation to the story, but the fact that he tells it in the course of a dispute over the meaning of his exorcisms suggests that Mark, at least, understands the exorcisms as evidence that Beelzebub or Satan (the strong man) is bound, and his household vulnerable to Jesus' attack. In Mark, only the image of the household is carried over into the second part of Jesus' argument; the image of the kingdom is dropped after Mark 3:24.

The parallel passages in Matthew and Luke proceed somewhat differently. Both evangelists expand the *ad hominem* portion of Jesus' argument with another "if" clause: "If I drive out demons by the power of Beelzebub, by whom do your sons drive them out; they shall therefore be your judges" (Matt. 12:27, Luke 11:19). Then, *before* the parable of the strong man guarding his house, they begin the serious and direct part of Jesus' reply with an important and memorable statement about the kingdom: "But if I drive out demons by the Spirit of God ("finger of God" in Luke), then the kingdom of God has come upon you" (Matt. 12:28, Luke 11:20). Then the parable of the strong man follows, with slightly different wording in Matthew from Mark, and in Luke with more substantial differences. Luke and Matthew thus carry over *both* the image of the household *and* the image of the kingdom from the satirical, almost playful first part of Jesus' argument to its deadly serious conclusion. In the process, the two images seem to go separate ways: "household" remains an image or metaphor, whether it is the "house divided" of the first part of the argument or the "strong man's house" of the second; "kingdom," on the other hand, shifts from being a metaphor in its first occurrence to being a straightforward designation of present reality in the second. Another difference is that while "household" is applied in both instances to Satan's sphere of power, "kingdom" is applied first to Satan's domain and then to God's.

Strictly speaking, of course, the phrase "kingdom of God" is metaphorical even in Matthew 12:28 and Luke 11:20. It is based on an analogy: God is *like* a human king or queen. But in these verses, and in most of its uses in the Gospels, "kingdom of God" tells not merely what God's actions are *like,* but what he actually *is* and what he *does.* Thus it no longer functions as a metaphor but has become fixed as a concept. As such it needs to be itself explained and elaborated by other metaphors and similes. Matthew and Mark, in the collection of Jesus' parables in the chapters that immediately follow, characteristically introduce the individual parables with the formula, "The kingdom of God [or heaven] is like. . . ." To the Gospel writers, the kingdom of God is a concept—*the* concept, in fact, that dominates the teaching of Jesus.

But is it only coincidence that there is also a parable or metaphor of a kingdom, paired in the Synoptics with that of a household? Kings or even kingdoms appear elsewhere in Jesus' parables (e.g., Matt. 22:1–14, Luke 14:31), though less frequently than images related to houses or households (e.g., Matt. 7:24–27, 10:25, 24:45–51, Luke 12:35–48, Mark 13:33–37). In Luke 19:11ff., there is a particularly close connection between "the kingdom of God" in the parable's introduction (Luke 19:11) and the "kingdom" that the nobleman in the parable itself goes away to receive (Luke 19:12).

It has generally been taken for granted that the kingdom of God in Jesus' teaching, being first of all a concept is only derivatively, perhaps even coincidentally, a metaphor or image. When kings or kingdoms appear within Jesus' parables (as in Luke 19:11ff.), they are often taken to represent the church's later allegorization, or dramatization in light of the finished Gospel story, of Jesus' pure concept of the kingdom's nearness. But the reverse is also possible: metaphor or parable may lie at the root of Jesus' proclamation itself. Just as earlier we made the observation that the voice at Jesus' baptism ("You are my beloved Son") sounded strangely like the interpretation of a parable about a son, so here it is possible to think of Jesus' proclamation, "the kingdom of God is at hand" as the concrete here-and-now application of a parable about a kingdom or a king. This is an avenue that cannot be explored until we have examined more closely the use of parables in Jesus' teaching and in the Gospels. But it is no accident that the kingdom of God and parables have been almost inseparable topics in many recent studies of Jesus and the Gospel tradition.[5] This link is grounded in the New Testament material itself, and must be respected.

The tendency of much modern scholarship has been to try to establish whether Jesus conceived of the kingdom abstractly (as the rule of God) or concretely (as the eschatological realm of salvation), and whether he regarded it as basically present or future. Then, when the nature and time of the kingdom are established as a framework, other aspects of Jesus' ministry are placed within this framework: his parables, his miracles, his exorcisms, his announcement of forgiveness to sinners, his call to discipleship, his ethical teaching. But careful surveys of the Gospel material have shown that the kingdom he proclaimed was *both* abstract and concrete, *both* present and future. Such a "both-and" way of viewing the kingdom of God, judicious and necessary though it may be as an assessment of the evidence, becomes a rather sterile and colorless matrix for Jesus' mighty works of healing and deliverance, his radical grace, and his radical demand. Somehow the questions of rule versus realm and present versus future in relation to the kingdom seem technical and pedantic, almost trivial, after one has sifted through the Gospel material and gained an impression of the kingdom's incalculable impact on the human situation. If the kingdom viewed in this way is the true framework for the rest of Jesus' teaching and his works, then it is a very skeletal framework indeed, for the real nature of the kingdom emerges not in its time reference nor in its degree of abstractness, but in what it accomplishes for those in need and what it requires of those it touches. If that is the case, then the quicker we move on to other topics, the sooner we will understand what the kingdom is.

The parables, however, are not simply one of these other topics to be fitted into the overall framework of Jesus' kingdom proclamation. Rather, they are essential to this framework. Together with the Old Testament background, Jesus' parables define for us the kingdom he proclaimed and bring it to life. They flesh out the skeletal framework and impart to it color and depth. They alone integrate the kingdom of God with the rest of Jesus' teaching and ministry. Jesus' message of the kingdom would not be what it is if it were not for the parables.

5.
IMAGES
OF THE KINGDOM

Both in Mark and in Matthew, very shortly after the controversy over the charge of being in league with Beelzebub Jesus begins to teach in parables (Mark 4:1ff.; Matt. 13:1ff.). The reason for this arrangement is perhaps Mark's understanding that the parables were a method Jesus used to conceal the truth from those who would not believe in him while at the same time revealing it to his followers. The Beelzebub controversy represents the crest of an early wave of opposition to Jesus. From this point on it was necessary to distinguish sharply between those around him (Mark 4:10, cf. 3:34), who possessed the "mystery of the kingdom of God" (Mark 4:11), and the "outsiders," who remained blind to its truth (Mark 4:11, 12). The official beginning of Jesus' practice of teaching in parables is therefore dated from a particular occasion when Jesus sat in a boat pushed out from the shore of the lake of Galilee and taught the curious crowds who had hardly given him room to breathe (cf. also Mark 2:1, 2, 3:20).

It is quite likely, however, that parables of some sort had a place in Jesus' proclamation and teaching from the very start of his ministry. Mark, as we have seen, uses the term *parables* in connection with the images of a kingdom and a household in the Beelzebub controversy itself. Luke uses *"parable"* in its traditional sense of "proverb" ("Physician, heal yourself," Luke 4:23) in the confrontation at

Nazareth with which he commences Jesus' Galilean ministry. Without using the actual term *parable,* the earliest controversy stories in Mark attribute to Jesus metaphorical language about a physician (Mark 2:17), a bridegroom and a wedding party (Mark 2:19), patches on clothing (Mark 2:21), and flasks of wine (Mark 2:22). These examples are not all of one kind (e.g., the "physician" sayings in Luke 4 and Mark 2 are probably traditional proverbs). None of them qualifies as a fully-developed parable of the kind typical of Jesus. Yet taken together they give evidence of the importance of metaphor in Jesus' speech from the beginning of his ministry. In each case, it is the metaphor that settles the controversy and puts the questioners in their places.

These early, simple metaphors could be called metaphors of *normalcy.* They appeal to what normally happens in everyday life. A physician is for sick people, not those who are well. A wedding is a time for rejoicing, not sadness. No one sews a patch of unshrunk cloth on a new garment. No one pours new wine into old wineskins. It just stands to reason!

Something similar is true of the parables told in connection with the Beelzebub controversy: there is no way a divided kingdom or a divided house can stand; no one can rob a strong person's house unless he or she first finds a way to bind that person.

With these metaphors, Jesus parades before his hearers a series of small inevitabilities or impossibilities. They are not stories of the surprising or unexpected, but reminders of what we can normally expect in several typical life situations. They serve, therefore, as invitations to the hearers to make the appropriate (i.e., the "normal") response to the new life situation Jesus brings.

Viewed in the light of these metaphors, "unorthodox" or "abnormal" actions on Jesus' part—eating with sinners, celebrating instead of fasting, spending time with the handicapped and the demon-possessed—are seen as entirely normal and appropriate. By the use of metaphor, Jesus turns contemporary standards of normalcy upside down and reveals some startling assumptions that his hearers must either accept or reject. Mark 2:17 makes a telling point—*if* Jesus is a physician. Mark 2:19 is a relevant comment—*if* Jesus is like a bridegroom and his disciples like a wedding party. Mark 2:21f. makes sense—*if* something new is beginning to take place in Galilee. Jesus' reply to the Beelzebub charge leads up to a bold assertion, one that reiterates his initial proclamation and carries it a step further: the kingdom that is at hand makes its presence felt in the very words and actions of the one who proclaims it (Matt. 12:28; Luke 11:20).

Despite the importance of metaphor in the Gospel records of Jesus' earliest controversies in Galilee, a clear difference can be seen when we come to the formal collections of kingdom parables in Mark 4 and Matthew 13 (it is not so evident in Luke 8, which really contains only one parable, that of the sower). Each parable in the collections, except the first, purports to tell what the kingdom of God (or heaven) is "like." In form, they appear to be expanded similes. Unlike the brief metaphors of normalcy described earlier, they are real stories with characters, plot, and denouement. They remind us of the story in Matthew and Luke about the wise and the foolish builder, with which both these Evangelists conclude their presentations of Jesus' Sermon on the Mount, (or plain; Matt. 7:24–27; Luke 6:47–49). The difference is that in the parable of the two builders Jesus does not need to append an interpretation, because the reference points of his simile are perfectly clear. The one being compared to the wise builder is "everyone who hears these words of mine and does them," and the one being compared to the foolish builder is "everyone who hears these words of mine and does not do them." The interpretation of the parable is thus contained in the very stating of the two analogies that comprise it. No further explanation is needed.

On the other hand, in Mark 4 and Matthew 13 the point of comparison for the simile is the "kingdom of God," itself basically a metaphor. Whereas in the parable of the two builders a one-to-one correspondence was at once apparent between the person doing Jesus' word and the first detail mentioned in the story (i.e., the wise builder), the same is not true here. The kingdom is not being compared with any *one* element in the story, as for example a person sowing seed rather than the seed itself, or hidden treasure in a field rather than its finder, or a grain of mustard seed rather than the full grown tree. Instead the whole story is viewed as in some way the story of the kingdom of God. As Joachim Jeremias has paraphrased the introductory formula, "It is the case with the kingdom of God as when a grain of mustard seed is planted in the ground" (or whatever the parable may be).[1] This means that, despite the use of "like" or "as," we are not dealing here with similes in the usual sense of the word, but with complete stories functioning as metaphors.

Jesus takes the single metaphor (i.e., the kingdom) that dominates his proclamation as a whole and juxtaposes it with various other metaphors. Instead of saying "the kingdom of God is at hand," he tells several stories that do not mention a kingdom at all, stories about life's familiar activities such as planting and harvesting, fishing, baking, buying, and selling. These things too, he says, proclaim the message of God's kingdom. Jesus, the herald of a new age, becomes for a while Jesus, the storyteller. But unlike the story of the two builders, these stories are not crystal clear. When we read the former, we know what the phrase "everyone who hears my words and does them" means before the story begins; the story simply adds its rich characterization of these wise listeners. But in the latter case (despite all that can be said about the Old Testament background of the kingdom), we do not *really* know what "kingdom of God" means.

The stories, therefore, do not merely characterize the kingdom of God; they *define* it. They are perhaps the definition for which modern scholars have looked in vain. It is as if Jesus is saying, "What I proclaim to you can be summed up in the one rich metaphor of the 'kingdom of God,' but I can express it in story form as well." The first way has the advantage of clarity, but it is a deceptive clarity. The hearers have traditional Jewish categories in which to understand "kingdom of God." If they forget its metaphorical character and treat it simply as an abstract concept, they will grasp a considerable part of the truth, but they may also jump to disastrously wrong conclusions. They may equate it with the theocratic hope of a Davidic king, or they may understand it in revolutionary political terms as armed resistance to Rome. Christian readers may so spiritualize the kingdom in terms of the individual's experience of justification or "new birth" that they find they can dispense with it altogether.

The better way requires, as Jesus puts it, eyes to see and ears to hear. The meaning of the kingdom in Jesus' message cannot be wrapped in a "concept." Nor can it be exhausted in a single metaphor with one agreed-on interpretation known to all. Instead, it emerges rather in story form, and not from one story alone, but from many. A number of crucial parables about the kingdom are grouped in a single collection. The first story has to do with a sower, four kinds of soil, and a harvest (Mark 4:1-9; Matt. 13:1-9; Luke 8:4-8). It is the only story in the collection that does *not* begin with the formula, "The kingdom of God is like. . . ." According to the interpretation supplied by all three Synoptists (cf. Mark 4:20; Matt. 13:23; Luke 8:15), the story has to do with the right and wrong ways of hearing "the word" (or, as Matthew puts it, "the word of the kingdom"). This emphasis corresponds to that of the story of the two builders, but instead of introducing the parable with a long formula such as "everyone who hears the word and accepts it is like good soil in which the sower sows his seed," Jesus simply tells the story from the beginning and allows it to raise its own questions in the minds of the hearers. Then he provides a key to its interpretation, along much the same lines as the parable of the builders. The point of the story is to reinforce and elaborate the warning with which Jesus punctuates so much of his teaching: "Whoever has ears to hear, let him hear" (e.g., Mark 4:23f.).

The story of the sower and the different kinds of soil is programmatic in this chapter and in the Gospels as a whole because it is a parable about parables, and especially about the need for attentive and obedient listening. The four classes of hearers described in the appended interpretations can be regrouped for all practical purposes into *two* classes: three wrong ways of hearing on the one hand (Mark 4:14-19), and the one right way, the way that bears fruit, on the other

(Mark 4:20). Between the parable and its interpretation we find in all three Synoptics a division of the hearers into precisely two classes: the disciples, who have been given the "mystery of the kingdom of God," and "those outside" who "see but do not perceive and hear but do not understand" (Mark 4:11f.; cf. Matt. 13:11ff.; Luke 8:10). This section could be regarded as a rudimentary interpretation of the parable of the sower, preliminary to the more formal interpretation that immediately follows. Together, they drive home the point that the parable divides the hearers inevitably into two groups, those who "get it" and those who do not. What makes the difference, apparently, is the "mystery [or mysteries] of the kingdom of God." Those who understand the kingdom will understand this parable, and those who understand the parable will understand the kingdom. Every parable in the collection *after* the parable of the sower will now be introduced with the formula, "The kingdom of God (or heaven) is like . . ." (Mark 4:26, 30; Matt. 13:24, 31, 33, 44, 45, 47; cf. vs. 52).

It is doubtful that the mysteries consist of the interpretive keys appended to the parable of the sower in the three Synoptics and to two of the other parables in Matthew (i.e., Matt. 13:36–43, 49–50). Although we have become accustomed to speak of these as the "interpretations" of the parables, the text never calls them that in so many words. When we examine them closely, we find that they do not actually tell what the parables they are supposed to be interpreting are about, or what each story as a whole means. They serve more as a kind of scorecard, or cast of characters. They assert one-to-one correspondences between some of the details in the stories and people or events in real life. They serve as a framework within which the hearer or reader may decide what each story means, but by themselves they do not yield a definite meaning or message.

Interpreters through the centuries have generally followed a correct instinct in refusing to settle for these appended interpretations. When they did not discard or circumvent them altogether, they often picked up elements in the parables that were not developed in the "interpretations" at all, and made these the main point of the story.

The best example of this is the element of growth that is common to so many of these stories. Nineteenth-century scholars in particular focused on slow growth, or gradual, unnoticed development as the teaching about the kingdom of God that emerged most clearly from the kingdom parables. Another example is the conclusion sometimes drawn from the Matthean parable of the wheat and weeds that church discipline is inappropriate because matters of right and wrong in the kingdom of God should be settled at the final judgment and not before. This rests on a questionable inference from a detail in the parable itself (Matt. 13:28f.), not from anything to be found in the appended interpretation.

Modern scholarship on the parables, from Adolf Jülicher through C. H. Dodd and Joachim Jeremias down to more recent writers has with few exceptions bypassed the interpretations entirely and gone directly to the parables themselves. At least this was the practice of those whose aim was to discover what the parables meant to Jesus. It was based on the assumption that the "interpretations" were added to Jesus' stories later by the Gospel writers or their predecessors. Obviously, those intent on determining what the parables meant to the Evangelists found the interpretations important for their purposes, but without any direct bearing on Jesus. But even if the historical-critical method had never been applied to the parables at all, interpreters would have had to agree that the appended interpretations were of very limited usefulness. Not only were they few in number—the vast majority of Jesus' parables leave interpretation up to the hearer—but, as we have said, they merely decoded certain details of each story without addressing the story in its totality.

METAPHOR AND INTERPRETATION

More helpful in determining what the stories are about are the introductory formulas. They have to do with the kingdom of God. But what do they tell us about the kingdom of God? What "mystery" do they bring to light? The reference point for all subsequent study of the parables is the work of C. H. Dodd *(The Parables of the Kingdom)* and Joachim Jeremias *(The Parables of Jesus)*. Dodd and Jeremias agreed that it was absolutely essential to interpret Jesus' parables within their original life setting *(Sitz im Leben)*, which, they maintained, was not the time of the early church and the Evangelists but the historical situation Jesus himself experienced. To that extent, their work was a defense of the parables as authentic Jesus-material.

They further agreed that Jesus saw this life setting as "eschatological" (having to do with the messianic "age to come"). Dodd considered the parables an expression of what he called the "realized eschatology" of the kingdom of God. Jeremias (like most of those who came after Dodd) modified this to an "eschatology in process of realization."[2] In either case, the parables became a key to Jesus' own understanding of the events taking place in his ministry, as well as to his intentions and his anticipations of the future. Since the work of Dodd and Jeremias, the parables have assumed crucial importance for any attempt to reconstruct the life and teaching of the historical Jesus. But at the same time, decisions already made about the historical Jesus are bound to affect one's approach to the parables.

The defense of authenticity implicit in the work of Dodd and Jeremias was not bought without price. Their work strengthened, almost to the point of consensus, the view that the "interpretations" appended in the Gospels did not fit the *Sitz im Leben* of Jesus, but reflected the situation and the interests of the post-resurrection church. The same was true of certain elements—sometimes major ones—within the parables themselves. A great deal of confidence was placed in the ability of the interpreter to disentangle these secondary elements from the original core. This core, when uncovered, would be found to reinforce the emerging eschatological picture of Jesus' ministry. This picture included the teaching that the kingdom of God, the day of salvation, had dawned, and that God's mercy was now being radically and unconditionally extended to sinners. Furthermore, what was now under way would move surely, but in its own time, toward consummation. It was imperative to seize the hour by responding to the crisis before it was too late. A proper response of childlike trust and obedience would mean for the disciple both untold joy and a new set of specific and radical obligations.[3]

Many Christian readers, even those uninitiated into the world of biblical scholarship, will find such a reconstruction very "biblical," and they will be right. For those who aspire to "doing" biblical theology, especially biblical theology that puts Jesus at the center, the parables represent a remarkably fresh and vivid way of saying things that are known already on other grounds.

But that, of course, is what gives us pause. If we think back for a moment to what is now almost the pre-history of the interpretation of parables (i.e., before Dodd and Jeremias), we are reminded that the church's understanding of Jesus' parables was plagued almost from the beginning by the tendency to regard them as *allegories.* Dodd records a classic example of allegorical interpretation on the very first page of his *Parables of the Kingdom,* that of Augustine on the Good Samaritan:

> *A certain man went down from Jerusalem to Jericho;* Adam himself is meant; *Jerusalem* is the heavenly city of peace, from whose blessedness Adam fell; *Jericho* means the moon, and signifies our mortality, because it is born, waxes, wanes, and dies. *Thieves* are the devil and his angels. *Who stripped him,* namely, of his immortality; *and beat him,* by persuading him to sin; *and left him half-dead,* because in so far as man can understand and know God, he lives, but in so far as he is wasted and oppressed by sin, he is dead; he is therefore called *half-dead.* The *priest* and *Levite* who saw him and passed by, signify the priesthood and ministry of the Old Testament, which could profit nothing for salvation. *Samaritan* means Guardian, and therefore the Lord Himself is signified by this name. The *binding of the wounds* is the restraint of sin. *Oil* is the comfort of good hope; *wine* the exhortation to work with fervent spirit. The *beast* is the flesh in which He deigned to come to us. The being *set upon the beast* is belief in the incarnation of Christ. The *inn* is the Church, where travellers returning to their heavenly country are refreshed after pilgrimage. The *morrow* is after the resurrection of the Lord. The *two pence* are either the two precepts of love, or the promise of this life and of that which is to come. The *innkeeper* is the Apostle (Paul). The supererogatory payment is either his counsel of celibacy, or the fact that he worked

with his own hands lest he should be a burden to any of the weaker brethren when the Gospel was new, though it was lawful for him "to live by the Gospel." (*Quaestiones Evangeliorum,* II, 19— slightly abridged.)[4]

Whatever else we say about the merits or demerits of Augustine's interpretation, it is clear that he says nothing about the parable of the Good Samaritan that he did not already know (or thought he knew) from other sources. The parable added nothing to the interpreter's fund of knowledge, but merely displayed it. In short, Augustine treated the parable as if it were an allegory. The difference between parable and allegory is not that a parable makes a single point while an allegory makes a number of points represented by the individual details of a story—though they often do just that. The difference is that an allegory depends for its meaning on a key external to itself, while a parable carries its meaning, or meanings, within itself. Dodd compares an allegory to a cryptogram that must be decoded.[5] The decoding takes place on the basis of a system of belief and terminology with which the allegorist and his readers are both familiar. Augustine wrote for people familiar with Adam, the devil, Christ, the church, and the apostle Paul. All he had to do was match up the details of Jesus' simple story with the great epic of salvation, so that the former would take on theological significance for his readers. For all practical purposes, the interpretation far outweighed the parable itself in importance.

Dodd recognized that such an approach effectively silenced the parables of Jesus. Their essential character as metaphor was denied, and the historical setting in which they were first told was completely forgotten. Alien categories were imposed on them so that they became the vehicles, not of revelation or of authentic teaching from Jesus, but only of the interpreter himself and his own traditions. By careful historical research Dodd and Jeremias believed they could put the parables back into their original settings in the ministry of Jesus. They detected traces of allegorization in the "interpretations" appended to one or two of Jesus' parables in the Gospel tradition—on a tiny scale, to be sure, in comparison with Augustine's efforts, but real nonetheless. Dispensing with these secondary interpretations (and other minor allegorical touches) was the price they paid for salvaging the parables as a whole as authentic stories of Jesus from radical form criticism. Although they were careful not to say that Mark or Matthew had *mis*interpreted Jesus, they clearly believed that their own interpretations were better than those of the Evangelists, i.e., closer to Jesus' original eschatological intent and to the proclamation and the ethical demand that most clearly expressed it.

But what is it that makes one interpretation better than another? Exactly what have we accomplished when we interpret a parable? It is necessary in answering these questions to remember that a parable is first of all an expanded metaphor. Unlike an allegory, it needs no external key to unlock its meaning. Metaphor and meaning are inextricably linked together. All we do when we "interpret" a metaphor or parable is to say it another way, a way with which we feel comfortable and find more understandable. It is often said that we understand something when we are able to put it into our own words. This is exactly what parabolic interpretation involves. Because we are the kind of people we are, this almost always means removing what we sometimes call the metaphorical wrapping and restating the truth conveyed by the parable in prosaic, nonmetaphorical language.

This is well and good, provided we keep in mind the limitations of such an interpretive method. If a metaphor were merely an attractive wrapping for an abstract idea or proposition, it would quickly become dispensable. Once the meaning had been extracted, the wrapping in which it had first been presented would have only an historical or literary interest. It would be laid aside and carefully preserved. But the real center of attention would be the meaning or message that scholarly investigation had managed to draw from it. In such a case, the process of interpretation becomes all-important because it penetrates *behind* the metaphor to the metaphor's true meaning.[6]

Modern research on the parables since Dodd and Jeremias has come more and more to recognize that assigning such a grandiose role to the interpreter violates the nature of parabolic language. For several decades Amos Wilder kept reminding the New Testament fraternity of the importance of respecting metaphor and figurative language as a distinct literary and rhetorical phenomenon with its own character and integrity. But only in the sixties did his admonitions begin to bear fruit in relation to Jesus' parables. The results are seen in the work of Robert Funk, Dan Via, Dominic Crossan, Norman Perrin, and others.[7] Common to all is the recognition that the metaphors of Jesus are not dispensable. The imagery cannot be separated from the message it is intended to convey, nor is the message quite the same when it is expressed abstractly, without imagery, or when different imagery is introduced. All the interpreter can do, therefore, is to "say it another way," and we should not pretend that our way is somehow "better," or closer to the life situation or the mind of Jesus than is the uninterpreted metaphor with which we began. All we can say is that our restatement of the metaphor is more convenient and understandable to us and our contemporaries.

A different kind of assumption, seldom articulated yet very real, underlies most of the work done on the parables until very recently and a good share of the work still being done even by the scholars listed above. It is a theological assumption, not one belonging to any particular theological tradition, but the common property of many. Once Jesus is regarded as the revealer of God, the assumption is that he brings to us from God a set of truths or teachings in the form of propositions (e.g., "The kingdom of God is at hand"; "Your sins are forgiven") and moral imperatives (e.g., "Repent"; "Follow me"; "Love your enemies"). He then considers how best to communicate these truths to his hearers, and decides on metaphors as one effective means of getting the message across. Parables thus become part of a *strategy* of communicating the Good News. They are seen as a form of Christian education, essentially as illustrations of propositional and nonparabolic truth. The metaphor becomes a mere wrapping for the truth, and therefore dispensable. When we remove the wrapping by saying it another way, we think we are somehow getting back to what it really means, i.e., to what the storyteller wished to express by the metaphor. Interpretation is viewed as the restoring of what was present from the start, in the mind of God, or Jesus, or any story-teller.

Because of this assumption, modern scholarship is often troubled by the obscurity of the parables. If their purpose was to communicate or illustrate definite "truths" that we by our hermeneutics can reconstruct, why were they so puzzling to Jesus' contemporaries? Why was the success of Jesus' strategy so mixed and ambiguous? His parables seem to have had the dual effect of revealing the truth to those who had "eyes to see and ears to hear" (whoever they may have been!), while concealing it from most of Jesus' contemporaries, and to a considerable degree from the disciples, the Gospel writers, and all modern readers who approach the Gospels uncritically! Ironically, modern scholarship on the parables has trapped itself in a contradiction: Mark is said to be wrong in his contention that the parables were given to conceal the truth,[8] yet his Gospel stands as proof that they did at least conceal it from him! Whatever we say about the "hardening theory" based on Mark 4:10–12, there is no escaping the element of mystery and obscurity in Jesus' parables. They resist all efforts to sum up their truths in a set of propositions, whether historical, theological or ethical.

To get back to what was originally intended, whether by the Gospel writers, or Jesus, or God, is surely a worthwhile undertaking. But what if the primal form, or at least one primal form, of divine revelation is the parable itself? Christian theology has always understood that "in the beginning was the Word," with the assumption that "word," or *logos* had to do with propositional, mostly abstract, truths and with logical discourse.

But what if the model becomes instead, "In the beginning was the Word" in the sense of narrative, so as to allow the application, "In the beginning was the story," or even "In the beginning was the image"?[9] Then the "Christian education" model for the defining of parables has to be turned upside down. Far from being mere illustrations, parables are now seen as belonging to the primal revelation itself. This means that to interpret a parable is not to get *back* to something more basic or profound than the parable itself, but solely and simply to say it another way. By putting it into our own words we try to get a handle on it so as to better apply it to our twentieth-century needs and circumstances. Instead of parables being an illustrative means of accommodating God's truth to human limitations and weakness, it is the other way around: the parable is itself the revelation, and our interpretations of it are the accommodation. Not merely the "interpretations" of Jesus' parables appended in the Gospel tradition by the early church (if that is what they are), but *all* interpretations are relativized: Augustine's, Dodd's, Jeremias', and our own. Parabolic interpretation draws closer to what used to be called application. The interpreter's role is a more modest one than he or she may have first assumed. The task is that of particularizing the revelation by bringing the parables to bear on specific situations that one's own community of faith may face in his or her own world. This demands that one take account of how the revelation was particularized and how it functioned in the past, whether in the situation of Jesus, or of the early church, or in subsequent generations. But as to "understanding" the revelation (i.e., the metaphor in itself) the interpreter may have to give place to the systematic theologian, or the poet, or even the child. One has, at least, no intrinsic advantage over any of these.

The parables thus equalize and relativize all our scholarly efforts. The refrain of Jesus with which they are laced, "Whoever has ears to hear, let him hear," invites the scholar to put aside his or her lexicons and concordances, to stop taking notes and just listen. Professionals are reluctant to do this because it means giving up the built-in advantages they think they have over other hearers—the preacher, the dramatist, the literary critic, and of course the much-despised "ordinary Bible reader." Very soon the scholar who "lets go" in this way will turn out to be no different in human reactions from a small child hearing Jesus' stories for the first time, or a bemused stranger to Christian faith pausing to listen to something oddly familiar, yet at the same time new and unsettling. But if the scholar is dissatisfied with the conclusions to which scholarship has led him or her or feels that there is more to be said, why not? Where is the risk? Traditional critical methods once laid aside can be quickly taken up again. At some stage of the interpretive process they will again be necessary. But perhaps there is a prior need to reflect on basics.

This is not to sell interpretation, or interpreters, short. There is a danger in some recent literary approaches to the parables of a pure aestheticism which regards *all* interpretation as somehow a betrayal of the primal metaphor. Such an approach could lead to a mere contemplation of metaphors as aesthetic objects without raising the question of meaning at all. It is doubtful that this can be reconciled with Jesus' challenge, "Whoever has ears to hear, let him hear!" To interpret a metaphor, that is, to find meaning in it and even lift up for a moment the meaning apart from the metaphor, is by no means a betrayal of the metaphor. We do it constantly in preaching and Bible study. If we did not, there would be no preaching and no Bible study, only public and private reading of the Bible as literature. Particularization is of the essence of interpretation. When we isolate one major point in a story for special attention, or even when we play the game of establishing one-to-one correspondence between characters or elements in a parable, and figures in real life or redemptive history (as in the allegorical method), we are not *necessarily* being untrue to the primal images. On the contrary, it is only by being particularized in the social context of a community that such images have the possibility of becoming "language events."[10]

Or, to use Perrin's terminology for a moment, the "tensive symbols" must become "steno-symbols"[11] over and over again in specific communities of faith in order to have an impact on the world. The betrayal comes only when we allow these interpretations or particularizations to usurp the place of the metaphors themselves. This we have sometimes done in our traditions, both ecclesiastical and academic. But the uninterpreted parables, the pure metaphors, are always there, waiting for us to return and start the interpretive process over when our situations change and our "steno-symbols" lose their force.

To attach to a parable one meaning, once and for all, is to frustrate a story-teller's intent. No wonder the parables of Jesus continually fascinate us, and will never let us go until we come back to them for yet another look.

STORIES HIS FATHER TOLD HIM

It is important at this juncture not to let our discussion of parable and metaphor in general distract us from our main concern, Jesus himself. What does Jesus' use of parables tell us about his self-understanding and his mission? A clue was dropped earlier in connection with the voice at Jesus' baptism, i.e., the impression that the words "You are my beloved Son" sound strangely like the interpretation of a parable, or at least like something that belongs in a parabolic context. We were reminded of Nathan's interpretation of the parable he told King David ("You are that man"), or Daniel's interpretation of King Nebuchadnezzar's dream ("You are the head of gold," and "You are the tree, tall and strong"). Both the figure of a son and the figure of a kingdom are conspicuous parts of Jesus' parabolic imagery, and, in line with the preceding discussion of metaphor, it is legitimate to ask if perhaps primal metaphors or parables may have given rise to these theological concepts rather than the other way around.

Another clue is furnished by a recurring type of remark in several recent works on the parables. Robert Funk writes:

> Jesus disposes himself to the parable as one who, like his hearers, is "listening" to what transpires in the narrative. . . . He thus accords the parable a certain measure of independence over against himself and, in so doing, moves to the side of his auditors vis-à-vis the parable. . . . He "responds" to the parable by entering in upon the world to which the parable points. The parable, it could even be said, is an implicit invitation to follow him.[12]

Both Funk and J. D. Crossan appeal to a distinction, made previously by C. S. Lewis, between a "master's metaphor" and a "pupil's metaphor."[13] The master's metaphor corresponds quite closely to what I have called the Christian education model for defining parables (i.e.,

illustrations used as part of the strategy for communicating concep-
tual truths).

In the case of the parables, Crossan opts rather for the "pupil's
metaphor," in which "the speaker is not the Master using metaphor
only for some pupil's sake. Rather the referent is Master, the speaker
too is pupil, and the necessary classroom is the metaphor. Remove the
metaphor and you lose the referent. The metaphor is body, not co-
coon."[14] Crossan also remarks that the parables were the means by
which Jesus "expressed his experience of God's advent," and that
"they proclaim and establish the historicity of Jesus' response to the
kingdom."[15] Amos Wilder speaks repeatedly of the creative "vision"
of Jesus that finds expression in the parables. He says that Jesus
imparts to his disciples "his own vision by the power of metaphor"
and that "the formal felicity and coherence of these parables reflect
the intensity of his own vision."[16]

Despite the ambiguity of such a word as "vision," which can refer
to either an artist's creative genius or the supernatural experience of
a prophet or seer, quotations like these point toward a startling, yet
wholly natural conclusion: that Jesus' parables (or at least some of
them) are a retelling of what he himself has heard, or seen, from God.
They may be described as stories his Father told him, or images his
Father showed him. Is not such a proposal the concrete and specific,
perhaps even naive, way of saying what Funk and Crossan and Wilder
and others have implied—that Jesus is the "listener," and that the
parables reflect his own unique experience or "vision"? Is it not also
the concrete and specific way of saying what many students of the
parables have said, and what the Gospel writers seem unmistakably
to have believed—that the parables are revelation?

The notion that what Jesus speaks is what he has heard from God,
or even seen in God's presence, is not strange to the New Testament.
It appears again and again in the Gospel of John:

> "He who sent me is true, and I declare to the world what I have
> heard from him" (John 8:26RSV).
> "I do nothing on my own authority but speak thus as the Father
> taught me" (John 8:28RSV).

"I speak of what I have seen with my Father" (John 8:38RSV).
"But now you seek to kill me, a man who has told you the truth which I heard from God" (John 8:40RSV).
"All that I have heard from my Father I have made known to you" (John 15:15RSV).

The opening lines of the book of Revelation place the words to be written by John on the island of Patmos in a similar context: "The revelation of Jesus Christ, which God gave to him to show to his servants what must happen soon, and having sent word by his angel he 'imaged' it to his servant John" (Rev. 1:1). In this case the prophet John is the visionary, but the first recipient of the revelation is Jesus himself.

What if this emphasis on Jesus' words as revelation from God is decisively brought to bear on the *parables* in particular? Such a possibility is allowed, if not actually raised, by the prophetic and apocalyptic traditions of the Old Testament, late Judaism, and early Christianity. Prophets who speak must first receive a revelation. They see visions and hear auditions from God. Often the form of what they see or hear is said to be a *mashal* (i.e., proverb or parable), or (whether or not *mashal* is used) is metaphorical in nature. Examples can be found in biblical books (Amos, Ezekiel, and Daniel), in late Jewish apocalyptic writings (Enoch and 4 Ezra), and in early Christianity (the Shepherd of Hermas).[17]

In a number of passages, the categories of parable and vision are very closely associated. Sometimes what is seen or heard is a colorful and splendid pageant of heavenly imagery—angels, thrones, trumpets, and the secrets of a distant past or future. But in other instances (Amos, Ezekiel, 4 Ezra, Hermas), the revelation is cast more in terms of everyday realities familiar to the prophet and his people. Jesus' parables belong in this second category, although the Gospel tradition shows him fully capable of apocalyptic imagery as well. He is concerned in the parables with farmers, travelers, sons, fathers, weddings, bread, houses, wheatfields, vineyards, and the like, yet these mundane images by no means exclude the parables from the category of vision or revelation. The terms are those of our common life, but they are put together in such a way as to make us ask new and searching questions about that life.[18]

The ambiguity of the word "vision" in describing what is expressed in Jesus' parables can now be seen as natural and inevitable. They may be described as visionary either against a prophetic-apocalyptic tradition of divine revelation that comes in images, or in the sense that they represent a deeper and more penetrating perception of the realities of rural and town life in first-century Galilee. Prophetic and artistic vision merge in such a way that historical scholarship long after the fact has no power to disengage them. Prophets repeat what they see or hear because God has revealed to them something otherwise inaccessible to human knowledge. Artists reproduce things which anyone can see or hear, but which they see or hear in arresting and provocative ways. The parables of Jesus can be studied profitably as artistic vision, even when we recognize that their biblical context defines them as revelation. What is inappropriate, however, is to describe them as works of the imagination or of "creative genius." If Jesus' parables are indeed stories his Father told him, then he did not create or invent them. He *experienced* them. In the same way, it can be argued that great artists do not "create"; they simply "see" and then try to reproduce faithfully what they have seen. That the same is true of prophets goes without saying.

Approaching Jesus' parables in this way means that we bring to them a new set of questions. If we return for a moment to the point at which the question of parable first came up (i.e., the voice at Jesus' baptism, and the possibility that the utterance had a parabolic context), we are reminded of the importance of audience identification in connection with parables. When one hears a story, it is natural to ask, whether consciously or not: Where do I fit into that story? What does it tell me about myself? A good story draws the hearer into the action so that he or she identifies with one or more of the story's characters, asking, "How would I feel if that happened to me?"[19]

In suggesting that the voice at Jesus' baptism may have a parabolic context, we may conjecture a story about a father (or mother), and a son, perhaps involving other sons and daughters as well—in short, a story about a household. Anyone hearing the story might find a point of audience identification with one particular member of the household. Can it be that the baptismal voice expresses Jesus' identification with a "son" (a "beloved son" in fact) in just such a story? The possibility seems far-fetched until we remember that the "son" *is* a notable figure in several of Jesus' parables: the prodigal son and his older brother, the two sons in Matthew 21:28–32, even a "beloved son" who was killed by the wicked tenants of the vineyard, to say nothing of a whole class of stories about "servants" who are held accountable by their masters for the quality and faithfulness of their service.

Critics have suspected at times that the church's christological interest in Jesus the divine Son of God have influenced the way some of these stories were handed down. But the reverse is also possible, i.e., that such parables were a genuine part of Jesus' religious experience, and that he found his point of audience identification in them in the figure of the servant or the son, so that he was impelled to ask, "Am I a good servant?" or "What are my responsibilities as a son?" If he experienced them as revelation, it would not have been surprising for him to define his servanthood and sonship in relation to God, rather than to a human master or father.

This line of thinking should not be confused with allegorical interpretation. Audience identification is a subjective thing, and for Jesus as listener to identify with the prodigal son, or the older brother, or with the son sent to deal with the wicked tenants, is no different psychologically than for anyone to find himself or herself drawn into a story as an imaginary participant. This is how we may conceive of imagination working in the mind of Jesus—not to create a story or invent a revelation, but to become involved personally and vividly in the story or revelation that he receives. A practical difference between such audience identification and the allegorical method is that a subjective conclusion such as "I am the Son" does not exclude other possible self-identifications. The listener may conclude on another occasion that "I am the older brother" or "I am the grieving (or joyful) father" or whatever the story may elicit from him as he hears it over and over again.

Far from being unduly influenced by later christology, parables may thus stand at the very root of christology itself. If parables were a mode by which Jesus heard God addressing him, then we might expect them to have powerfully shaped his self-understanding. A number of British scholars (C. H. Dodd, Barnabas Lindars, John A. T. Robinson) have pointed out parabolic forms underlying certain christological statements in the Gospel of John. For example:

> "Truly, truly, I say to you, the Son can do nothing on his own, but only what he sees the Father doing. For whatever the Father does, the Son does likewise. For the Father loves the Son and shows him everything that he himself does, and greater works than these he will show him, that you may be amazed" (John 5:19–20).
> "The slave does not remain in the household forever, but the son remains forever. So if the Son sets you free, you will be free indeed" (8:35f.).
> "I no longer call you slaves, because the slave does not know what his master is doing, but I have called you friends, because all that I heard from my Father I have made known to you? (15:15).[20]

The first passage in its present context is a doctrinal passage about "the Son" (Jesus) and "the Father" (God), but seems to be based on a story drawn from everyday life in which a son works as an apprentice with his father. Except for the last part about the "greater works," the whole passage is comprehensible in such a story setting. Only the larger Johannine context gives it its deeper theological and christological import.

The second passage is even more clearly based on a story about a household. Like the parables of the household and of the kingdom in Mark 3:24f., it is a parable of normalcy. A slave can be sold; he has no rights of inheritance, and is no permanent member of the household he serves. A son, on the other hand, has such rights; he belongs to the household permanently. The theological application comes abruptly in the last sentence: "So if the Son [of God] sets *you* free, you will be free indeed."

The third passage moves within the same story world of slaves and masters in a household, and makes a similar point about the limitations of a slave's privileges: a slave has no real knowledge of the master's affairs. The son is not mentioned, but Jesus' statement that "all that I heard from my *Father* I have made known to you" implies his sonship and gives his "friends" a privileged status. Again, the passage is not a parable, yet presupposes a parabolic story world reminiscent of the household parables of the synoptic Gospels.

In each of these passages a transition can be seen from a story to one or more theological assertions about "the Son," "the Father," and Jesus' disciples. A wider look at the imagery of John's Gospel shows how fully this imagery has been pressed into the service of christology. Such expressions as "I am the true vine," "I am the good shepherd," and "Unless the seed of grain falls to the ground and dies, it remains alone," recall the world of Jesus' parables as known to us from the Synoptics. It has often been assumed that the "world" presupposed by these images is rather that of the Old Testament Scriptures (Isaiah 5 for the vine, or Ezekiel 34 for the shepherd). There is no denying that this is the case with the assertion "I am the bread of life" in John 6:35, 48 (cf. the quotation in 6:31). But if parables, like Scripture, are for Jesus a given, the possibility exists that parabolic forms as well as biblical texts have contributed to the christological imagery found in John. As we saw in connection with the temptation story, Jesus is represented as quoting biblical texts with a definite point of self-identification: he is himself the man who shall "not live by bread alone"; he is the one called to worship, and not to tempt, the Lord his God. A principle of self-identification with reference to scriptural texts is not so different from a principle of audience identification in relation to parables. A reader or hearer is drawn into a story and identifies himself with the one acting or being acted upon, the one speaking or the one being addressed.

The remarkable feature of the Johannine images is that Jesus' point of identification can be not only with a person, such as a shepherd, but also with inanimate objects such as a vine, a seed planted in the ground, a door, or a loaf of bread. Is audience identification with such impersonal objects in a story (richly symbolic though they may be) a real possibility? We have noted already the precedent of Nebuchadnezzar, who in visions was explicitly identified with a head of gold and with tall trees (Dan. 2:38, 4:22). Jesus himself had no hesitation in addressing his enemies as "offspring of serpents" or "white-washed tombs," and his disciples as "salt" or "light." There is no reason to think that a mind that was drawn to images, as was Jesus' mind, would have declared itself off-limits to its own image-making. The more extravagant and incongruous the image, in fact, the more easily is it remembered and passed on.

A reading of the Gospels suggests that Jesus could have endorsed the famous remark of Flannery O'Connor:

> When you can assume that your audience holds the same beliefs you do, you can relax a little and use more normal means of talking to it; when you have to assume that it does not, then you have to make your vision apparent by shock—to the hard of hearing you shout, and for the almost-blind you draw large and startling figures.[21]

Yet Jesus' images are not mere strategy. He sketched his images in bold and exaggerated strokes because he saw them that way. When he found himself drawn as a participant into a vision that he had seen, a parable that he had heard, or a Scripture that he had read, it was not always in the obvious or natural ways, but on occasion also in incongruous, almost violent ways. He can be the keeper of a vineyard, or a servant or son sent to collect rent from the tenant-farmers (which we might expect), or he can be a vine (which we would not expect were it not for our familiarity with the fourth Gospel). He can be the sower (which we might expect), or he can be the seed that falls to the ground (which we do not expect). But can he also be the soil on which the seed falls? Or the full-grown plant? He can be the shepherd caring for the sheep (which we might expect), or he can be the door of the sheep (which we do not expect). But can he also be one of the sheep? Or perhaps a housewife looking for a lost coin? And where is his point of audience identification in the story of the lost son?

These examples suggest that there is no reason why a hearer would be drawn into a story at only one point. As he or she meditated on the story (or vision, or passage of Scripture), its meaning would become apparent again and again in different ways. If we seriously press the theory that Jesus is in either sense (artistic or prophetic) the first "audience" of the parables he tells, this ambiguity (with the many interpretive questions it raises) must be kept in mind. And is the transition from parable to christology the work of Jesus himself, or of the church after his resurrection? Did the early church transform Jesus' parables into christology, or did this process begin with Jesus himself?

The issue of the authenticity of the christological images of the fourth Gospel is now put into a new light. Among all who contributed to the Gospel tradition, Jesus himself was the image-maker par excellence. It is of course possible that early Christians extended and developed the "rebirth of images" that took place in his ministry,[22] and brought it decisively to bear on their confession of him as a divine person. Thus "I am the vine" would be their way of saying "He is to us a vine"; "I am the door" would mean "He is to us a door," and so on. But if the principle of audience identification is already at work in Jesus with relation to what he sees and hears, then the burden of proof is on those who would attribute these "I am" statements to the church, or post-resurrection Christian prophets rather than to Jesus himself. Explicit identifications of this kind are in any case somewhat rare in Gospel tradition, being limited mostly to John's Gospel and to such crisis incidents in the Synoptics as the baptism or the transfiguration ("You are . . ." or "This is my beloved Son"). Even if it could be established that such identifications only became explicit after Jesus' resurrection, the strong likelihood would still remain that they were implicit in Jesus' parabolic teaching from the start.

6.

THE PARABLE COLLECTIONS:
A CLOSER LOOK

It is necessary to return to the programmatic parable of the sower. There has been considerable agreement among students of this parable that the emphasis lies either (a) on the different portions of seed that fell on different kinds of soil, with the implied question to the hearer, "What kind of soil are you?" or (b) on the greatness of the harvest despite the wasting of so much of the seed.

The first of these represents the meaning of the story as it emerges from the interpretive key supplied in each of the Gospels (Mark 4:13–20; Matt. 13:18–23; Luke 8:11–15). This meaning is limited to an insistence on the simple necessity to hear the message in the right way.[1] But what exactly is the message we must hear? The question is not answered by this first interpretation, which is simply a strong exhortation to listen well and *find* the correct interpretation. Again the analogy with the parable of the two builders in Matthew and Luke is helpful. This story too has as its meaning simply the necessity to "hear these words of mine and [do] them" (Matt. 7:24; Luke 6:47), the "words" being the immediately preceding collection that we call the Sermon on the Mount (Matt. 5:1—7:23; Luke 6:20–47). The story of the builders does not purport to *interpret* the Sermon on the Mount, only to encourage the hearing and obeying of it. The story of the sower also functions as an exhortation to hear, but in this case a question arises. Is it an exhortation to hear and rightly interpret *something else* that precedes or follows (as in the story of the two builders), or is it an exhortation to hear and rightly interpret *this parable itself?* Is there another meaning latent in the story beyond the simple imperative of obedient listening? The answers to these questions must take into account the distinction between the story of the sower in itself, and the story in its present context in Mark and Matthew introducing a collection of stories (Luke is somewhat different, as we shall see).

MARK 4

In Mark, the parable of the sower is presented as a sample of the "many things in parables" (Mark 4:2) that Jesus taught the crowds who surrounded him by the sea of Galilee. The story begins and ends with an invitation to hear (Mark 4:3, 9), suggesting that Jesus' parabolic teaching as a whole was punctuated by this same invitation. When they are alone with him, Jesus' disciples do not ask about the parable of the sower in particular but about the parables in general (Mark 4:10). In reply, he reminds them of what they (in contrast to "those outside") have been given: the capacity to hear and understand (Mark 4:11f.). He applies the parable of the sower specifically to three wrong ways and one right way of hearing (Mark 4:13–20), and invites the disciples to exercise their gift of hearing. They are not meant to be kept in the dark, but to perceive the hidden things Jesus has come to reveal. Light, after all, comes in order to shine, not to be hidden under a peck measure. Though some are blind and deaf to the truth, revelation, and not concealment, is the norm (Mark 4:21–25).

The kingdom of God is a "mystery" only in an abnormal world. For those who grasp it, it is as normal and natural as a growing plant. For Mark, the parable of the sower and its interpretation, as well as Jesus' sayings about parabolic teaching in general and about concealment and revelation, are all *preliminary* to the two brief parables of growth found in Mark 4:26–29 and 30–32. Strictly speaking, the Markan collection of parables numbers only two! The thrust of Mark 4:1–25 is "Hear!" and these two parables supply the *content* of what we are to hear. Mark makes it clear that these two stories, like the story of the sower, are mere samples from a larger collection (Mark 4:33f.). Unlike the parable of the sower, they are not furnished with interpretations, at least none in the text, but Mark concludes that Jesus explained everything privately to his disciples (Mark 4:34). The reader is left to imagine what these private explanations might have included; the history of parabolic interpretation yields nothing close to a consensus.

Instead of a "scorecard" identifying individual details in each story, the reader of the latter two parables has something he does not have in the parable of the sower: introductory formulas telling what each parable as a whole is about. Jesus begins the parable of the seed in the earth with the words, "Thus is the kingdom of God" (Mark 4:26) and the parable of the mustard seed with the words, "How shall I compare the kingdom of God, or with what kind of parable shall I present it?" (Mark 4:30). These are the Markan "parables of the kingdom" in a very specific sense. They seize the hearer's attention by juxtaposing two radically different metaphors, a kingdom and a sprouting seed, with the startling assertion that one is "like" the other. The two metaphors express the same reality. In this way, Jesus reveals new things about the kingdom of God, which, because of its dominant place in his teaching, has been all along the hearers' (and readers') fixed point of reference. Here, if anywhere in the chapter, the mystery of the kingdom of God is made known. The surprise is that the secret behind the kingdom metaphor is revealed in . . . another metaphor! The "mystery" is not a riddle or code requiring the proper key, as some have inferred from Mark 4:13–20. It is rather something expressed most faithfully in images.

What then do these two short parables of growth contribute to our understanding of the kingdom? The first (Mark 4:26–29) describes a process independent of all human efforts that in its early stages is imperceptible to the human eye. A seed is planted, the earth does its work, and before the farmer knows it the harvest is ready. A person familiar with all of Jesus' parables will recall the story of the thief who comes when he is not expected, or the master of a household returning from a journey to surprise his careless servants. The time, and in fact the whole process, lies outside the control of the story's main character. The second parable (Mark 4:30–32) lays emphasis on the smallness of the seed in contrast to the considerable size of the grown plant, and to this end specifies the seed as that of the mustard plant. A comic touch appears in the concluding reference to the "birds of the air" nesting in the tree's shade, for the language comes from Nebuchadnezzar's vision of the "great tree reaching up to heaven."[2] The mustard plant would have seemed an incongruous and feeble parody of this grandiose vision.

These details have been variously interpreted, but the impression they leave may be summarized as follows: The kingdom is not what you expect. It comes imperceptibly, not with a clash of thunder. It comes without your efforts and when you are not looking for it. Its beginnings are so small as to be almost invisible. Even when it is fully present you may be disappointed, for its splendor will seem pale in comparison to the kingdoms of the world. God's kingdom is not simply the world's kingdom raised to a higher degree, but something of a different kind altogether.

This is not unlike the impression left by Jesus' reply to the messengers from John the Baptist in prison, reminding them of what they have heard or even seen: "Blind receive their sight and lame walk; lepers are cleansed and the deaf hear; the dead are raised and the poor receive good news." Then he significantly adds "Blessed is anyone who does not take offense at me" (Matt. 11:6; Luke 7:23). Jesus' miracles are signs that he is the "Coming One" and that the long-expected messianic age has dawned; but they are no more than signs. They do not measure up to the glorious expectations. Only faith can perceive what they signify.

Something of this kind is what Mark's readers must infer from the two parables of growth in Mark 4:26–32. Mark's reference in verse 34 to private explanations for the disciples admittedly implies something resembling more closely the interpretation attached to the para-

ble of the sower, but we should not forget that for Mark the readers
and the original disciples are not in the same situation. The disciples
will later show themselves hardened in heart and slow to understand.
Whatever private explanations they receive will do them no good, for
Jesus will say to them "Do you not comprehend or understand? Your
heart has been hardened; having eyes, you do not see, and having ears,
you do not hear . . ." (Mark 8:17, cf. 6:52). The readers, on the other
hand, are given a private explanation only to underscore their obligation to listen carefully. From then on, it is their responsibility to
interpret Jesus' imagery for themselves. Mark assumes that they can
and will.

MATTHEW 13

The picture is somewhat the same in Matthew. The formula, "The
kingdom of heaven is like" appears in connection with every parable
except the parable of the sower, which again serves to introduce the
collection. The Markan emphasis on the necessity to hear is retained,
but is made more specific in terms of "understanding" (Matt. 13:13,
14, 15, 19, 23). At the end of the discourse, Jesus asks, "Have you
understood all these things?" and characterizes the person with understanding as a "scribe trained for the kingdom of heaven" (Matt.
13:51f.). As in Mark, a sharp distinction emerges between those who
understand and those who do not (Matt. 13:10–17). The latter are
described twice as those who seeing do not see and hearing neither
hear nor understand, first (as in Mark) paraphrasing Isaiah 6:9ff., and
then formally quoting the same passage in its entirety (vss. 13, 14, 15).
The former, by contrast, are pronounced blessed because their eyes
have seen what no one has ever seen before, and their ears have heard
what no one has ever heard (vss. 16–17). This beatitude is not from
Mark, but from the Q material. It reinforces the Markan indications
that the kingdom has already dawned, but shifts the emphasis away
from hiddenness in the direction of something now clearly visible.

Among the things that the disciples' ears are blessed for hearing
is the parable of the sower itself: "You then, hear the parable of the

sower" (Matt. 13:18). This story is therefore not simply preliminary (as in Mark) to the real message that must be heard, but is itself part of that message. Jesus grants the disciples a formal interpretation of it (Matt. 13:18–23) even though none has been asked. Nor is this the only such interpretation in the Matthean collection. The story of the wheat and the weeds in Matthew 13:24–30 is explained to the disciples in verses 36–43, while the story of the net full of fish (vss. 47–48) is explained in similar fashion immediately (vss. 49–50).

Another distinctive Matthean feature is that in the first two of these interpretations an explicit title is attached to the story being interpreted. Jesus speaks of "the Parable of the Sower" in Matthew 13:18, while in Matthew 13:36 his disciples ask about "the Parable of the Weeds of the Field." This suggests that the stories with their interpretations were well known in the Matthean church and classified as "parables." Nothing in the text sets the parable of the sower apart from the rest except the absence (carried over from Mark) of the formula, "The kingdom of heaven is like." That Matthew simply wants to record a series of parables broadly sharing a common theme is shown by the phrase "another parable" in Matthew 13:24, 31, and 33, and the repetition of the word "again" with the kingdom formula in verses 45 and 47.

In all, there are seven parables in the Matthean collection, arranged as follows: Jesus tells one parable ("the sower") and interprets it; then he tells three more ("the weeds of the field," the mustard seed, and the leaven) and interprets the first of these. Then he tells three more (the treasure hidden in the field, the costly pearl, and the net full of fish), and again interprets one of the three, this time the last. The impression is that all seven of these comprise (or at least exemplify) the revelation that Jesus' disciples are privileged to hear and called upon to understand. Though the parable of the sower retains its Markan function of spotlighting the obligation to hear, it also stands with the other parables as part of the revelation proper.

The grouping of the seven parables in Matthew, the themes and vocabulary that they have in common, and the peculiar ratio of interpreted to uninterpreted stories (one out of one interpreted, then one out of three, and one out of three again) all suggest that Matthew intended them in some way to shed light on each other. For him they have a cumulative meaning that, when grasped, qualifies the hearer to be a "scribe trained for the kingdom of heaven." Still in a parabolic vein (as a kind of eighth parable), Matthew compares such an "honor student" to the head of a household, bringing new things and old from his storeroom (Matt. 13:52). It is not surprising that the Gospel which portrays Jesus as the authoritative teacher (Matt. 7:28) and teaching as the primary task of the church (Matt. 28:19) also groups some of Jesus' parables in such a way as to exhibit his "school" in operation. Matthew 13 is an appropriate sequel to Matthew 11:28–30, in which Jesus, like personified Wisdom in the Old Testament, invites students to come and learn from him, and refresh themselves by assuming his yoke. In the parables of the kingdom, the school of Jesus has begun, as the disciples are guided toward true understanding.

But what is the cumulative meaning Matthew intends for these stories, and how do they, with their explanations, mutually interpret each other? The first four stories have the theme of growth in common, or, in the case of the leaven, a process resembling growth. In each of them, there is a planting of some kind that initiates the growth, a process that produces one or more results, and a harvest, or similar denouement in which the results are clearly displayed. In the parable of the sower there are three bad results and one good result. The point of the story in Mark was an individualistic one: "Make sure that in your case the result is good" ("make sure that you hear and obey the message").

The Matthean form of the story can be read in much the same way: ("Make sure you understand what you hear"). In retaining the Markan identification of the details in the story, Matthew has preserved, to a great extent, Mark's perspective on the story as a whole. But in Matthew the grouping of this parable with the other parables of growth suggests another dimension as well. It appears that even though there are three instances in which the seed fails to bear fruit, and only one instance in which it yields a good crop, nevertheless, the good results outweigh the bad. Despite all the wasted seed and wasted effort, the story ends with the successful harvest. The implication is that whether the harvest is a hundredfold, sixtyfold, or thirtyfold, it is worthwhile, even when weighed against the apparently wasted seed and labor.

This is an interpretation that the reader might come to see, with or without the appended private explanation to the disciples. It is only a short step between an individualized "harvest" of good works in the life of one person, and the harvest as an image for the end of the age as it affects the whole world. Although Matthew has retained the former from the appended Markan interpretation of the parable of the sower, he has explicitly introduced the latter in his own interpretation of the parable of the weeds (Matt. 13:39). This eschatological and more universal application of the harvest image is consistent not only with these two parables, but with the harvest imagery of John the Baptist (Matt. 3:12; Luke 3:17) and with Mark's own parable of the seed growing unnoticed in the earth (Mark 4:26–29), as well as with Matthew's implication that all seven parables he has assembled here are parables of the kingdom of heaven. It is also fully consistent with what we know of the eschatology of Jesus.

When the parable of the sower is separated from its Markan application (even partially, as in Matthew) and allowed to function as a kingdom parable in its own right, it has a meaning that could be summarized as follows: "Despite rejection, misunderstanding, and ignorance among many who hear the message of the kingdom of heaven, the kingdom will surely come. When it comes, it will be worth the waiting, and worth all the failures and frustrations, for the sake of those few who accept it."

Understood in this way, the parable embodies a "theology of failure." The sower himself is the natural point of audience identification. One unsuccessful sowing after another makes us wonder if all the sower's work is going to be in vain? Is no one going to respond and understand? But the final rich harvest provides the happy ending that makes everything else worthwhile.

It is perhaps no accident that the kingdom parables in Mark and Matthew are placed shortly after the Beelzebub controversy, with its expression of sudden bitter opposition to Jesus and willful misunderstanding of his words and works. Both accounts begin with indications of a wave of popularity surrounding Jesus (Mark 3:21 and Matt. 12:15, 23; Mark 4:1 and Matt. 13:2). Against such a background, Jesus and his disciples need to be prepared to experience failure, and yet confirmed in their sense of the kingdom's presence and their hope for its full realization.

Such a reading of the story suggests that it is told for the benefit of the sower, i.e., for the benefit of those who proclaim the word of the kingdom. It represents precisely what Jesus himself might have drawn from the story if he was, as we have suggested, its first audience. If he had a sense of personal mission to proclaim the kingdom of God to his generation, it is almost inevitable that his point of identification would have been with the sower. He would have heard the story as a word of consolation in the face of such incidents as the Beelzebub controversy, and in the face of misunderstanding even on the part of his own family and his disciples. A parallel can be drawn once again between parables and Old Testament Scripture in the way they functioned for Jesus. Just as we can imagine him reading Isaiah 6:9ff. and identifying his own situation with that of the prophet Isaiah in a blind, deaf, and hard-hearted generation, so we can imagine him hearing the story of the sower and identifying with its protagonist, as one effort after another seems to go for nought. Matthew's understanding of the parable of the sower is thus entirely appropriate as the understanding of Jesus as well.

The notion that he might instead have identified himself with the soils in which the seed was scattered, or asked, "What kind of soil am I?" seems (when phrased that way) banal by comparison. Yet in a more general way, the Markan use of the parable, as a preliminary reinforcement of the admonition to hear, has its own kind of plausibility when applied to the situation of Jesus. For Jesus too such parables as the sower or the wise and foolish builders could have served, in much the same way as the three temptations in Matthew and Luke, to underscore the necessity of hearing the word of God before (and as) he went out to proclaim it. There is, as we have seen, no reason why Jesus could not have related the same parable to himself in different ways at different times in his ministry.

Matthew's second kingdom parable, known as the "Parable of the Weeds in the Field" (Matt. 13:36), is also supplied with a point-by-point interpretation. Seven details in the story are identified: the sower, the field, the good seed, the weeds, the enemy who sowed them, the harvest, and the harvesters. Then the last judgment is described in terms of these details. The identification of the sower in this story with the Son of man confirms what the previous story led us to expect, even though the sower himself is the one figure not explicitly identified in the parable that bears his name! The identification of the field as the world has no precise equivalent in the parable of the sower, but is crucially important here. The mixed results attributed in the first parable to different kinds of soil are here attributed to different kinds of seed. The seed accordingly represents, not the message of the kingdom, but contrasting types of people, the "children of the Kingdom" and the "children of the Evil One." The "anti-sower" responsible for the weeds is, therefore, the devil. The tacit understanding within much of the Gospel tradition that the harvest represents the end of the present age as the time of judgment, and of separation of good from evil, is here made explicit, along with the almost superfluous added touch that the harvesters are angels.

Despite this abundance of detail, the interpretation tells us no more of what the story is about than did the interpretation of the parable of the sower. It provides a framework for understanding, but nothing beyond that. The story revolves around two exchanges between the householder who sowed the good seed, and his servants. The servants ask two questions: first, "Lord, did you not sow good seed in your field? Why then does it have weeds?" and second, "Do you want us to go and gather them out?" Strangely enough, these servants are never identified in the interpretation. Their first question, with the sower's answer that "an enemy has done this" (Matt. 13:28), is illuminated by identifications of the weeds and of the enemy in verses 38–39, but the second question is ignored altogether.

This is particularly strange because the second question is one that elicits from the sower a rather long and careful response: "No, lest in gathering out the weeds you uproot the wheat along with them. Let both grow together until the harvest; and in the time of the harvest I will say to the harvesters, 'First gather out the weeds and bind them in bundles for burning, but gather the wheat into my granary.' " Thus in the story the detailed description of the harvest is simply part of the householder's long reply to his servants. The harvest itself is not even part of the narrative. The householder merely tells his servants what he will say when the time comes. The real thrust of his reply to the servants is "Sit tight for now. Don't rush things. Wait for the harvest." But the interpretation skips the question and the admonition to wait. It ignores the main point of the story in order to capitalize on certain of its details.

Here we should avoid jumping to the conclusion that the interpretation of the parable of the tares in the field has therefore missed the point of the story. Such a judgment assumes that the interpretation intends to reveal what the story is about in such a way that nothing is left to the reader or hearer. But if its purpose is simply to provide a framework within which the reader may form his or her own impressions of the story, the charge is unwarranted. Here as in the interpretation of the parable of the sower, we have merely a cast of characters for the story, not an explanation of its meaning. Whoever is responsible for this listing (whether Jesus or Matthew or the pre-Matthean tradition) has taken the opportunity to sketch in vivid detail a sequence of events to take place at the "consummation of the age," but this sequence is only marginally related to the story recorded in verses 24–30. Similarities to Matthew 13:49f., 16:27, 24:31, 25:31ff., and 7:23 suggest that much of the language of the "interpretation" may belong to Matthew, but this does not necessarily make him responsible for its existence. In any case, we should not expect more from a mere "scorecard" than it is intended to provide.

What it does provide in this case is a clue. Sometimes the persistent tendency of scholars, even conservative ones, to ignore altogether these appended interpretations misleads them. The clue is the second of the seven identifications: "the field is the world." Interpreters of the parable have frequently assumed that the field is the church and that the story has to do with church discipline, specifically with the impossibility or uselessness of church discipline. But despite his interest in the church and its discipline, Matthew makes it clear that this is not the meaning he intends here. Nor is the "ecclesiastical" interpretation conceivable as the meaning Jesus intended. Though there is nothing implausible about Jesus' having anticipated an ongoing community of his followers, it is hard to imagine him speaking in advance to such procedural issues as how *not* to deal with the church's hypocrites! There is every reason to take the statement, "the field is the world," seriously as an important clue to the original frame of reference of this parable.

The late Jewish apocalypse known as 4th Ezra, which dates from a little less than a century after the time of Jesus, provides an example of similar imagery. The visionary who represents himself as Ezra asks God about Israel's suffering and is told:

> For the evil about which you ask me is sown, but the ingathering of it has not yet come. Unless, therefore, what is sown is reaped, and unless the place where the evil is sown shall have passed away, the field where the good is sown cannot come. For a grain of evil seed was sown in the heart of Adam from the beginning, and how much ungodly fruit has it produced up to now, and shall yet produce until the threshing-floor comes!
>
> Consider now in your own mind: if a grain of evil seed has produced so much ungodly fruit, when once the ears of the good seed shall be sown without number, how great a floor shall they be destined to fill? (4 Ezra 4:28–31).

There are obvious differences between the two passages: 4 Ezra has placed the imagery in the context of creation and of Adam's sin. The seed represents not people but respective good and bad tendencies within the human heart. The evil and the good seed are apparently sown in two different fields, probably representing this world and the world to come.

But there are similarities as well: the dualism of the good and evil seed; the emphasis on the "threshing floor" (i.e., the harvest), and on the fact that it will not come until the evil seed reaches its full growth; and especially the global context of all that is described. In 4 Ezra too the field is the world, whether seen as the present world of evil and suffering, or as the new world in which the good seed will spring up. This dualism based on the co-existence of the wicked and the righteous in the world is as conceivable in the life situation of Jesus as it is in 4 Ezra, or anywhere else in the apocalyptic or sectarian Judaism of Jesus' day.

The point of audience identification for a Jewish reader of 4 Ezra would be the inquiring prophet himself. Like Ezra, the reader wants to know from God, "How long and when shall these things come to pass? For our years are few and evil" (4 Ezra 4:33). In a somewhat similar way, the point of audience identification for Jesus' disciples, or for Christian readers, in the story of the weeds in the field would be the servants who asked, "Where did the weeds come from?" and, "Do you want us to go and gather them out?" Like the visionary of 4 Ezra, they need to learn a lesson of patience. Ezra was told, "Your haste may not exceed that of the Most High; for you are in a hurry for your own sake, but the Exalted One on behalf of many" (4 Ezra 4:34). The servants in the story are told not to gather out the weeds, but to let weeds and wheat grow together and ripen for the harvest. The story thus becomes a warning not to get ahead of God's timetable, not to rush the consummation, and especially not to be overzealous for judgment on one's enemies. Though the kingdom is at hand and is even now dawning, it has not yet come in its fulness. Therefore patience is required.

Is such an interpretation also a credible picture of what Jesus might have learned from the parable? There is every reason to think so. Despite the Matthean identification of the Son of man with the householder, it is more plausible that if the story came first as a revelation to Jesus, his own point of self-identification would have been the same as that of his disciples: namely, with the servants who asked the master about the weeds. His inclination, like that of any dedicated preacher of righteousness (his predecessor, John the Baptist, for instance) would have been to hasten the harvest and purify the world of its evil right away. For him, as for those to whom he passed the story along, it was necessary to learn the lesson of patience. From the time of Israel's slavery in Egypt to the anguished cries of the Psalmist and of apocalyptists like the author of 4 Ezra, the people of God had cried out for vindication against their adversaries and attempted to hasten the day of judgment on the ungodly.

This was the tradition to which both John the Baptist and Jesus belonged. It would not be surprising if one who announced, "The kingdom of God is at hand" had to be reminded that the harvest would not take place until good and evil had reached their full growth. Thus Jesus is likely to have found his point of identification in the story of the weeds with the impatient inquiring servants. Later, when the parable came to be viewed through the eyes of the church, the readers saw themselves in this role. Therefore, the interpretation of the story, in its final Matthean form, leaves the inquiring servants unidentified and assigns to Jesus (perhaps on the analogy of the parable of the sower) the role of the householder who planted the good crop. This is not, after all, such a great modification: the householder and the impatient servants face the same problem; the difference is that the householder, like the *risen* Jesus, knows the solution. The parable of the weeds in the field, like the parable of the sower, can thus be understood as an expression of a theology of failure. If the point of the first story was to teach Jesus (and after him, his followers) that the kingdom he proclaimed would come despite apparent setbacks, and would be worth all his efforts even for the sake of a few, the point of the second is to teach that it will come despite the continuing presence of evil in the world. Both stories are told to encourage the hearer.

Encouragement can be found in what is presupposed in the parable of the weeds as well as in what is directly asserted. In contrast to the parable of the sower, the farmer does not plant the seed haphazardly along a path or in rocks or thorns, but rather "in his field" (Matt. 13:24). If "the field is the world" (vs. 38), then the story as Matthew understood it presupposes that the world belongs to "the Son of man." It is in fact *already* his kingdom, for when he carries out the harvest he gathers "out of his kingdom all who give offense or commit wrongdoing" (Matt. 13:41). The latter have been trespassing in a field that is not theirs. The world belongs even now to the Son of man and his followers. There is no reason why a similar emphasis may not have been present in the parable for Jesus himself: the world belongs to God despite all appearances to the contrary. Such a confidence underlies Jesus' recorded ethical teaching at certain points. His most characteristic ethical demand on his disciples is to "love your enemies," and he undergirds this demand on at least one occasion with the reminder that God causes his sun to rise both on the evil and good people, and causes rain upon righteous and unrighteous alike (Matt. 5:45; cf. Luke 6:35).

The implication of the parable of the weeds is that precisely *because* God rules the world and is bringing his rule to perfect realization, there is no need to "jump the gun" by repaying evildoers in kind. Let God mete out his own rewards and punishments in his own time. The end is not yet, and the watchword of an ethic that keeps this in mind is "Love your enemies." The clearest statement of such a "preconsummation" ethic is perhaps found in Paul:

> Do not take vengeance, my friends, but leave room for the wrath of God, for it is written, "Vengeance is mine, I will repay," says the Lord. But if your enemy is hungry, feed him; if he is thirsty, give him a drink; for by doing this, you will heap coals of fire on his head. Do not be overcome by evil, but overcome evil with good (Rom. 12: 19–21).

The parable of the mustard seed in Matthew requires little comment beyond what it received in the discussion of Mark. The two main differences are slight but noteworthy. The first is attributable to a difference of context, the second to Matthew's avoidance of Markan irony.

First, Matthew speaks of a man who sowed the mustard seed "in his field" (Matt. 13:31), much like the man who sowed good seed "in his field" in the preceding story (Matt. 13:24). Mark describes the seed as sown "on the ground" (Mark 4:31), like the seed sown "on the ground" in *his* preceding parable (Mark 4:26).

Second, Matthew heightens somewhat the sizeable mustard plant by making it into a tree, with birds nesting in its branches instead of merely under its shade (Matt. 13:32). He has thus assimilated the image more closely to its traditional form in such passages as Daniel 4:10–13, 20–22 and Ezekiel 17:22–23, 31:3–9. Mark's comic touch has disappeared. Instead of a parody of the traditional image, we have an example of the image itself. There is no hint in Matthew that the kingdom, when it comes in its fullness, will be other than what the hearers expect.

The parable of the leaven is a companion piece to that of the mustard seed, both in Matthew and in Luke, though Luke has placed the two of them in an entirely different context. The collection of sayings in the Gnostic Gospel of Thomas, on the other hand, separates them widely, while Mark retains only the mustard seed, coupling it with another parable about a growing plant. Thus there were collections of Jesus' sayings that placed the two stories together, and other collections that did not. The principle by which they were kept together seems to have been the pairing of a man who took the seed and planted it in his field (Matt. 13:31, Luke 13:19), with a woman who took the leaven and hid it in three measures of meal (Matt. 13:33, Luke 13:21). The collector (the so called Q source) may have wished to express the idea that the kingdom of God realizes itself not apart from the common life of humanity, but in and through that life.

This common life was seen exemplified in a characteristic activity of a man planting a field, and then of a woman making a loaf of bread. There are hints of a similar man-woman division in the Q account of the coming of the Son of man: two men working in the field and two women grinding at the mill (Matt. 24:40f.).[3] One might also compare the twin Lukan parables of a shepherd seeking his lost sheep (Luke 15:1–7), and a housewife searching for her lost coin (Luke 15:8–10).

It appears that the stories of the mustard seed and the leaven, when placed together, were meant to express the same, or almost identical meaning. The first story accents a contrast between a tiny, almost imperceptible, beginning, and an impressive conclusion. The tree has become large enough to give shelter to the birds of the sky. The second story accents a contrast between leaven that is hidden and therefore works imperceptibly in three measures of meal, and its very obvious and visible later effects on the whole mass of dough. In the same way, the kingdom of heaven is at work in the world, even though its scope and its far-reaching effects are not yet apparent. Its working is beyond human perception and human control. Men and women go about their business from day to day, and before they know it the kingdom of heaven is upon them, whether for good or ill. Possibly Mark omitted this story from his very limited collection because his parable in 4:26–29 seemed to make the same point without departing from the imagery of seeds and plants.

The *Gospel of Thomas* separates the story of the leaven (Logion 96) from that of the mustard seed (Logion 20), linking it instead with another story centering on a woman:

> The kingdom of the [Father] is like a woman who was carrying a jar full of meal. While she was walking (on a) distant road, the handle of the jar broke (and) the meal spilled out behind her on the road. She did not know (it); she did not perceive the accident. After she came into her house, she put the jar down (and) found it empty. (Logion 97).

In one instance, a gain or benefit is first hidden and then finally perceived; in the other a loss is similarly hidden and then perceived. Implicit in many or most of Jesus' kingdom parables is the insistent question to the hearer, "Will it be gain or loss for you?" The next-to-last saying in the collection called the Gospel of Thomas reads almost like an application of the parable of the spilled jar of meal. "It does not come when one expects it. They will not say, Lo, here! or Lo, there! But the kingdom of the Father is spread out upon the earth, and humans do not see it" (Logion 113).

The parable of the leaven belongs to this same world of imagery. Though it lacks the comic element found in the earlier form of the story of the mustard seed, it achieves a comparable result by the use of ambiguity. Interpreters have frequently pointed out that leaven appears consistently in Scripture as an image for some kind of evil influence. Jesus warns his disciples against the leaven of the Pharisees, or the Sadducees, or of Herod (Mark 8:15; Matt. 16:11f.).

Paul twice quotes a proverbial expression remarkably similar to this parable—"A little leaven ferments the whole lump of dough" (1 Cor. 5:6, Gal. 5:9)—both times in the context of combatting false teaching and/or immoral practice in the churches. He contrasts the "old leaven, the leaven of malice and evil," with the "unleavened bread of sincerity and truth" (1 Cor. 5:8). In view of this it is striking that Jesus also employs leaven as one of his images for the kingdom of God. The effect of this is to shock the hearer, and to call into question his or her own moral stance with relation to the kingdom. If I hear God's kingdom presented to me as leaven, something my tradition has identified as an image for evil or corruption, what does that say about me? Why do I perceive as evil what I have always believed to be the supreme good? Do I doubt the validity of the presentation, or do I doubt myself? The ambiguity forces the hearer to break through old assumptions to view God's supreme good in a new way. God is doing a new thing in the world, quiet and unseen though it may now be.

The shock value of this little story is lost when we move from the first century to the twentieth. Interpretation has made it tame and commonplace by fostering the image of leaven as a benevolent influence slowly permeating a denomination or a social institution, or even the whole world. Despite its strangeness, the story has become one we can live with because it reinforces most of our assumptions about how change should take place—gradually, without trauma, and without cost. The story's original impact and purpose have been thwarted by overfamiliarity, by the long history of its interpretation, and by the very cultural "progress" it is said to describe!

The case is somewhat the same here as with the Lukan example story we call the parable of the good Samaritan (Luke 10:29–37). When we hear that story today, we do not think of the five hundred or so Samaritans who still practice their religion in Israel and on the West Bank, nor do we think of the intense hostility between Jew and Samaritan in Jesus' day. Instead of the story itself, we remember the title (which is never found in the text of Luke!) and use the noun *Samaritan* only in connection with the adjective *good.* When we want to compliment someone who does us a favor, we call him or her a *good Samaritan*—there is, apparently, no other kind! But as Crossan has pointed out, the conjunction of *good* with *Samaritan* was precisely the element of shock in the original telling of this story.[4] To achieve a comparable effect in, for example, present-day Israel, we might as easily speak of a *good* PLO terrorist! The adjective and the noun together were simply intolerable for many hearers.

The association of "kingdom of God" with "leaven" is a different kind of shock—not as intense or personal, perhaps, since we are dealing with a parable rather than an example story[5]—yet comparable nonetheless. Again the question presents itself, "Who was the first to experience the shock of such stories?" and again the intriguing possibility exists that it was Jesus. There is every likelihood that he, like his disciples after him, needed to learn not to be bound by his tradition or the symbolism inherent in it. God, who had revealed himself to Israel in all the imagery surrounding the law and the temple cult, was still Lord over both, and over the imagery as well. He was free, when necessary, to use old images in new and shocking ways—another example, perhaps, of Flannery O'Connor's "large and startling figures" for an almost-blind generation. The reason the parable of the leaven strikes us as so brief, bare, and perplexing is probably that Jesus passed it on to his disciples just as he received it, without elaboration or comment. He thus preserved the shock value it had for him, but in the course of time it has become for modern readers merely curious and abrupt.

Matthew's four parables of growth combine to make the point that the kingdom of heaven is breaking in upon the hearers, and that it will come in spite of many things: small and unnoticed beginnings, a mixed response to the message of its coming, acceptance by only a few, and the continuing presence of evil in God's world. There is nothing we can do to hasten or control the kingdom's coming; we cannot observe it and time its growth. It is God's kingdom, not ours. But we can take comfort in knowing that even now he is bringing it to realization, and that when this kingdom comes it will be worth all the waiting, all the frustration and disappointment, for the sake of those who accept its gifts and obey its demands.

On completing the sequence of four parables of growth, Matthew pauses to recapitulate (Matt. 13:34–35). The repeated expression, "another parable" (vss. 24, 31, 33) prepares for the summary statement: "Jesus spoke all these things to the crowds in parables, and he said nothing to them without a parable" (vs. 34). Matthew finds in this teaching method a fulfillment of Old Testament prophecy: "I will open my mouth in parables; I will utter things hidden since the creation" (vs. 35; cf. Ps. 78:2). The quotation and its fulfillment are linked by the phrase "in parables" in vs. 34 and again in vs. 35.

The other significant term in the quotation is "things hidden." By itself the quotation is noncommittal about these hidden things. The statement is neither that they will be revealed nor that they will remain hidden, only that they will be uttered. If "parables" and "things hidden" stand in parallelism to one another (as the poetry of the quotation suggests), the point is simply that Jesus' parabolic teaching fulfills this prophetic psalm. Jesus utters hidden things in parables with a two-fold result: for some hearers the hidden things are revealed, while for others the utterance of them merely reinforces their hiddenness. Matthew appends no general statement about private explanations for the disciples (in the manner of Mark 4:34b). Instead he provides an immediate example of such an explanation (Matt. 13:36–43) as Jesus leaves the crowds and identifies details of the parable of the weeds for his disciples in "the house" (vs. 36). For Matthew's readers, as we have seen, this becomes a partial clue to the understanding of all the preceding parables.

The last three stories in Matthew 13 are not parables of growth, though they continue to portray what the kingdom of heaven is like, and to set forth the same alternatives of good and evil implicit or explicit in the first four stories. The last of the three is supplied with an interpretation (Matt. 13:49f.) that closely matches the latter part of the interpretation of the parable of the weeds (i.e., the description of the last judgment), and is in fact introduced with the very same phrase ("so it will be at the consummation of the age," vss. 40b, 49). The other two (Matt. 13:44–46) form a pair in somewhat the same sense in which the stories of the mustard seed and the leaven are a pair. In the canonical Gospel tradition, the twin parables of the hidden treasure and the pearl occur only in Matthew. Versions of them appear in the noncanonical Gospel of Thomas, but separately. In addition to the common introductory formula, "The kingdom of heaven is like," two elements in the plot of these stories bind them together in Matthew: in each of them something is "found," and in each someone "sells all that he has" in order to "buy" it.

It is perhaps the similarity between the latter feature and Jesus' command to a rich man on one occasion (Mark 10:21 and parallels) that has prompted most modern interpreters to identify both the hidden treasure and the pearl with the kingdom of heaven. The kingdom is seen as the supreme good the hearer must acquire at all cost, without regard to the risk. The two parables are thus understood as parables of discipleship. This interpretation is reinforced by the opening words of the first story: "The kingdom of heaven is like a treasure hidden in a field" (Matt. 13:44). Yet the second story does not say that the kingdom is like a precious pearl, but that it is like "a merchant looking for good pearls" (Matt. 13:45). Once again it must be kept in mind that the kingdom is not necessarily represented by whatever detail happens to be mentioned first. The comparison is inherent in the story as a whole. But whose story is it? Who does the finding and what does he find?

Every other parable in the Matthean collection has to do with God bringing his kingdom to pass despite all appearances to the contrary. It is plausible, therefore, that the twin parables of the hidden treasure and the pearl also tell the story of how God finds us rather than how we find him. If God's kingdom is worth all the disappointments and the ambiguity for the sake of a few, is it worthwhile even for one? An interpretation along this line brings the two stories very close in their meaning to the three parables about lost things in Luke 15. A shepherd who leaves ninety-nine sheep to look for one that is missing, a housewife who sweeps her whole house to find a missing coin, a father who rejoices over the return of his lost son—all these tell the story of "joy before the angels of God over one sinner who repents" (Luke 15:7, 10). So too the man who unexpectedly discovers a treasure buried in his field sells his possessions and buys the field out of joy (Matt. 13:44).

Although the second parable does not explicitly mention joy, the pearl merchant (like the shepherd and the housewife in Luke 15) is seeking something (in this case "good pearls"), and his find far exceeds his expectations. The mention of good pearls recalls the good seed in the parable of the weeds (Matt. 13:37f.) and anticipates the good fish in the parable of the net (Matt. 13:48), two images used to represent God's people as the objects of his redemptive activity.

The difficulty in imagining God in the role of the man who gains the treasure or the merchant who acquires the beautiful pearl stems from the very human ways in which the main characters are described. The difficulty in imagining ourselves as a hidden treasure or a precious pearl is obvious! But these difficulties arise in part from the persistence of an allegorical outlook that, ostensibly at least, we have put behind us. The idea of God selling all that he has in order to gain a people is no more to be taken literally than the notion of his buying of the field as atonement or world redemption. The profit motive of both the pearl merchant and the buyer of the field, as well as the latter's outright deception about what the field contains, are no more models for a doctrine of God than for the behavior of a true disciple. Just as God is not in every respect like a wealthy shepherd or a thrifty housewife worried about financial losses, so he is not like a shrewd merchant or a crooked investor. The parables remain real-life stories, not coded messages. Still it is legitimate to ask what these stories are *about*. Are they more appropriately seen in relation to God's act or our response?

A comparison of the story of the pearl with several early Christian Gnostic texts is instructive. A version of it appears in the Gospel of Thomas 76. After telling the story in somewhat the same way as in Matthew, Jesus is represented as saying to his disciples, "You also must seek for the treasure that does not perish, that abides where no moth comes near to eat and (where) no worm destroys." Though the Gospel of Thomas has its own distinctive version of the parable of the treasure in Logion 109, it speaks of a treasure here as well in connection with the pearl. By the use of a saying similar to Matthew 6:19ff. or Luke 12:33, Thomas removes the apparent ambiguity of the canonical parable, and settles the matter in favor of what has become the traditional interpretation—that the parable has to do with human beings seeking God and his kingdom, rather than the opposite.

Thomas gives a similar slant to two other parables that are not ambiguous in the canonical Gospels, but that unquestionably refer to the activity of God: the parable of the net and the parable of the lost sheep. According to Logion 8,

> Man is like a wise fisherman who cast his net into the sea; he drew it out of the sea when it was full of little fishes. Among them the wise fisherman found a large, good fish. The wise fisherman cast all the little fishes down into the sea (and) chose the large fish without difficulty. He who has ears to hear, let him hear.

The implication is that the hearer should put aside all secondary matters in favor of the supreme good, whether expressed as knowledge or as the "kingdom of the Father." The contrast to Matthew's story of the net, as well as the similarity to the prevailing interpretation of the stories of the pearl and the hidden treasure, is striking. The same meaning seems to be intended in Logion 107: "The kingdom is like a shepherd who had a hundred sheep. One of them went astray; it was the largest. He left the ninety-nine (and) sought for the one until he found it. After he had exerted himself, he said to the sheep, I love you more than the ninety-nine." Formally the story is close to its canonical cousin. But the curious reference to the hundredth sheep being the "largest," and the concluding statement about loving it more than the rest, are clues that here again we are dealing with a choice human beings must make between secondary things and the highest good. In this respect the Gospel of Thomas has not moved away from biblical ethics or from Jesus' teaching about the high cost of discipleship. But it has moved a long way from the parables of the net and of the lost sheep as we know them in the Gospels. These tendencies make its interpretation of the parable of the pearl suspect.[6] It is possible, of course, that Thomas has used the latter as a model by which to transform the other two, but it is equally possible that all three have undergone a similar transformation at his hand.

Surprisingly, perhaps, a trace of the God-centered orientation of the parable of the pearl also survives in Christian Gnostic literature. Logion 48 of the Gospel of Philip is not a retelling of the story, but at most an allusion to it:

> When the pearl is cast down in the mud, it does not become dishonored the more, nor if it is anointed with balsam oil will it become more precious. But it has its worth in the eyes of its owner at all times. So with the sons of God wherever they may be. For they have the value in the eyes of their Father.

Here the pearl represents the people who belong to God. If the Matthean story of the pearl is understood in this way, the passage in Philip helps to explain why the pearl is described as precious. The few who say yes to Jesus' message of the kingdom are worth everything to God. Such a high view of repentant sinners is also made easier to understand by the Lukan parables of a shepherd who risks the safety of ninety-nine sheep for the sake of one stray that is very important to him, a woman who turns her house upside down to find one small coin, and a father who forgets the past and his dignity to run and embrace a returning, wayward son. Again and again Jesus tells the story of how God risks everything for the sake of those who respond to his love, no matter how many or how few, and of his boundless joy over even one sinner who repents.

The apocalypse of 4 Ezra provides another helpful parallel. In a vision, Ezra learns that things that are plentiful, such as iron, lead, or clay, are of less worth, but things that are rarer, such as gold, silver, or brass, are precious (4 Ezra 7:56ff). "So also shall be my promised judgment," God concludes.

> I will rejoice over the few that shall be saved, inasmuch as it is they who make my glory prevail now already and through them my name is now already named.
>   And I will not grieve over the multitude of them that perish, for it is they who now are made like vapor, counted as smoke, and are comparable to the flame. They are fired, burn hotly, and are extinguished! (4 Ezra 7:60f.).

The closest New Testament parallels are the Matthean application of the parable of the royal wedding ("Many are called, but few are chosen," Matt. 22:14) and the saying about the narrow door or gate that few will enter (Matt. 7:13f. and Luke 13:23f.). But the equating of what is precious with what is rare also illumines the parables about lost things in Luke 15, and the twin parables of the treasure and the pearl in Matthew. At least, they do when the latter two are understood as stories of God's reckless love for those who repent.

This interpretation is especially plausible in the Matthean context of the two stories, for it subsumes them under the familiar category of the theology of failure. The kingdom of heaven is worth all the obstacles that surround its coming—the small beginnings, the seemingly wasted efforts, the disappointments and ambiguities—even for the sake of a very few. It is worth it, in fact, for even one, as precious to God as an unexpected treasure, a priceless pearl, the hundredth sheep, or a beloved child. A man or woman who repents and believes the good news of the kingdom is worth everything to God, and for such a person God will risk everything. His love is indeed as reckless and impulsive as a person who sells all that he has to invest in a very special field or to acquire a very special pearl.

If such an interpretation is plausible for Matthew, does it also represent what *Jesus* would have heard in these stories? This raises once more the issue of audience identification. The question, "Where would Jesus find his point of identification in these stories?" is merely a particular instance of the question, "Where would anyone find his or her point of identification in them?" "With the seeker/finder who sold his possessions to gain a prize," is the answer that comes to mind. It is more natural to identify with a person than with an inanimate object, and perhaps easier to identify with the experience of finding than of being found. This helps to account for the prevailing interpretation of the two parables as stories of how human beings find the kingdom.

Yet a person may also be intended to identify with a certain character in a story in order to see things from God's perspective. This appears to be the case in the Lukan parables of the lost sheep and the lost coin. Hearers would be unlikely to identify first of all with a sheep or a coin; but on putting themselves in the place of the frantic and then joyful shepherd and housewife, they would learn "that's how it is in heaven. That is how God feels when a sinner repents!"

Such considerations make it difficult to decide the interpretation of the stories of the treasure and the pearl either way on the basis of audience identification. We have argued that the Matthean context tilts the scales toward what we have called the God-centered interpretation. But the two stories in themselves, whether taken separately or together, are open to either application: God finding sinners or sinners finding God.

A similar ambiguity is present when we try to establish Jesus'

own point of audience identification. Like anyone else, he presumably put himself in the role of the seeker/finder, but did these parables come to him as a challenge to seize the supreme good for his
own life (i.e., the kingdom or the will of God), or as a reminder of
the enormous value of each individual person to whom he was sent?
It is difficult to say. The answer depends on how large a place we
assign to a consciousness of mission in the mind of Jesus, and therefore perhaps on the period in Jesus' life when he first heard these
stories.

Jesus' own choice of God's kingdom over all others can be seen
in the account of the temptations, whereas John's Gospel shows him
probably near the end of his ministry, speaking of his disciples
as a gift or treasure "that the Father gave me" (cf. John 6:37, 39;
10:29, 17:6). There is in fact no reason why he may not have applied these parables to himself in both of these ways. The twin
images of the hidden treasure and the pearl provide an excellent
example of the ambiguity of metaphors. No single meaning can be
extracted from the metaphors and presented as the solution. Both
interpretations are relativized by the primal revelation, which is
the metaphor itself. Tracing the stories back to their first audience,
Jesus, does not remove the ambiguity, but reinforces it. The situation today is not that the traditional application to finding the kingdom needs to be set aside, but that the alternative application to God
and his reckless love for even one sinner deserves consideration alongside it.

The last parable in the Matthean collection, the parable of the net,
is accompanied by an interpretation similar to that of the parable of
the weeds (Matt. 13:49f.). Unlike the other two interpretations in the
chapter, this is unsolicited, and follows the parable without a break.
But like the others it comes far short of explaining what the story is
truly about, for this is not its intention. It is not even a very complete
scorecard by which to identify particular details in the story. For
example, the net itself has no precise equivalent in the interpretation.
The fisherman is anonymous in both the story and the interpretation.

Neither the shore to which the fish were brought nor the containers in which the good fish were stored, are identified. On the other hand, the angels who in the interpretation separate the evil from the righteous correspond merely to an impersonal "they" in the story itself (Matt. 13:48). The weeping and gnashing of teeth at the very end have no direct equivalent in the story. Virtually the whole interpretation, simply expands on the brief mention in verse 48 of the bad fish being thrown away.

Verses 49 and 50 are nothing more than a schedule of the events by which good people and bad are to be separated at the "end of the age," nor do they purport to be anything else. As far as the story is concerned, they are largely beside the point. One is therefore tempted to assign them to Matthew, whose interest in the sequence of end-time events is undeniable (Matt. 13:40–43, 24:29–42, 25:31–46). Yet if Jesus was influenced by the preaching of John the Baptist, there is no reason why he too may not have been fascinated enough with the details of final judgment for their own sake to introduce them even in connection with parables that did not wholly prepare for them. We should guard against a tendency to expect perfect consistency from Jesus when we expect it from no one else, or to make it a criterion of authenticity. The fact that something is beside the point in its immediate context has in itself nothing to do either with who said it or with its validity.

What then is the story of the net really about? Despite the change in subject matter, the previous stories provide clues. The parables of the treasure and the pearl have to do with radical or extreme measures taken in order to realize an all-consuming purpose. Two men liquidate their assets to possess an object of supreme value; one of them buys a whole field he does not particularly want in order to gain a treasure he has buried there. The parable of the net is also a parable about extreme measures, yet at the same time a parable of normalcy! These are two things we do not expect to go together, but Jesus is saying to his disciples, "Look, there are examples even in everyday life of going to extremes to gain some desired end. You do it every time you fish.

You fill your nets with fish indiscriminately. You don't worry about which ones you can use and which ones you can't. You bring them all to shore. Only when they are safe on shore do you separate the good from the bad."

So it is with the kingdom of heaven. God's forgiving love knows no restraints or limits; it seems to embrace good and bad indiscriminately. Not all will respond to it. Subsequent events right up to the judgment itself will distinguish between those who do and those who do not. But for the present, the net is spread as wide as the sea, as Jesus invites good and bad alike to the kingdom of heaven.

The closest similarities to the parable of the net occur in kindred stories about banquets in Matthew 22:1–14 and Luke 14:15–24. After unsuccessful efforts to persuade the invited guests to come, the host resolves to fill the banquet hall at any cost. In one account he sends for the poor and blind and lame and is told "still there is room." Then he tells his servant, "Go out to the highways and hedges, and compel people to come in, that my house may be filled" (Luke 14:21–33). The host in the other story (a king giving his son a wedding feast) sends out his servants with similar instructions. They "went out into the streets and gathered all whom they found, both bad and good; so the wedding hall was filled with guests" (Matt. 22:9–10RSV).

In these parables the extreme measures are not normal procedure, as in the parable of the net, but striking examples of socially eccentric behavior. The question of how Jesus himself would have heard the story of the net is best answered by a closer look at these two other parables in their own contexts.[7]

Of immediate interest, however, is the fact that Matthew is not content to end his parable of the wedding feast on the note of unqualified universality. He balances the indiscriminate acceptance of bad and good strangers into the banquet hall with a brief appendix about a guest without a wedding garment (Matt. 22:11–14). He is as conscious here as in chapter 13 of the need to sort out the recipients of grace on the basis of their moral conduct. He ends with a saying that in some respects could summarize his chapter of parables as well:

"Many are called, but few are chosen" (Matt. 22:14). The tension between God's reckless, indiscriminate love on the one hand, and his demand for repentance and the bearing of fruit on the other is not, however, something Matthew has created. It permeates the Gospel tradition back to Jesus, and back before him to John the Baptist.

LUKE 8

Luke's equivalent of the Markan-Matthean chapter of parables requires little comment because it is not a collection of parables at all. Luke 8 contains only one parable, that of the sower. It is told not while standing in a boat offshore in the sea of Galilee, but in the course of a Galilean journey, prior to the decisive journey to Jerusalem that begins at Luke 9:51. Jesus is traveling from one city and village to another, proclaiming the good news of the kingdom of God (Luke 8:1,4). When Jesus tells the story, his disciples ask only what that particular story means, not about parables in general (Luke 8:9). Though he mentions parables in his answer, there is no hint that he told more parables on this occasion. He grants their request by interpreting the parable of the sower, but without implying that this is a key to a whole genre.

Roughly, the Lukan material (Luke 8:4–18) parallels Mark 4: 1–20, omitting Mark's latter two parables (Mark 4:26–32) and summary (Mark 4:33f.). There is no reason to think that Luke's point differs substantially from that of Mark's first twenty verses. Both passages are essentially exhortations to "hear" (Luke 8:8,12,14,15, 18). The difference is that in Luke the two parables of the kingdom that specifically must be heard (Mark 4:26–29,30–32) are missing! Whereas in Mark the command to hear is preliminary to these two key stories, in Luke it stands on its own. The command is, however, brought to full force by the addition of an incident (found one chapter earlier in Mark and Matthew) in which Jesus' mother and brothers try to see him (Luke 8:19–21). In response to their effort, Jesus says, "Those who hear the word of God and do it are my mother and my brothers" (Luke 8:21). What must be heard is not a particular set of parables, but the "word of God" in general, just as in the parable of the sower (8:11) and frequently in Luke-Acts (Luke 5:1, 11:28, Acts 4:31, 6:2,7, 8:14, 11:1, 12:24, 13:5,7,44,46,48; 16:32, 17:13, 18:11). If the Lukan parable of the sower is leading up to anything, it is leading up to the statement that Jesus' true family ties are with those who "hear the word of God and do it" (Luke 8:21). These sentiments are important enough for Luke to repeat three chapters later. When an unidentified woman calls out to Jesus, "Blessed is the mother who gave you birth and nursed you," he replies "Blessed rather are those who hear the word of God and obey it" (Luke 11:27f.).

Luke's purpose is not to pass judgment either way on the faith or obedience of Jesus' earthly family (his mother's faith was a matter of record, Luke 1:38,45–55) but to use natural kinship as a foil for the new priority of hearing the word of God and the new community built around that word. The fixity of the term "word of God" or "word of the Lord" in Luke-Acts suggests that it means much the same as what the author of the Epistle to the Hebrews calls the "salvation, which was first announced by the Lord" and "was confirmed to us by those who heard him" (Heb. 2:3). This good news of salvation is what renders even the natural ties of family obsolete (Luke 20:34f.). Unlike Mark 4 and Matthew 13, Luke 8 provides neither a collection of parables nor a theology of the kingdom, but simply a call to recognize the supreme importance of hearing the "good news of the kingdom of God" that Jesus was bringing to the towns of Galilee (Luke 8:1).

7.

THE PARABLES
AND THE PASSION

When taken together, the parables of Jesus define the kingdom he proclaimed. Though the metaphor of the kingdom of God was rooted in the prophetic and apocalyptic traditions of Israel as mediated to Jesus through John the Baptist, it had to find its decisive realization in Jesus' own religious experience. His mission was to tell a story he had heard—or seen—from God, a story of conflict between two kingdoms or two households, one belonging to a strong man, and another to someone even stronger. Jesus knew that the strong man was Beelzebub or Satan, the ruler of the demons, and that the stronger one was God. He knew the ending: the stronger one would win, in fact had won. But if he knew how this would take place, he was not telling.

The story as we find it in the Gospels is incomplete. Like the revelations of the past mentioned in the Epistle to the Hebrews, it is told "in many parts and in many ways" (Heb. 1:1). The one metaphor fragments into many: the story of a kingdom or a household can also be the story of a growing plant, or of a farmer raising a crop, a woman baking bread, an investor looking for a good deal, or a fisher trying to make a living. Every story is different, the images are used in different ways, yet the hearer gets the impression that they are somehow all the same story.

Beyond telling what "the kingdom of God is like," what do they

have in common?" In one way or another, they all embody an element
of conflict or ambiguity, or explore the alternatives of good and evil.
They give varied expression to the clash between the two kingdoms
or households. Yet they are comedies and not tragedies; their endings
are happy. God realizes his kingdom despite the conflict and ambiguities, despite temporary setbacks, delays, and apparently wasted
efforts. His love knows no shame, and his ingenuity in reaching his
goals knows no bounds. The endings of the stories are inevitable, yet
always a surprise. The kingdom comes, yet not in the way we expect
it. Most of the parables exemplify what Tolkien calls *eucatastrophe*—
the unexpected happy ending.[1]

But we still have an unanswered question: "Why are the parables
not related more explicitly to the death and resurrection of Jesus?"
The crucifixion of the king is a totally unexpected way of realizing the
kingdom, and when the cross and resurrection are viewed together we
have a perfect example of eucatastrophe. Surely the passion is the
most appropriate occasion in the whole Gospel tradition for a theology of failure! Yet the parables (at least the ones considered so far)
are in no sense miniature passion stories.

If the church wrote them, or rewrote them, after Jesus' death and
resurrection, it is hard to understand why these redemptive events
have not been made explicit. The absence of this kind of theologizing
suggests that the parables of the kingdom originated before Jesus'
death, and that whatever recasting of them has been done after the
fact has been very minor. The few possibly secondary features have
to do with establishing a firm sequence of events surrounding the last
judgment, not with reflecting on the meaning of Jesus' death.

This does not say that none of Jesus' parables point to his death
and resurrection. At least one story the Gospel writers have placed
near the end of Jesus' ministry has been frequently thought to contain
an allusion to his death. It is the parable of the wicked tenants (Mark
12:1–12 and parallels), in which an absentee landlord fails to collect
what his tenant farmers owe him even after sending a number of his
servants as collectors. The servants are mistreated, and finally he

resolves to send his son (a "beloved son" according to Mark) in the hope that the heir of the estate will at least have their respect. Instead they kill the son, hoping to gain the whole estate for themselves. In all the Synoptic Gospels, this story comes *after* Jesus has predicted his passion three times.

There is little doubt that the Gospel writers understood it as a kind of passion story in miniature. But does this mean that it was first told for this purpose, and that the Gospel writers created it? These questions cannot be answered apart from the broader question of whether or not Jesus anticipated his own death. If he did, there is no reason why he might not as easily have reflected on it in story form as in direct predictive assertions. If any part of the story goes back to Jesus, our method demands that we ask our standard questions: "How would Jesus himself have heard the story? With whom in the story would he find his point of self-identification?"

The hint dropped earlier in the Gospel accounts of his baptism suggests that he might indeed have identified himself with the beloved son. Again it must be stated that this is not to turn Jesus into a maker of allegories. It cannot be argued that he identified himself *only* with the son in the story world of his parables. But if he identified himself with servants, or a sower, a fisherman, a pearl merchant, or a housewife, why not also with a son? And once he enters into the world of that particular image—the world of the household, and in this case also of farming, crops, and money—to what conclusions about himself will the imagery lead him? Perhaps to a confirmation of the voice he once heard at his baptism? Or was this the very world of imagery that first provided a context for that voice? In either case, the logic of the story sooner or later points toward a violent and shocking denouement: the son must die!

The same logic is inherent in the brief parable (not identified as such) about fasting at a wedding celebration (Mark 2:18–20). Unlike the story of the wicked tenants, it comes early in the Gospel accounts, before any predictions of the passion. The first part of the story is a typical illustration of normalcy: guests at a wedding rejoice; they do not fast or mourn. But then comes a startling departure from the norm: the bridegroom is "taken away"—by sudden death, apparently, not by a normal end to the festivities, and clearly not to his honeymoon!

This second stage of the parable is widely believed to reflect the church's later awareness of Jesus' death. It may do just that, and yet there is nothing in the logic of the story that excludes the possibility of a sudden tragic turn of events. There is just such a turn of events in the late Jewish story of a wedding celebration found, significantly, among the apocalyptic visions of 4 Ezra. The vision is of a woman in mourning for her dead son (4 Ezra 9:38ff.). She tells the seer of his birth after thirty years of waiting (vss. 43–46), of the wedding celebration she prepared for him when he was grown, and of his sudden death on his wedding day (4 Ezra 9:47—10:1). She consequently resolves "to mourn and fast till I die" (4 Ezra 10:4). Her story is interpreted later as the story of Zion (4 Ezra 10:44ff.), and the death of her son as "the fall of Jerusalem that has now come to pass" (4 Ezra 10:48).

The similarities between the two narratives suggests that there is nothing necessarily contrived or artificial about the ending of the Markan parable. A story of this kind is capable of widely divergent applications. There is no reason why Jesus may not at some point have heard the story in much the same way that the author of 4 Ezra did: i.e., as an intimation of Jerusalem's impending doom, and, in 4 Ezra, a doom already accomplished. In this case, the first part of the story becomes simply a foil for the implicit prediction to follow. This perception would not have prevented Jesus, at another point in his career, from identifying himself with the stricken bridegroom in the story. The emphasis on mourning and on the bridegroom's absence is difficult to explain otherwise, if the story's ending is purely a creation of the church after Jesus' death. Where precisely in that case is the joy of the resurrection, and the sense of Jesus' presence in the eucharistic meals of the ancient church? The prospect of being "taken away," and of the mourning and fasting to follow, is more naturally understood as an individual's vision of his own impending death.

While it is true that in 4 Ezra we have a later community looking back on the destruction of Jerusalem, there are few apparent similarities between the way second-century Jews viewed Jerusalem's fall and the way first-century Christians viewed the death of Jesus! Jesus' ministry is a more plausible life setting not only for the first part of the parable in Mark 2:18–20 ("the time for celebration is here!"), but for the last part as well ("the time for mourning will be here soon").

The parables of growth are susceptible to a passion interpretation. They may not be so understood in the programmatic Markan-Matthean collection, but they are in the fourth Gospel, in which Jesus' identification is with the growing plant itself, not with the farmer who plants and harvests it. This self-identification is most explicit in John 15:1,5: "I am the true vine, and my Father is the vineyard keeper . . . I am the vine, you are the branches." In this passage the image is applied to Jesus' corporate existence in and through his disciples, and not to his passion. There is no allusion to Jesus' redemptive death until John 15:13f., *after* the imagery of the vine has been put aside. The vine is never cut down; only its fruitless branches are taken away to be burned (John 15:2,6). It can be argued that the eucharistic overtones of the vine imagery presuppose the cross, and that the notion of dwelling corporately in Jesus presupposes his resurrection. Such theological implications, however, belong to the larger context the Evangelist has given to the imagery, not to the imagery itself.

It is different in John 12:24, the one other Johannine parable of growth: "Truly, truly, I say to you, unless the seed of grain falls to the earth and dies, it remains alone, but if it dies, it bears much fruit." The saying's closest kinship is with Paul's comment in the course of his argument for resurrection: "You fool! The seed you sow does not germinate unless it dies, and what you sow is not the full-grown plant, but only a seed, whether of grain or of something else" (1 Cor. 15:36f.). The principle is that even in nature, radical transformations take place and, specifically, that life comes through death.

The Johannine context suggests that the "seed of grain" represents, first Jesus, the Son of man who is to be glorified (John 12:23) and, derivatively, the disciple who "hates his life in this world" and follows Jesus even to death (John 12:25f.). In either case, the principle of life through death comes to clear expression. But the brief metaphor in John 12:24 has its sequel in vs. 32. The symmetry of these two statements is seen when they are placed together:

(a) "Truly, truly I say to you, unless the seed of grain falls *to the earth* and dies, it remains alone; but if it dies, it bears much fruit . . . (vs. 24).

(b) And I, if I am lifted up *from the earth,* will draw everyone to myself" (vs. 32).

The key to the symmetry is the contrast between *to the earth* in the first stanza and *from the earth* in the second. The contrast is accentuated by a certain similarity of form between the two stanzas. Both are built around "if" clauses. The first begins with a negative "if" (i.e., "unless") clause of a kind found three times before at crucial junctures in the fourth Gospel with the same "Truly, truly, I say to you" formula that occurs here:

"Truly, truly, I say to you, *unless* a person is born from above he cannot see the kingdom of God" (John 3:3)
"Truly, truly, I say to you, *unless* a person is born of water and Spirit, he cannot enter the kingdom of God" (John 3:5)
"Truly, truly, I say to you, *unless* you eat the flesh of the Son of man and drink his blood, you do not have life in yourselves" (John 6:53).

In addition to the formal similarities, all of these sayings involve metaphors. Salvation is characterized in terms of birth, eating and drinking, and the germination of a seed. In John 12:24 there is a double metaphor. Salvation is compared to the germination of a seed, which in turn is likened to dying in such a way as to suggest human death. The Evangelist reinforces these overtones with the sayings he appends to the metaphor in verses 25 and 26. The negative "if" clause in John 12:24 also differs from John's previous ones in that it is immediately followed by an equivalent positive "if" clause. In chapter

3 there was no explicit statement that "if" someone was reborn, he or she would enter the kingdom. Chapter 6, contains just such an equivalent positive statement (John 6:54), but it is not in the conditional form. In chapter 12, the positive conclusion is explicit, and the conditional form is retained: "but if it dies, it bears much fruit" (John 12:24b).

This positive conditional form is carried over into the second stanza: "And I, *if* I am lifted up from the earth, will draw everyone to myself." This stanza not only completes the parable of growth, it at the same time interprets it. The plant that begins as a seed of grain is now, by the emphatic "I," explicitly identified with Jesus. The fruit-bearing is defined as drawing everyone to himself. The image of the seed falling *to* the earth comes to completion in the image of the growing plant rising *from* the earth. A basic Synoptic-like parable of growth has become a vehicle for proclaiming the death and resurrection of Jesus! The drawing of everyone to himself is then most naturally understood in relation to the future general resurrection and judgment.

But the question still remains whether this interpretation goes back to Jesus' own self-identification with the growing plant in the story, or whether it is an after-the-fact creation of the church. In any case, it is not the creation of the Evangelist. John's Gospel has separated the two stanzas so as to downplay the fact that they originally went together. The kinship of the first stanza with the Synoptic parables of growth is still readily apparent, but the second has been put to a different purpose. John intends his readers to recall the earlier statement in 3:14f.: "And just as Moses lifted up the serpent in the desert, so must the Son of man be lifted up, so that everyone who believes in him may have eternal life." The biblical allusion is to Numbers 21:8f., which becomes a sign of the crucifixion. Jesus, like the serpent, is lifted up so that those who look to him in faith can be saved.

The connection in John's mind between John 3:14f. and 12:32 is so close that when the crowd in John 12:34 challenges Jesus' statement, the people sound as if they are quoting John 3:14: "How can you say that the Son of man must be lifted up?" Neither the term "Son of man" nor the emphasis on necessity ("*must* be lifted up") are part of the pronouncement in John 12:32; they come from John 3:14. To the Evangelist, *lifting up* means crucifixion, not resurrection. He says as much in verse 33: the statement signifies the kind of death Jesus will die (cf. John 18:32, 21:19).

Commentators have inferred that the drawing of everyone to Jesus refers to the church's mission to the Gentiles, made possible by Jesus' death. This serves as an appropriate answer to the request of the Greeks, with which the narrative began (John 12:20f.). It also corresponds rather well to the bearing of much fruit mentioned in John 12:24. The Evangelist's interpretation, in fact, assigns to verse 32 much the same significance as verse 24: the Gentile mission cannot take place until the Son of man is "glorified" (vs. 23) or *lifted up* on the cross. Verses 24f. make it clear that he (and, derivatively, his true followers) must die, while verse 32 specifies *how* he will die.

The parabolic understanding outlined above is more sequential. The first stanza asserts that a seed (i.e., Jesus) must die in order to live and bear fruit; the second stanza specifies not how it dies (by falling to the earth, vs. 24), but rather how it *lives* and bears its fruit. It is lifted up from the earth. This interpretation is also more eschatological, for a lifting up that is *subsequent* to death is nothing other than resurrection. The term "lifted up" comes not from the terminology of plant growth but from that of exaltation or resurrection (cf. Acts 2:33, 5:31). But the Evangelist cannot resist the opportunity to point out again (cf. John 3:14, 8:28, 18:32) the appropriateness of this term to the gruesome manner of Jesus' death. The two-stanza parable in John 12:24, 32 is thus older than the fourth Gospel, having undergone significant modification at the Evangelist's hand.

Moreover, echoes of the Synoptic context of the parable of the sower may be detected in the Johannine context. The quotation from Isaiah 6:9f., familiar to the reader of the Synoptics from Matthew 13:14f., appears prominently in John 12:39f. as part of the Evangelist's verdict on Jesus' public ministry: "He has blinded their eyes and hardened their heart, lest they see with their eyes and understand with their heart, and turn, and I heal them." There are even hints of the several classes of response to Jesus' message found in the Synoptic interpretation of the parable of the sower: those who could not believe (John 12:39), those who believed in Jesus but did not confess him (John 12:42), and those who believed and came out of their darkness (John 12:44ff.). Jeremias' argument that the so-called Markan hardening theory should be applied to Jesus' teaching as a whole rather than to the parables in particular[2] thus unexpectedly finds a degree of support in the Gospel of John.

The Johannine evidence suggests that at some point between its original telling and its use in the fourth Gospel, a parable of growth similar to Mark 4:1–9 or 4:26–29 came to be applied to the death and resurrection of him who first told it. Some scholars will continue routinely to assign any such interpretation to the post-resurrection church. Nevertheless, all that we have come to know of Jesus' own sense of the grotesque and his penchant for large and startling figures suggests that he was himself fully capable of making this application.

The same goes for the image of the snake on the pole mentioned in John 3:14. It is plausible that the Gospel writers arranged and rearranged the primal images and their major applications, but not so plausible that they created them. Jesus himself, above all others in the New Testament, is the image-maker and storyteller. He tells his stories and shapes his images in the light of his own peculiar vision. If the church after his death and resurrection applied his "large and startling figures" to those two redemptive events, it could only have done so by a vision that was a continuation and extension of his own.

At any rate, the Synoptic collection of kingdom parables found in Mark 4 and 13 does not yet know of any explicit connection between the parables and the passion. The opposition is there, the failure and the mixed response are there, the hope is there, but the end of the stories remains to be told. Before it can be told, Jesus must be seen as more than a storyteller, more than a man of words. The stories he told have as their unspoken center *the story that he lived.* The ending of this story is what resolves all the others. "The Son of man has come not to be served, but to serve, and to give his life a ransom for many" (Mark 10:45). Between the image of the seed and the reality of the cross there is the ministry of Jesus, the healer and servant of the poor, the sick, and the oppressed.

JESUS AND THE
UNCLEAN SPIRITS

The good works attributed to Jesus in the Gospel tradition can be divided into four main types: exorcism of the demon-possessed, healing of the sick, forgiveness of sinners, and symbolic actions. The first three are specific acts of helping people, whether spiritually or physically. They may be called acts of salvation, or of liberation—setting people free from what enslaves them. The fourth type includes all actions of Jesus that represent symbolically this same liberating activity—eating with sinners; providing bread for the hungry, wine for celebration, or a great catch of fish; and even walking on water to rejoin his frightened disciples.

It is important to observe that we have established no separate category called "miracle." When we discuss Jesus' miracles as a distinct aspect of his ministry—especially when we speak of the *problem* of his miracles—we are dealing with a category of our own creation. The fact that they may be a problem for some, and therefore in an identifiable class by themselves, tells us nothing of how they were viewed by Jesus or the Gospel writers. And the fact that Jesus and the Gospel writers viewed them as exceptional or miraculous does not necessarily mean that they regarded this quality as the most conspicuous or important feature of these deeds.

It is arguable that the importance of some of the miracles lay in the specific good they accomplished, whereas the importance of others was in what they represented or symbolized. By the same token, even Jesus' non-miraculous acts often had the effect of setting people free from what bound them (e.g., calling disciples to follow him), or of representing truth in symbolic form (e.g., washing the disciples' feet). In short, Jesus' acts are not defined by whether or not they are miraculous, but by their purposes and what they accomplished. Some of his miracles fall under the heading of exorcism or healing. Some can be classified as symbolic acts. A few combine elements of both, or are hard to classify. Even though "miracle stories" are a category long familiar to the form critic and the student of comparative literature, they do not require special treatment as a distinct class of phenomena in the Gospels.

Wherever one looks in the Gospel tradition, the fact stands out that both Jesus and his contemporaries saw him as an exorcist and healer. When messengers from the imprisoned John the Baptist challenged Jesus about his identity, he replied by pointing to his deeds: "Blind people receive their sight, lame people walk, lepers are made clean, deaf people hear, dead are raised, and poor people receive good news" (Matt. 11:5; Luke 7:22). The account in Luke of the opening of the Galilean ministry in the synagogue at Nazareth seems to pick up where the answer to John the Baptist leaves off: "He has anointed me to preach good news to the poor. He has sent me to proclaim release to the captives and recovering of sight to the blind, to set at liberty those who are oppressed, to proclaim the acceptable year of the Lord" (Luke 4:18f.RSV). In these verses the concept of healing has been widened to include the forgiveness of sins and the liberation of the oppressed—all that was represented in the Old Testament by the traditional year of the jubilee (Lev. 25:8ff.). But Jesus' words are still heard in the context of healing. He anticipates that his hearers will say to him, "Physician, heal yourself," and challenge him to do what he had done in Capernaum—presumably heal the sick (Luke 4:23).

Both of these references to the works of Jesus draw on the Old Testament. The passage in reply to John alludes indirectly to Isaiah

29:18, 35:5f., and 61:1. At Nazareth Jesus quotes Isaiah 61:1f. directly. In part, his ministry of healing is seen as a fulfillment of prophecy: the blind will see, the deaf will hear, and the lame will walk. Such things are marks of the messianic age foretold by Isaiah. In another passage, Matthew summarizes Jesus' cures and exorcisms as the fulfillment of what Isaiah had said about the servant of the Lord: "He bore our infirmities; he endured our sufferings" (Matt. 8:17; cf. Isa. 53:4). But the correlation between Jesus' healing ministry and Jewish messianic expectations is a very general one at best. Though biblical precedent could be cited for the cleansing of lepers (2 Kings 5), there is no indication that this was expected to happen as part of the messianic age. Resurrection of the dead was, of course, a familiar hope in some circles, but not in the way in which Jesus speaks of it in his reply to John's messengers—as simply one kind of healing among many. Again, there are precedents for raising someone from the dead only to die again (1 Kings 17:7–24; 2 Kings 4:32–37, 13:21), but it is not part of the messianic hope.

The other major aspect of Jesus' healing ministry that has no obvious basis in the Old Testament is the exorcism of those who were demon-possessed. It is true that later Judaism read back into the lives of its biblical heroes the power to drive out demons. Solomon is a conspicuous example.[1] But the New Testament makes no attempt to find in the Old Testament either prophecy or precedent for Jesus' exorcisms. Only by being lumped together with his healings as an example of how he "bore our sufferings" (Matt. 8:17) are they seen foreshadowed in the Scripture. They are not directly mentioned in either the summary of Jesus' activities in Matthew 11:5 and Luke 7:22 or the Lukan summary of the Nazareth confrontation.

Luke prefaces the answer to John the Baptist with a notice that Jesus had just "healed many people of their diseases, afflictions, and evil spirits, and had given sight to many who were blind" (Luke 7:21). Matthew anticipates the summary with an earlier one given when Jesus sent out the disciples on their first preaching tour: "Heal the sick, raise the dead, cleanse lepers, drive out demons" (Matt. 10:8).

When challenged by the Pharisees, Jesus appeals to his exorcisms as evidence of the kingdom's presence (Matt. 12:28f.) in much the same way that he had appealed to his other healings when responding to John in prison. In Luke, as he heads toward Jerusalem, Jesus sends word to Herod: "Today and tomorrow, I drive out demons and perform healings, and on the third day I reach my goal" (Luke 13:32). Here Jesus' life up to his passion is wrapped up in the twin activities of exorcism and healing. Even after the resurrection, when Peter preaches to Cornelius at Caesarea, he tells how Jesus "went around doing good works and healing all who were enslaved by the devil, because God was with him" (Acts 10:38).

Exorcism is clearly an integral and essential part of Jesus' ministry. References to demon-possession and exorcism are embedded in every stratum of the Gospel tradition—Mark, the Q source, the distinctive material in Matthew and Luke, and the Gospel of John. But the main source of descriptions of the actual occurrence of exorcisms is the Gospel of Mark. The Markan evidence consists of four incidents (Mark 1:23–28, 5:1–20, 7:24–30, 9:14–29) and a number of summary statements that include among Jesus' characteristic acts the driving out of demons (Mark 1:32–34,39, 3:7–12).

THE DEMONIAC IN THE SYNAGOGUE

In Mark Jesus' first miracle after the call of his first disciples is an exorcism. As soon as he enters Capernaum on a Sabbath, he goes to the synagogue and begins to teach (Mark 1:21). His teaching caused wonder among the people, Mark says, because he was teaching them as one having authority, and not as the scribes (Mark 1:22). In Matthew this impressive statement becomes the conclusion and response to the Sermon on the Mount (Matt. 7:28–29), but in Mark it is included with the first, programmatic example of Jesus' power over the demonic world. After Jesus heals the demoniac in the synagogue, the people give voice to their wonder: "What is this? A new teaching with authority! He commands even the unclean spirits, and they obey him" (Mark 1:27). For Mark, the exorcism underlines this point about Jesus' teaching authority, a point Matthew makes in a very different context and without reference to demons at all. The story in Mark is not told for its own sake or to satisfy curiosity about the phenomenon of demon possession, but to say something about Jesus and his authority.

Mark narrates the incident with classic brevity and simplicity. Five basic elements stand out: the situation (a demon-possessed man appears in the synagogue); the demon's challenge to Jesus; the rebuke and exorcism; the departure of the unclean spirit; and the response of the onlookers. The demoniac is described as "a man in an unclean spirit," an expression that occurs only in Mark (here and in 5:2). The other Synoptists change it in both cases. The only parallel to this passage refers somewhat elaborately to "a man having a spirit of an unclean demon" (Luke 4:33RSV). The parallels to Mark 5:2 mention "a certain man . . . having demons" (Luke 8:27), or "two [!] demoniacs" (Matt. 8:28). The phrase, "a man in an unclean spirit," is strikingly reminiscent of Paul's strange reference to himself in 2 Corinthians 12:2 as "a man in Christ." The latter passage refers not simply to the continuing "in Christ" relationship of which Paul speaks frequently, but to an exceptional prophetic or ecstatic experience of being totally possessed by the risen Lord so as to see visions and hear supernatural words of revelation.

In somewhat parallel fashion the demoniac in Mark 1:23 is also "inspired." He knows something about Jesus, and speaks what he knows "in a spirit." The difference is that the spirit by which he speaks is unclean. He is in fact the precise opposite counterpart to the inspired Christian prophet. The words recorded in Mark 1:24, "What have we to do with you, Jesus you Nazarene? Have you come to destroy us?," are not the words of a man but of "a man in an unclean spirit." The use of the plural "we," or "us" makes it clear that the demon is indeed the real speaker. It is important, however, not to read the situation of Mark 5:1–20 back into this account. The plural does not indicate that the man is possessed by more than one demon (as in Mark 5:9). It indicates only that the demon speaks as one of a class of beings sharing a similar attitude toward Jesus and common fears of destruction at his hands. The demon also addresses Jesus with a singular verb, *"I* know who you are . . ."* and is in turn addressed in the singular (Mark 1:25).

It is the demon, and not Jesus, who initiates the confrontation. His opposition to Jesus, even as he utters a kind of confession, is seen in the contrast between the words "unclean" (he is an *unclean* spirit, vs. 23) and "holy" (Jesus is "the Holy One of God," vs. 24), as well as in the formula "What have we to do with you?" His recognition of Jesus as "the Holy One of God" is not equivalent to the Christian confession, "Jesus is Lord," which according to Paul can be uttered only at the impulse of God's Holy Spirit (1 Cor. 12:3). If it were, Mark's narrative would stand in contradiction to the Pauline principle.

Yet the similarities are unmistakable. It appears that Jesus' silencing of the demons has something to do with the fact that for them to acknowledge him as God's unique messenger seems inappropriate, whether to Jesus or the Gospel writer, or both. But instead of suppressing the fact that such things took place, Mark has faithfully recorded the tradition, while being careful to append to it Jesus' commands not to speak.

This explanation fits the formal insistence on secrecy mentioned in Mark 1:34 and 3:12, though too much should not be read into Jesus' simple command to the demon in Mark 1:25 to "shut up." The latter is preliminary to the key phrase of exorcism that follows, "Come out of him." The silencing of the demon is reminiscent of Jesus' rebuke to the storm in Mark 4:39, and is merely Jesus' way of commanding the demon to cease his outcry and relinquish his victim. And at Jesus' word the demon does just that. With one last shudder and cry he disappears. The reader learns nothing of his fate or the fate of his former victim. The conclusion of the narrative focuses rather on the amazement of the witnesses and the spread of Jesus' fame throughout that part of Galilee (Mark 1:27–28).

The parallel between this first Markan exorcism and the stilling of the storm is not accidental. A more extensive comparison between Mark 1:23–28 and 4:35–41 shows a cluster of similarities.

1:25	4:39
"And Jesus sternly commanded him, saying 'Be quiet and come out of him' "	"And he got up and sternly commanded the wind and said to the lake, 'Be still. Keep quiet' "

1:27	4:41
" 'What is this? A new teaching with authority. He even gives orders to the unclean spirits and they obey him' "	" 'Who then is this, that even the wind and the lake obey him?"

Clearly Jesus addresses the storm in much the same language with which he had earlier addressed the unclean spirit. And the chorus-like response of the onlookers to the miracle is remarkably similar in the two incidents. Though the text never quite makes it explicit, the stilling of the storm functions in its own way as an exorcism. The wind is a kind of demon, and the lake is possessed. Jesus' authority over the spirits extends also to chaotic natural elements, and they obey him. Once again Jesus "binds the strong man" and releases his captives.

This reminder of the first exorcism serves as an appropriate preface to the second, which follows immediately in Mark 5:1–20.

THE GERASENE DEMONIAC

The longest and most remarkable account of an exorcism in the New Testament takes place in the region of Gerasa, across the sea of Galilee from Capernaum and its synagogue. This is the nearest thing we have in the New Testament to a case history of demon-possession and its cure. The same five elements are present here as in the simpler story of exorcism in the synagogue: the situation is sketched, this time in considerable detail (Mark 5:1–5). The "man in an unclean spirit" challenges Jesus in much the same way as before (vss. 6–7). Jesus commands the unclean spirits to depart (vss. 8–12). And they finally do so (vs. 13), but only after an exchange unparalleled in any other Gospel incident. Finally, the reaction of those affected by the miracle is described (vss. 14–20).

Mark has preserved this order of narration even while offering at the same time a clue that the actual sequence of events may have been different. Mark 5:8 appears to be an explanatory insertion moderating the abruptness of verse 7. Running to Jesus and falling prostrate before him, the man shouts, "What have I to do with you, Jesus, son of the Most High God? I implore you in God's name, do not torment me!" (vs. 7). Verse 8 is a kind of flashback, explaining that Jesus had earlier said to him "Come out of the man, you unclean spirit." Whether Jesus said this before the demoniac fell at his feet or at the moment he did so is uncertain. In any event the initiative in this case (unlike that in Mark 1:23ff.) lies with Jesus. He is the first to speak. Verses 9 and 10 seem to resume the main thread of the narrative. Jesus asks, "What is your name?" and receives the reply, "My name is Legion, for we are many." Then the demons plead with Jesus "not to send them out of that region."

It is perhaps significant that Matthew 8:28–34 lacks any parallel to Mark 5:8–10. We know that Mark is capable of working backward from an incident or saying in order to describe parenthetically the circumstances that led up to it. He has done this, for example, in Mark 6:17–29, in which a series of explanatory statements introduced by "for" (Mark 6:17,18,20) supplies the background to Herod's references to John the Baptist in Mark 6:14,16. Mark introduces 5:8–10 in much the same way, as if these verses were also intended as a flashback. But he actually assigns this function only to verse 8, picking up in verses 9–10 the flow of the narrative and the time frame of verses 1–7.

The insertion has the effect of explaining why in verses 12–13 the demons are suddenly plural. The demoniac is first described as a "man in an unclean spirit" (singular) in verse 2, and when he speaks in verse 7, he speaks in the singular ("What have you to do with me . . . *I* implore you . . . do not torment me . . ."). The only preparation for a shift to the plural ("They begged him . . . 'Send us . . .' and he permitted them . . .") is verse 9 ("My name is Legion, for we are many"). Matthew, by contrast, has already used plurals in Matthew 8:29, his parallel to Mark 5:7. There are, after all, *two* demoniacs in Matthew's version of the story! The plurals in the verses that follow in Matthew therefore come as no surprise, even though the alert reader may notice that the first reference is to a plurality of *demoniacs* and the second to a plurality of *demons.* Because plurals are used throughout, Matthew needs no parallel to Mark 5:8–10, and he has none.

Luke follows Mark's procedure rather closely, except that he weaves into his version of the Markan flashback (Luke 8:29, parallel to Mark 5:8) some additional material, more or less parallel to Mark 5:4f., about the man's personal history. The following verses in Luke, like those in Mark, pick up the thread of the story that was momentarily interrupted (Luke 8:30–31; cf. Mark 5:9–10).

Another function of Mark 5:8–10 is to indicate the way the unclean spirits feared Jesus would torment them. The words "Do not torment me" in verse 7 are explained by verse 10: "And he pleaded with him earnestly not to send them out of that region." They feared that Jesus would expel them from the country of the Gerasenes, which appears to be their home for the time being and in that sense a haunted place. They ask to be sent into the bodies of a nearby herd of swine, and Jesus grants their strange request (vss. 11–13). It is difficult to determine whether this solution is to be regarded as an act of mercy or of judgment. At the very least, the narrative has the effect of stressing the multiplicity of the demons. The *Legion* of verse 9 is dramatically displayed in the picture of two thousand swine drowning in the lake. There were enough demons in this one man to galvanize two thousand pigs and send them to their deaths!

Again the reader's attention is gripped by "large and startling figures," this time not in Jesus' metaphors, but in his actions. Who can visualize this scene in Mark's Gospel and soon forget it? We are not

intended to speculate about the immediate fate of the unclean spirits
in Mark 5:11–13. What matters is that their power over the demoniac
has been broken and their days are shown to be numbered. Beyond
this, the fact that unclean spirits are sent into unclean animals is
hardly accidental. They take possession of swine because swine (according to biblical and Jewish tradition) are unclean. Unclean spirits
thrive in the region of the Gerasenes and the Decapolis because this
is a region inhabited mainly by Gentiles, also considered unclean by
pious Jews. They ask to be allowed to go to a place that is natural for
them, and there is no need to draw the conclusion that Jesus has
somehow tricked them or sent them prematurely to their final destruction.

The drowning of the swine in the lake is just that; there is no
evidence that spirits are vulnerable to such natural disasters. The
narrative has no interest in where they may have gone next. The
drowning does, however, illustrate for the Gospel writers the destruction that awaits the unclean spirits when the kingdom of God over-
turns the kingdom of Satan. Matthew has the demons themselves
anticipating this final turn of events in their initial question to Jesus:
"Have you come here to torment us before the time?" (8:29). The
story as a whole illustrates, especially for Mark, the abolition of the
old distinctions between clean and unclean, particularly when these
distinctions are applied to people as well as animals and food. This
will be dramatized in Mark's next exorcism account, the story of Jesus
and the Syro-Phoenician woman (Mark 7:24–30).

The reaction of the Gerasenes to the cure of the demoniac (Mark
5:14–17) is contrasted with that of the man who has been set free (vss.
18–20). The people are afraid, and plead with Jesus to leave the area.
Their behavior is strangely reminiscent of the demon's behavior in
verses 7 and 10. The whole region, being Gentile, is unclean and, in
its own way, demon-possessed. Jesus is unwelcome because he has
threatened its uncleanness and its old mode of existence. The man
who had been possessed also pleads not to be rid of Jesus but to join
him on his way. He is told to return to his home and family and "tell

them what the Lord has done for you and how he has had mercy on you." So the man goes back, "proclaiming in the Decapolis what *Jesus* had done for him, and all were amazed"(Mark 5:20).

The implicit identification of Jesus with "the Lord" (or "God" in Luke 8:39) is a striking note on which to end. Even more striking, however, to anyone who recalls other New Testament accounts of exorcism is the contrast between what the demons are told in Mark 1:34 and 3:12 and what the cured demoniac is told here. They are not permitted to speak, but this man is encouraged to extol the Lord and thus, implicitly, to extol Jesus. Part of the reason is the inappropriateness of a messianic confession on the lips of demons or the demon-possessed, but an additional factor is perhaps the fact that Jesus is on Gentile soil, where there is little danger that he will become the victim of his own popularity and is in any case about to leave.

Before leaving the story of the Gerasene demoniac, it is useful to reflect on what it might have meant to Jesus to hear himself addressed as "Son of the Most High God" (Mark 5:7) or "the Holy One of God" (1:24) by people who were (of all things) demon-possessed. What feelings would such a hideous parody of the voice at his baptism have called forth? As in the case of the parables, Jesus is drawn into a story, and finds a specific role thrust upon him. But this time it is no imagined story of a household with the stock characters of son and father, but a vivid real life drama unfolding before his very eyes. Jesus is drawn into the story not by meditative reflection on something he has seen or heard, but suddenly and violently, by the very seeing and hearing itself.

Even more to the point is a comparison of these exorcisms with the three temptations in Matthew and Luke. The baptismal pronouncement that Jesus is God's Son echoes and reechoes in the frenzied cries of the demoniacs no less than in the reasoned and calculated proposals of Satan, introduced by "If you are the Son of God. . . ." A wry comment of Geza Vermes about "the excellence of the demonic intelligence service"[2] gets at the strange parallelism between the demons' confession of Jesus in the exorcism stories and Satan's testimony, in the desert and elsewhere, to Jesus' sonship. The exorcisms confirm the theory that temptation was for Jesus a continuing experience, and not something limited to the forty days after his baptism and an hour or so in the garden of Gethsemane. To hear from the pit of hell the very same verdict on himself that had come to him from heaven at his baptism and in the household imagery of the parables must have been an unnerving experience, a temptation to end all temptations.

In the light of this, Jesus' abrupt silencing of the demons (whatever its deeper motivation) is a rather natural and understandable response to their grim confession. The cries of the demon-possessed, like the voice of God at the baptism and Satan in the desert, and like the images displayed in Jesus' parables, go to the very heart of Jesus' self-consciousness. He is a son, the very Son of God. But who is telling him this, God or Satan? And how should God's Son act in the world? His response is to silence the voice of the Enemy, and to begin setting free the Enemy's victims!

Reflecting on this activity, Jesus sees it not as his own work but the work of God: "If I, by the finger of God, drive out demons, then the kingdom of God has reached you" (Luke 11:20; cf. Matt. 12:28). For Jesus, the controlling word in the title "Son of God" is not *Son* but *God.* The household imagery of the parables is but a pointer to the one to whom Jesus is accountable. His replies to the Tempter's three questions in the desert all focused on "God" or "the Lord your God," not on his own sonship. And when he sends home the cured demoniac, he tells him to "announce to them what things *the Lord* [in Luke, "God"] has done for you, and what mercy he has shown you." (Mark 5:19; cf. Luke 8:39).

The fact that the man proceeds to testify to "Jesus" is not viewed by the Evangelists as something contrary to Jesus' own intentions, but as a reflection of the precise sense in which Jesus was, and is, the Son of God. What Jesus does, whether teaching or healing or freeing people from the grip of Satan, is the work of God himself. God speaks and acts uniquely through this man whom He has acknowledged as "son." Any acknowledgement of Jesus as "Son of God" that does not begin and end with God, and makes of Jesus a hero or some kind of semidivine superstar with whom the forces of evil may bargain, is only formally a confession. In reality, it is a blasphemy from hell.

THE SYRO-PHOENICIAN WOMAN

Some may question whether the third Markan exorcism story (Mark 7:24–30) really belongs in that category at all. Jesus has no direct contact with any demon-possessed person, and consequently faces no demonic outburst bearing on his own identity or calling. Instead, a woman comes to him asking help for her daughter, who had an unclean spirit (Mark 7:25).

This incident, like that of the Gerasene demoniac, takes place on Gentile soil, in what we would call southern Lebanon ("the region of Tyre," Mark 7:24, or of "Tyre and Sidon," Matt. 15:21). The woman, according to Mark 7:26, is "a Greek, a Syro-Phoenician by birth." Matthew calls her a Canaanite (Matt. 15:22). Emphasis is thus placed on the fact that she was not a Jew but a Gentile.

Again, the connection can be seen between an unclean spirit and unclean people. The Jewish perception of non-Jews as unclean comes to expression on the lips of Jesus himself, as he voices his hesitation about granting the woman's request: "Let the children first be fed, for it is not right to take the children's bread and throw it to the dogs" (Mark 7:27).

The honesty of the Gospel writers in attributing to Jesus a particularism that was already being overcome in their own churches is indeed startling. Today we have become so accustomed to think of any kind of racial or religious particularism as prejudice that we find it extremely difficult to deal with such a presentation of Jesus. Either these traditional Jewish attitudes are being read back into the incident by the Gospel writers, we are told, or else Jesus is playing games with the woman in order to elicit from her the kind of faith on the basis of which he can grant her request. But why would Mark, with his Gentile interests and orientation, make Jesus a more particularistic

Jew than he actually was? And for Jesus to voice objections that he
did not truly feel in order to test the woman's persistence or ingenuity
is as questionable morally as the objections themselves.

The better course is to take the Markan narrative at face value.
Jesus speaks at first to the Syro-Phoenician woman exactly as a first-
century Jewish teacher might be expected to speak. In doing so, he
stands wholly within the framework of Old Testament law. Those
who did not follow the Jewish laws of purity were by definition
unclean. But the woman's ingenuous response—"Yes, Lord; yet even
the dogs under the table eat the children's crumbs"—breaks through
Jesus' Jewish particularism and causes him to act. Her honesty appears to take him by surprise, and he responds in kind with an honest
acknowledgment that she is right: "For this saying go your way; the
demon has left your daughter" (Mark 7:29). She goes, and finds her
daughter cured.

Matthew uses the word *faith* to characterize the woman's attitude
(Matt. 15:28), thus linking the incident with an earlier one in which
Jesus heals from a distance the servant of a Gentile centurion (Matt.
8:5–13). The structural similarities of the two stories are remarkable.
First, a Gentile makes a request of Jesus (Matt. 8:6; Mark 7:25f.).

Second, Jesus raises an objection to granting the request; this is
clear in the story of the woman, but can be seen in the incident of the
centurion only if Jesus' words are taken as a question: "You expect
me to come and heal him?!"

The emphatic pronoun indicates that this is indeed the correct
understanding.[3] Jesus is hardly volunteering his services in the pomp-
ous and melodramatic way suggested by the alternate rendering: "I,
for my part, will come and heal him." Rather, Jesus the Jew is
expressing the same reservations about close contact with Gentiles
that he shows in the incident of the Syro-Phoenician woman.

The third similarity is that the Gentile's wise answer overcomes
Jesus' hesitation (Matt. 8:8f.; Mark 7:28).

The fourth is that Jesus commends the Gentile for his/her answer, and the cure is accomplished from a distance (Matt. 8:10–13; Mark 7:29f.).

These parallels are especially striking when we remember that the one incident is a healing whereas the other is an exorcism. The two stories function in almost exactly the same way. The account of the Syro-Phoenician woman is told not to illumine the practice of exorcism as such, but to show how Jesus' mercy reaches beyond Judaism to the Gentile world. The placing of the incident between the feeding of the five thousand on Jewish soil and the feeding of the four thousand in a predominantly Gentile region graphically illustrates for Mark and Matthew the woman's point about the dogs being entitled to the crumbs that fall from the children's table.

The issue of clean and unclean food in relation to clean and unclean people is also intimated by placing the incident immediately after Jesus' polemic against the Pharisaic food laws (Mark 7:1–23; cf. Matt. 15:1–20). Mark wants us to understand that Jesus comes to make all things clean (Mark 7:19). By his words he abolishes the distinction between clean and unclean foods, and by his ministry of exorcism he does the same thing to existing distinctions between groups of people. The reader cannot help but be reminded of Peter's vision at Joppa of clean and unclean animals (Acts 10:9–16), with the subsequent inference that "God has shown me not to call any person common or unclean" (Acts 10:28). Mark and Matthew are thus using traditional material about Jesus to address issues in the churches regarding Gentile inclusion and food laws.

The meaning the Gospel writers find in the story of Jesus and the Syro-Phoenician woman is not, however, a meaning imposed after the event. Mark and Matthew have not suppressed the fact, for example, that Jesus acts from within the limitations of his Jewish heritage. The initiative lies almost wholly with the woman (as with the Gentile centurion in the other story). Her quick thinking and spontaneous answer make her, like the centurion, a fitting example of "the violent" who in one of Jesus' most memorable sayings seize the kingdom of

God and take it by force (Matt. 11:12; Luke 16:16). Jesus is more the observer in this drama than the actor. He perceives the wisdom of the woman's answer and, in Mark at least, does not so much perform an exorcism as simply recognize that, because of what the woman has said, the demon is now gone (Mark 7:29f.). Just as Jesus does not invent parables but hears them, so he does not make the miracle happen but simply watches it happen.

It is somewhat different in Matthew's Gospel. There Jesus' word becomes the decisive factor in the exorcism: "Be it done for you as you desire" (Matt. 15:28; cf. 8:13). Yet Jesus is not presented as the active forerunner of the Gentile mission, but rather as one who recognizes genuine faith where he finds it. The removal of the distinction between clean and unclean is not something he deliberately brings about but something he experiences as he confronts human need. Jesus remains essentially within a Jewish framework with all its restrictions. He goes neither to the home of the centurion nor of the Syro-Phoenician woman, and he ministers to them only under protest. Though the Evangelists have recorded these stories with later situations in mind, there is no evidence that they have bent the facts to their purposes. And what is striking is that the story of the Syro-Phoenician woman and her daughter shows no interest in the phenomenon or symptoms of demon possession as such. It could just as easily have been a case of leprosy or blindness or anything else that required a cure.

THE BOY WITH A DEAF-MUTE SPIRIT

The last of Mark's exorcism narratives (Mark 9:14–29) has in common with the story of the Gerasene demoniac the characteristics of a case study. Jesus, returning with Peter, James, and John, to the rest of the disciples from the mountain of the transfiguration, finds a crowd gathered around them, in the center of which was a man whose son was possessed by a "mute spirit" (Mark 9:17). The man describes the boy's symptoms for Jesus: "Wherever it seizes him, it dashes him down; and he foams and grinds his teeth and becomes rigid," (Mark

9:18). In answer to Jesus' question, "How long has he had this?" the man said: "From childhood. And it has often cast him into the fire and into the water, to destroy him" (vss. 21f.; cf. 5:3–5).

Two features differentiate this case from that of the Gerasene. The first is that the unclean spirit is mute (vs. 17), deaf-mute in fact (vs. 25). Presumably these terms are applied to the demon on the basis of the symptoms it produces in the boy—when he is possessed, he cannot speak and appears not to be able to hear or respond to what is being said. This demoniac, therefore, cannot confess Jesus as "Son of God" or "Son of the Most High."

Mark perhaps focuses on this detail in order to explain and underline the difference between this case and those recorded in Mark 1:23–28 and 5:1–20. The point is hardly that the demon itself is physically handicapped, though the strange paradox of having Jesus say, "You deaf-mute spirit, I command you . . ." (vs.25) may have been what caused Matthew and Luke to drop the whole matter. Instead of a mute or deaf-mute spirit, Luke speaks merely of a "spirit" (which in fact causes the boy to cry out!), or of a demon or unclean spirit (cf. Luke 9:39,42). Matthew either avoids mention of a spirit altogether (Matt. 17:15) or instead refers to a demon (Matt. 17:15,18). It should be noted in passing, however, that Matthew and Luke have their own traditions about "mute" (Matt. 9:32; Luke 11:14) or even "blind and mute" (Matt. 12:22) demoniacs. In these passages, when the demon is expelled the victim's faculties are restored (Matt. 9:33, 12:22; Luke 11:14), but in this Markan incident nothing is said about the boy hearing or his tongue being loosed when the spirit is driven out, even though the logic of the story implies that these things happened. The boy simply appears lifeless until Jesus raises him up.

Mark's chief reason for retaining the doubtless primitive terminology of "deaf-mute spirit" seems to have been to explain the absence of a confessional outburst like those in Mark 1:24 and 5:7, and therefore of any silencing of the demon. No such explanation was needed in Mark 7:24–30 because the actual exorcism is never described. Mark seems to have had several kinds of exorcism accounts in his tradition, and he tries to do justice to each without forcing them all into the same mold.

A second distinctive feature of this incident is the emphasis on the inability of Jesus' disciples, and everyone else except Jesus, to drive out the unclean spirit. The assumption is that others as well as Jesus, have the power to expel demons, at least theoretically, so that when they fail to do so, Jesus sees it as symptomatic of a faithless generation (Mark 9:19). When the father of the possessed boy says to Jesus, "If you can do anything, take pity on us and help us," Jesus replies, "What do you mean 'If you can'? Everything is possible for the one who believes" (Mark 9:23).

After the exorcism, the disciples ask Jesus privately why they were unable to drive out the demon. His answer is that "this kind can come out only by prayer" (Mark 9:29). Mark's purpose is to emphasize not only what Jesus did in one instance but what every disciple can do through faith and prayer.

Mark brings out the same point two chapters later, in connection with Jesus' only destructive miracle, the cursing of the fig tree:

> Have faith in God. Truly I say to you, whoever says to this mountain "Be taken up and cast into the sea," and does not doubt in his heart, but believes that what he says will come to pass, it will be done for him. Therefore I tell you, whatever you ask in prayer, believe that you have received it and it will be yours (Mark 11:22–24).

Matthew omits the exchange between Jesus and the boy's father, as well as the final saying about prayer (Mark 9:23,29), but he accomplishes much the same result by introducing into the exorcism story from its later Markan context the statement about faith moving a mountain (Matt. 17:20; cf. 20:21). Only Luke allows the exorcism to speak for itself, with little of Jesus' comment or application.

The closing Markan reference to prayer may suggest that what Mark is commending to his readers is not exorcism in the strict sense of the word, but simply individual and corporate prayer by Christians for those who were sick or demon-possessed in the author's own day.

The implication is that Christians after the resurrection of Jesus can succeed where the original disciples failed.

The four major exorcism stories in Mark thus serve a variety of purposes for the Evangelist. Only the first two center upon the exorcism itself and on the authority of Jesus over the demonic world, whereas only the second and the fourth show a clinical interest in the symptoms of demon possession. The fourth subordinates the exorcism itself to teaching about the necessity of faith and prayer, whereas the third is only peripherally an exorcism story at all. One such incident would have been sufficient to illustrate this aspect of Jesus' ministry (Mark 5:1–20 would have done nicely), but Mark has at least four in his tradition and finds reasons to work them into his Gospel without seeming repetitious.

In similar ways, Matthew and Luke have made room for three exorcisms. But historically, the most important thing about the exorcism accounts is not that they illustrate some theological or ethical point, such as abolition of the food law, or grace to the Gentiles, or the power of prayer, but the sheer fact that the accounts exist, and that there are several of them. Far from creating them, the Gospel writers seem to have had more stories of demon possession than they knew what to do with.

By far the easiest explanation of this abundance is that Jesus actually and repeatedly performed what his contemporaries took to be genuine exorcisms. His enemies claimed that he drove out demons by the power of Beelzebub but never denied that he drove them out! Modern scholarship, even in its more radical expressions, has generally admitted the historicity of Jesus' role as an exorcist. The nature and the validity of this ministry is another matter. Many scholars have tended to regard the belief in demons and demon possession as an ancient explanation of abnormal behavior that psychology can now explain in more "scientific" ways. This view admits that Jesus, like others before and after him, had the gift of calming certain kinds of emotional disturbance by a touch, a word, or his mere presence. Observers of what he did, as well as subsequent Gospel tradition, interpreted the symptoms as demonic and Jesus' acts as the driving out of demons.

These scholars stand in a long tradition, but one that is going out of style. In almost every other area they have given up the attempt to explain biblical miracles in rational or scientific terms. Not only those who denied the possibility of the miraculous, but even those who professed to believe in it very strongly, had, for a century or more, grasped at almost any alternative to taking the miracle stories at face value.[4] Historicity was more important to them than wonder. Non-miracles that really happened were preferable to true miracles that happened only in story or legend.

But scholars have increasingly come to realize that it is better to let the biblical narratives be what they are and say what they say. Either the events happened or they did not. It will not do to say that something of a different kind happened and was then interpreted as an exorcism. The interpretation in this case is part of the story, and if it goes, the story goes. The phenomenon of the victims speaking with other voices and confessing Jesus as Son of God is not easily explainable in terms of emotional disturbance. It belongs rather to a class of phenomena that happen even in the twentieth century and that, when they do, are still labeled "demonic" by a sizeable body of medical and psychological opinion.[5]

The shocking fact that the unclean spirits sound like strangely twisted Christian candidates for baptism flies in the face of anything we might have expected from reading the New Testament—1 Corinthians 12:3, for example! It is scarcely possible to imagine a milieu in the early church in which such details could have been invented. They are not in good taste. They belong to that violent element we encounter in the Gospels again and again, an element that startles us and cuts across all our logical expectations. The most plausible reason for their presence in the text is that they were a shocking, awesome, and very real, part of Jesus' own experience. There is no alternative to accepting such details as integral to the Gospel story, and no good alternative to accepting them as fact—apart from a cultured will to disbelieve.

THE SUMMARIES

In addition to the four specific incidents of exorcism (five if we count the stilling of the storm), Mark includes three generalized summaries that confirm the observation that he probably had access to more stories of demon-possession than he could use. These summaries, in both Mark and the parallel passages of Matthew and Luke, shed light on the relationship between exorcism and healing in Jesus' ministry and in the early church.

The first Markan summary places Jesus' exorcisms and healings side by side, yet manages to keep them distinct: "That evening at sundown they brought to him all the sick and the demon-possessed ... and he healed many who were sick with various diseases and drove out many demons, and he did not permit the demons to speak, for they knew him" (Mark 1:32–34).

The second summary, though it immediately precedes the cleansing of a leper, speaks only of exorcism: "And he went throughout all Galilee, preaching in their synagogues and driving out demons" (Mark 1:39).

The third mentions healing and exorcism together and in somewhat similar terms, but still without blurring the distinction between them: "For he had healed many, so that those with diseases were falling down before him to touch him, and the unclean spirits when they saw him, fell down before him and cried out, saying 'You are the Son of God.' And he commanded them sternly not to make him known" (Mark 3:10–12).

It is somewhat different in Matthew, where demoniacs are listed along with epileptics and paralytics among "all who were sick with various diseases and suffering severe pain" (Matt. 4:24). All these groups together are "healed." Mark never in so many words speaks of demoniacs as being healed. The summary in Matthew 8:16f. begins with exorcisms: "They brought to him many who were possessed with demons; and he drove out the spirits with a word." Then it extends the range by referring to healings in general: "and he healed all those who were sick." The latter is evidently taken to include the former, for Matthew appends a quotation from Isaiah to cover both: "He bore our sicknesses and carried our diseases" (Matt. 8:17; cf. Isa. 53:4,11).

In much the same way, Matthew's parallel to Mark 1:39 replaces Mark's reference to "driving out the demons" with "healing every disease and every infirmity among the people" (Matt. 4:23). And in Matthew 10:1, "authority over unclean spirits" results in "healing every disease." The tendency of Matthew is to put demon possession under the general heading of illness and therefore to classify exorcism simply as a type of healing.

Luke exhibits a similar tendency but not to such a marked degree. The Lukan parallel to Mark's first summary statement is content to leave exorcism and healing side by side much as Mark has done (Luke 4:40f.), but Luke 6:18 moves in a direction not unlike that taken by Matthew. Luke mentions a large crowd near Jesus who had come "to hear him and to be healed of their diseases; and those who were troubled by unclean spirits were healed." Here as in Matthew, healing pertains almost interchangeably to disease and demon possession. Elsewhere, in a passage uniquely his own, Luke describes a woman who had a "spirit of infirmity" for eighteen years (Luke 13:10). Jesus tells her, "Woman, you are set free from your infirmity" (Luke 13:12). Later he defends his action by saying, "Then should not this woman, a daughter of Abraham, whom Satan has kept bound for eighteen long years, be set free on the Sabbath day from what bound her?" (Luke 13:16). Is this a healing or an exorcism? The line between the two is difficult to define. When Peter in the book of Acts tells how Jesus "went around doing good and healing all who were under the power of the devil, because God was with him" (Acts 10:38), he similarly groups exorcism and healing under a single rubric.

The summaries, as we move from Mark to Matthew and Luke, show how the phenomenon of demon possession underwent interpretation, or at least classification, even within the synoptic tradition itself. It simply became one category of disease, while exorcism, came to be classed as a specific kind of healing. This helps to explain why the lists of spiritual gifts in 1 Corinthians 12 include healing and miraculous powers but not exorcism as such (1 Cor. 12:9f., 28f.).

This tendency cuts two ways. Subsuming demon possession under the broader heading of illness may serve to explain the demonic in medical terms, or it may broaden the definition of the demonic itself, reflecting a belief that all sickness is in some sense demonic, and that therefore all healing is exorcism. The question arises as to which category is the more inclusive. The Markan passage about the deaf-mute spirit (Mark 9:14–29), as well as similar incidents in Matthew (Matt. 9:32–34, 12:22–24) and Luke (Luke 11:14f.) seem to attribute handicaps of speech, sight, and hearing to demon possession in some instances at least. The Lukan account of the woman with a "spirit of infirmity" (Luke 13:10–17) implies a similar belief about a physical deformity.

As we have seen, Mark can even describe the stilling of the storm (Mark 4:35–41) as if it were an exorcism!

The material resists simplistic explanations. Clearly Matthew subsumes exorcism under healing. Mark in his summaries attempts to keep the categories distinct, but implies at points in his narratives that demonic activity is behind all sickness or misfortune. Luke's evidence, although inconclusive, points in the same general direction as Mark's. John has no exorcism accounts, but describes Jesus' victory on the cross as one great act of exorcism: "Now is the judgment of this world; now is the ruler of this world driven out" (John 12:31). John's *ruler of this world* is strongly reminiscent of the Synoptic Beelzebub, the ruler of the demons.

The evidence of the Gospels, complicated as it is, suggests the following conclusions:

1. There were in Jesus' ministry specific encounters with demon possession. These are described almost clinically in Mark 5:1–20, 9:14–29, and to some extent 1:23–28, and their symptoms are unmistakable: confusion, multiple personality, and panic occasioned by the presence of Jesus, whom the demons call "Son of God." Whether classified under a more general heading or not, these incidents have

certain features in common that set them apart from all other types of healing.

2. These encounters were such a conspicuous part of Jesus' ministry that they imposed some of their distinctive characteristics on descriptions of other aspects of his work: i.e., healing of afflictions such as deafness or physical deformity that had no obvious demonic aspects, a nature miracle (the stilling of the storm), and his conflict with Satan generally from the desert temptations to the cross. This tendency is only partly attributable to a first-century world view that assigned to demons a major role in a wide spectrum of human activities and experience. It arises also out of the actual historical character of Jesus' ministry. He did perform many exorcisms, and he did attribute to them special significance as signs of the kingdom he proclaimed: "If I by the finger of God drive out demons, then the kingdom of God has come upon you" (Luke 11:20; cf. Matt. 12:28).

3. This tendency to demonize various kinds of conflict in Jesus' ministry happens some of the time but not always. Jesus is not depicted as encountering Satan or the demonic at every turn. Often a healing is simply a healing, and is either told for its own sake or else to illustrate some other aspect of Jesus' ministry (e.g., his attitude toward the Sabbath) that has no direct relation to the demonic world at all. This will be seen from a consideration of the healing stories in the Gospel tradition.

9.

THE
MESSIANIC HEALINGS

Five types of healing are set forth in Jesus' classic answer sent to the imprisoned John the Baptist: "Blind people receive their sight, lame people walk, lepers are made clean, deaf people hear, dead are raised, and poor people receive good news" (Matt. 11:4; Luke 7:22). These may be divided into messianic (the blind see, the lame walk, the deaf hear), and non-messianic (lepers are cleansed and the dead are raised) healings. The first group can be designated as messianic healings because of certain prophetic passages that seem to have influenced Jesus' summary: for example, Isaiah 35:5f., "Then the eyes of the blind shall be opened, and the ears of the deaf unstopped; then shall the lame man leap like a hart, and the tongue of the dumb sing for joy" (cf. Isa. 29:18). The Gospel narratives, therefore, present instances in which Jesus gave sight to the blind, hearing and speech to deaf-mutes, and strength to those who were lame.

THE BLIND

In one instance blindness is attributed to demon possession (Matt. 12:22). This is the exception and not the rule, however. Mark records two examples of the blind receiving their sight. The first (Mark 8:22–26) is found only in his Gospel, whereas the second (Mark 10:46–52) is also found in Matthew and Luke. The incident in Mark

8:22–26 is strategically placed to illustrate the gift of spiritual sight (i.e., understanding). Jesus has just rebuked his disciples for their failure to grasp the meaning of his two miracles of the loaves: "Do you not yet perceive or understand? Are your hearts hardened? Having eyes do you not see, and having ears do you not hear? And do you not remember? . . . Do you not understand?" (Mark 8:17f., 21).

Jesus at almost every turn has encountered spiritual blindness and hardness of heart. Then the anonymous blind man appears on the scene abruptly as Jesus' party reaches Bethsaida. He becomes the positive counterpart to the disciples and all in Mark's Gospel who have shown themselves spiritually blind. Those who had sight had failed to perceive the reality of Jesus. It took a blind man to "see everything clearly" (Mark 8:25)! His experience sets the stage for the Markan climax, as Jesus begins to reveal his own death and resurrection and the nature of true discipleship (Mark 8:27–9:1). The promise that "there are some standing here who will not taste death before they see the kingdom of God come with power" (Mark 9:1) follows.

The unnamed blind man is a pivotal figure in Mark's literary purpose. He represents a glimmer of hope when everything is dark, the promise of a pure vision to come. At the same time, his presence in Mark's account is not simply a literary device. His story is told vividly and realistically, as an eyewitness would tell it—too realistically, perhaps, for Matthew and Luke, who omit the story altogether and realize their literary intentions in other ways. The blind man begs for the touch of Jesus, but Jesus does more. He takes him by the hand and leads him from the village, then spits on his eyes and lays hands on him for healing. Such earthy, almost indelicate, details are unnecessary for Mark's literary and theological purposes. They simply represent the way Mark heard the story told, and probably the way it actually happened.

The same is true of the two-stage healing described in verses 23–25. At Jesus' first touch the man saw people "like trees, walking" (Mark 8:24), whereas at the second he "was restored, and saw everything clearly" (vs.25). Mark's purpose is not to illustrate how spiritual enlightenment takes place, but again merely to describe what he understood to have happened. He does not allow his literary goals to override his concern for accuracy in detail. Matthew and Luke may have chosen to omit the story because its picture of Jesus spitting on a man's eyes and making two attempts at the same healing raised more questions than it answered about Jesus the Son of God. Only John's Gospel preserves an echo of a somewhat similar method of healing a blind person. Jesus spits on the ground, applies mud to a man's eyes, and sends the man off to wash in the pool of Siloam (John 9:6f.; cf. vss. 11,15). John also draws an analogy, but more explicitly than Mark, between physical and spiritual blindness (John 9:39–41).

The second healing of a blind person in Mark (Mark 10:46–52) is less vivid and more conventional, though some graphic details remain. Jesus enters Jericho, as he had entered Bethsaida earlier, but he is now on his way for the last time to Jerusalem. Mark passes over the visit to Jericho itself to speak of an encounter on the road out of the city with a blind beggar named Bartimaeus. The account is a curious variation on the exorcism stories. Like the demoniacs, the beggar addresses Jesus with a kind of confession: "Son of David, have mercy on me!" But instead of silencing him, as many try to do, Jesus has him summoned, and asks him what he wants (Mark 10:48). "Master," he replies, "let me receive my sight." Then Jesus dismisses him, redemptively, as he had dismissed the Syro-Phoenician woman and the inquiring Roman centurion: "Go your way; your faith has saved you." The man's sight is restored. Jesus accepts the role of messianic healer that the man's initial outcry had thrust upon him. He carries out his role almost passively, on the basis of the blind man's faith, much as he did in the incidents of the woman and the centurion. But in this case there is no hesitation on his part; he is "Son of David," ministering in mercy to a Jew.

The differences in Matthew's and Luke's accounts are mostly matters of factual detail. Matthew has two blind men rather than one (Matt. 20:29–34), probably by virtue of assimilation to a very similar story involving two blind men in Matthew 9:27–31. The latter is a separate incident in a very different context, but the telling of it seems to have affected Matthew's version of the healing at Jericho. Luke has one blind man but does not call him Bartimaeus. He places the incident on the way into Jericho instead of on the way out (Luke 18:35), perhaps to smooth over Mark's abrupt silence about the Jericho visit itself and set the stage for his own story of Jesus' encounter with Zacchaeus in passing through the city (Luke 19:1–10). Such differences offer a worthy challenge to harmonists. More to the point, however, is the tendency in both Matthew and Luke for Jesus to assume at least a slightly more active role in the healing. In Matthew he touches the man's eyes (Matt. 20:34), a detail that may reflect the influence of Matthew 9:29. In Luke he does not simply dismiss the man and announce the healing, but specifically tells him, "Receive your sight" (Luke 18:42). Apart from these features, Matthew and Luke tell essentially the same story as Mark.

The several basic Synoptic accounts of healings of the blind resist easy generalizations. Mark 8:22–26 is graphic and earthy, assigns to Jesus a very active role, and uses physical blindness as a foil for spiritual blindness. The same is true of John 9; but Mark 10:46–52, Matthew 9:27–31 and 20:29–34, and Luke 18:35–43 are more stereotyped. Jesus' role is a more passive one, and physical blindness is not tied in with spiritual blindness. Mark has a few vivid details, but even these (e.g., Mark 10:50) seem to fall away in the other Gospels. The narratives of the giving of sight to the blind fit no discernible pattern.

THE DEAF

Aside from the cures of deaf-mute demoniacs[1] there is only one account in the Synoptic tradition of the healing of a deaf or deaf-mute person, and that is in Mark 7:31–37. Where this incident would normally come in his Gospel, Matthew simply supplies a general summary:

> And there came to him great crowds bringing with them lame, deformed, blind, deaf-mutes, and many others. They laid them at his feet and he healed them, so that the crowd was amazed to see the

deaf-mutes speaking, the deformed made whole, the lame walking, and the blind seeing. They glorified the God of Israel (Matt. 15:30f.).

Mark tells a specific story about *one* deaf-mute who was healed. A deaf man with a speech impediment was brought to Jesus so he would lay his hands on him. Taking the man aside, Jesus put his fingers in the man's ears, then spat on his own hands and touched the man's tongue. Finally he looked up to the sky with a groan and said "Ephphatha," or "Be opened!" At once the man's ears were opened; he was able to hear, and his speech impediment was gone. Jesus warned the onlookers to tell no one, but the more he warned them not to, the more they proclaimed what had happened: "He has done everything well! He makes the deaf hear and the mute speak" (Mark 7:37).

The resemblances between this incident and the healing of a blind man in Mark 8:22–26 are striking. In both cases an afflicted person is brought to Jesus with a request that he touch or lay hands on him (Mark 7:32 and 8:22). In both cases, Jesus takes the initiative and leads the man away from the crowds. In both cases he touches and spits on the affected parts to accomplish the healing (Mark 7:33 and 8:23). In both cases the healing is total, whether in one stage or two (Mark 7:35 and 8:25), and in both there is a concluding prohibition (Mark 7:36 and 8:26). The two stories are almost a matched pair, framing and offsetting the grim indictment of those who have eyes but do not see, and ears, but do not hear (Mark 8:18).

Presumably the same factors that led Matthew and Luke to omit Mark 8:22–26 were at work in the case of Mark 7:31–37 as well. They may have felt that the dignity of the Son of God was not enhanced by the image of Jesus poking his fingers into a man's ears, touching the man's tongue with saliva, and groaning as he stared up at the sky! But once again the graphic details give evidence of a story that rests on the report of eyewitnesses.

Like Mark 8:22–26 (and unlike Mark 10:46–52) this is an active rather than a passive healing. Confronted by a request for help, Jesus takes charge of the situation as any healer of his time might do, and does not disdain the use of whatever secondary means are available to him, whether words or the direct contact of touching or spitting. It is a very different kind of incident from one in which he simply dismisses the seeker with an assurance that the request is already granted, perhaps even from a distance. There is no basis for arguing that the one kind of healing is authentic while the other is not. Both are firmly rooted in the Gospel tradition. But it does appear that the active type of healing reported in Mark 7 and 8 (and in John 9) was too materialistic for some tastes in the ancient church and tended to be played down in some circles. Mark serves as a necessary reminder that the one who has done everything well (Mark 7:37) does not always do everything *easily.* In some instances Jesus works hard and groans in the completion of his tasks. In others he seems more like an observer watching the work of God unfold and simply announcing to his hearers the mysteries that have taken place.

THE LAME

The distinctive feature of Gospel narratives about the healing of the lame is that in every case but one they become the occasion for theological controversy, and all but one of these controversies have to do with the Sabbath. The only such cure that does not give rise to a controversy is the healing of the centurion's servant in Matthew 8:5–13.

Two factors enter in here. First, only in Matthew 8:6 is the servant said to be "paralyzed." The Lukan version simply states that he was "sick to the point of death" (Luke 7:2) while the story in John 4:46–54 tells of a royal official's son whose life is in danger from a fever (John 4:47, 52). Second, if the centurion was a Gentile, as Luke 7:5 makes clear, the Sabbath issue in any case was irrelevant.

The first account in Mark of the healing of a lame person is Mark 2:1–12. Here the theological issue is not the Sabbath (as in each subsequent account) but the authority to forgive sins. The stage is set for the healing by the graphic picture of the paralytic's four friends lowering him through the roof of Jesus' house to avoid the crowds in the house and around the door (Mark 2:1–4). But there is an interruption. Just when we expect Jesus to lay hands on the man for healing or to say "Your faith has saved you," instead he makes a statement that invites controversy: "Your sins are forgiven" (Mark 2:5). And the actual healing is delayed as attention focuses on Jesus' authority to forgive sins (Mark 2:6–10). Only when he has firmly asserted that "the Son of man has authority on earth to forgive sins" (Mark 2:10) does he command the paralytic: "Stand up! Pick up your bed, and go home." He does so, and the amazed onlookers give their praise to God (Mark 2:11–12).

Despite the difference in setting, there are certain similarities between the healing of this paralytic and the fourth Gospel's account of the healing of the lame man at the pool of Bethesda in Jerusalem. There, amid a group of "the sick, the blind, the lame, and the disabled" (John 5:3) Jesus focuses his attention on an individual who had been almost helpless for thirty-eight years. With the others, the man waits for the stirring of the intermittent spring that fed the pool (presumably because he believes in its healing properties), but without help he cannot avail himself of whatever benefits the pool may have. Jesus heals him with words, virtually the same words used in Mark 2:9 and 11: "Stand up! Pick up your bed and walk" (John 5:8).

This time there is no interruption; Jesus heals the man immediately. But there is a controversy. No sooner is the paralytic healed than the Evangelist reminds the reader that it was the Sabbath (John 5:9). Jesus' conduct is challenged, not because of the healing itself, but because he had told the man to carry his bed, thus assuming responsibility for someone else's unlawful work on the Sabbath day (John 5:10–16).

Jesus defends his conduct on the basis of an analogy between his work and the work of God (John 5:17). God must "break" every Sabbath or the universe will collapse! Is it so strange, then, that one who sees himself as God's Son will feel free to do the same? This shifts the debate to the matter of sonship (John 5:18–30). The language of verses 16 and 18 suggests that John intends these exchanges to be typical examples of recurring issues in the early days of Jesus' ministry: "And that is why the Jews began persecuting Jesus, because he was doing such things on the Sabbath . . . so therefore the Jews tried all the harder to kill him, because he would not only break the Sabbath, but he kept saying that God was his Father, making himself equal with God." If this tradition is historical, it suggests that Jesus' identification of God's kingdom as a household, with God as Father and himself as Son, led him to attempt the work of God regardless of times, circumstances or traditions (cf. John 4:34, 9:4f., 11:9f.).

The pattern of healing intertwined with controversy is maintained in the three remaining accounts of the healing of the lame. The usual definition of "lame" must be widened somewhat to "maimed" so as to include the incident of the man with the shriveled hand (Mark 3:1–6), but the basic elements of that story suggest that it belongs here. The atmosphere of controversy is grim indeed in this instance, and pervades the entire narrative. The immediate background of the incident is the Sabbath controversy of Mark 2:23–28, ending with Jesus' sweeping pronouncement, "The Sabbath was made for man, not man for the Sabbath" (Mark 2:27), and a personal claim of authority: "So the Son of man is lord even of the Sabbath" (Mark 2:28).

The claim is as startling as that of divine sonship in John 5:17, or of the authority to forgive sins in Mark 2:10. It cannot fail to arouse opposition. Thus when Jesus first encounters the man in the Capernaum synagogue, Mark immediately alerts the readers that some "were keeping an eye on him to see if he would heal the man on the Sabbath, hoping to bring an accusation against him" (Mark 3:2). Jesus makes the man stand up in front of everyone, but, as in Mark 2:1–12, the actual healing is delayed.

Again it is a theological issue that causes the interruption, and again it is Jesus who initiates the controversy: "Is it permitted to do a good deed on the Sabbath—or an evil one? To save life or destroy it?" (Mark 3:4). When the potential accusers are silent, Jesus looks around in anger and grief at their hardened hearts. Only then does he invite the man to reach out his shriveled hand and pull it back restored. There is no praise or wonder at this miracle. Instead Mark notes that the Pharisees went out and "began to plot with the Herodians how they might destroy him" (Mark 3:6). This story thus plays a role in the overall plan of Mark's Gospel somewhat comparable to the role played by John 5:1–18 in John's Gospel.

Matthew's account of the man with the shriveled hand (Matt. 12:9–14) differs in a few details from that in Mark. The onlookers, not Jesus, initiate the controversy. Instead of merely watching to see what Jesus will do, they ask him, "Is it permitted to heal on the Sabbath?" Their motive, says Matthew, is the same; they are looking for evidence against Jesus (Matt. 12:10). Jesus' reply is not a general statement, as it is in Mark, about the alternatives of doing good or evil on the Sabbath, but a parable formulated as a rhetorical question: "Suppose one of you has a sheep and it falls into a pit on the Sabbath. Will he not take hold of it and pull it out?" (Matt. 12:11).

This is one of Jesus' characteristic parables of normalcy, inviting the hearer to identify with the shepherd, so as to reply, "Of course I would rescue the sheep. After all, it's my property, and it's worth a lot of money!" Then, without resorting to allegory, Jesus makes an argument from the lesser to the greater: "Think how much more precious a human being is than a sheep" (Matt. 12:12a). "Precious in the sight of God" is the implication, but there is no need to labor the point. On the basis of the parable, Jesus answers his opponents' question in his own terms: "Yes, *good* deeds are permitted on the Sabbath" (Matt. 12:12b). Then he proceeds with the healing, and the Pharisees begin plotting against him.

Luke's version of the incident (Luke 6:6–11) follows Mark's account closely. As in the latter account, the opponents wait to see what Jesus will do, but they do not raise the question of the Sabbath. Jesus himself raises it, as he does in Mark's version, and then goes ahead with the healing. Luke softens somewhat the harshness of the confrontation (omitting Mark's references to anger and hardness of heart), and leaves the opponents merely deliberating instead of hatching a specific plot against Jesus. Otherwise the impact of the story is much the same—healing gives rise almost inevitably to conflict.

Luke records no parable in connection with this incident, but later includes something similar to Matthew's parable of the sheep in the pit in a healing story of his own (Luke 14:1–6). The circumstances are much the same, even though the afflictions are different. The stage is set for controversy: Jesus is eating in the home of a leading Pharisee on the Sabbath, and being closely watched, just as in the earlier story, to see what he will do. A man with swollen arms and legs appears before them (as candidates for healing have a way of doing in the Gospels) without explanation as to where he came from or how he got there. Jesus again lays down the gauntlet: "Is it permitted to heal on the Sabbath or not?" (Luke 14:3). When there is no answer, he heals the sick man and sends him away. After the healing, he answers his own question with a question—more precisely, a parable in the form of a rhetorical question: "Suppose one of you has a son, or an ox, that falls into a well on the Sabbath. Will you not pull him out at once?" (Luke 14:5; cf. Matt. 12:11).

The hypothetical situation is the same as in Matthew's parable of the sheep in the pit, and the response expected from the hearer is the same. The odd combination, a son or an ox, suggests that Jesus is not attempting a coherent story, but is simply drawing almost randomly on the stock characters of his story world in order to make a point. If something is valuable or dear to us, whether a farm animal on which our livelihood depends, or a child whom we love, we are not going to let even the traditions that structure our existence prevent us from safeguarding its welfare. The hearers are again drawn into the hypothetical situation. Of course they will rescue their property, or their own flesh and blood from the well, Sabbath or no Sabbath! So once more they are silent. The small parable serves much the same function here as in Matthew 12:9–14.

In both cases it is helpful to push the situation one step back and imagine Jesus himself confronted with a brief hypothetical story of this kind. What if it were *his* sheep? *his* son? *his* ox? Would he not rescue it immediately? And if it happened to him, would he not want to be rescued? It should be remembered that these are parables of normalcy, even as far as the law is concerned. The law allowed that what was otherwise abnormal might become normal in case of emergency. Things forbidden on the Sabbath might be permitted in situations of drastic need. If Jesus found himself drawn into short parables or imagined life situations of this kind, it is easy to see how they might have dramatized for him the crisis he himself had been proclaiming. It *was* an emergency! The old legal restrictions did not apply. But oddly enough, this emergency situation meant for Jesus precisely a return to normalcy and everyday common sense, not a departure from it. If people are in trouble, rescue them, and don't ask what day it is.

Jesus saw himself in relation to the Jewish people of his day in such earthy images as a shepherd looking for his confused and straying sheep (Matt. 9:36, 15:24), or a mother hen spreading her wings over her panicky brood (Matt. 23:37; Luke 13:34). Here the same sense of personal responsibility for his people, individually or collectively, underlies his imagery of immediately pulling a sheep from a pit, or a son or an ox from a well. Once again Jesus' use of metaphor provides an important key to his self-consciousness, this time as healer and helper. The same images that inform the faith of Jesus govern his actions as well.

The last remaining cure of a lame person (Luke 13:10–17) is presented as an exorcism, but is relevant also to the present discussion because it involves a controversy over the Sabbath. As he teaches in a synagogue, Jesus meets a woman who has been bent over for eighteen years, and is unable to straighten up. She is said to have a "spirit of infirmity." Jesus lays hands on her, her body is made straight, and she praises God. The ruler of the synagogue rebukes Jesus in front of the people for healing on the Sabbath, and Jesus replies, "You hypocrites! Does not each of you on the sabbath untie his ox or ass from the manger, and lead it away to water it? And should not this woman, a daughter of Abraham whom Satan bound for eighteen years, be loosed from this bond on the sabbath day?" (13:15f.).

There is a surface resemblance between his reply here, and the brief parables in Matthew 12:11f. and Luke 14:5. This time, however, Jesus' does not appeal to a hypothetical or parabolic situation, but to a common and customary procedure. This is not a parable, nor is Jesus speaking of a normal response to an abnormal occurrence (e.g., a person or an animal falling into a pit). Rather, he is speaking of a normal response to a normal situation: Animals need water every day. The Sabbath law allowed a person to care for the basic needs of his livestock even when there was no actual emergency. One could not carry water in vessels to the animal, but at least one could loose the animal and lead it to water. Why, then, should a human being, a "daughter of Abraham," not be loosed from the deformity with which Satan had bound her? The argument is from the lesser to the greater.

The link between the two very different situations, and the key to the argument, is the play on the word "loose," or "untie" (Luke 13:15, 16). It is as normal and natural for a human being to be free all the time as it is for an animal to be loosed for a few moments to quench its thirst. Conventional wisdom says that if the woman has waited eighteen years, why not wait one more day so as not to break the Sabbath? But common sense replies, "She is here now; she is in need of healing. Now is the time to act." We have become so accustomed to a tragically distorted world that we have learned to regard it as inevitable and therefore normal. When Jesus restores real normalcy, we are taken by surprise, and overjoyed—or else put to shame (Luke 13:17).

10.

THE
UNCLEAN

The remaining elements in the summary given to the messengers from John the Baptist are that "lepers are made clean . . . the dead are raised, and poor people receive the good news" (Matt. 11:5; Luke 7:22; the last of these activities does not involve physical healing and will be discussed in the next chapter). What of the cleansing of lepers and the raising of the dead? They are not messianic miracles in the sense that the healing of the blind, the deaf, and the lame are. But do they have anything in common, or are they merely samples from a large miscellaneous class of healings? On the contrary, Matthew singles them out along with exorcisms in Matthew 10:8, whereas he combines all the *other* kinds of cures under the miscellaneous category of healing the sick.

It is difficult to assess the relevance of the fact that in the Old Testament both lepers (Lev. 13–14) and the dead (Lev. 21:1–4; Num. 19:11–22) were regarded as unclean. Aside from the basic Markan account of the cleansing of a leper (Mark 1:40–45), nothing much is made of this in the Gospels. But it is perhaps worth noting that the story of the raising of Jairus' daughter from the dead is interwoven with another healing of an uncleanness—a woman's issue of blood (Mark 5:25–34; cf. Lev. 15:25–30). With only two exceptions,[1] in fact, Gospel healings that do not fit the preceding categories of exorcism or messianic healings (i.e., of blind, deaf, and lame) have to do with the unclean.

There is biblical precedent for the cleansing of lepers and the raising of the dead, even though there are no biblical prophecies that such things would happen in the messianic age. Old Testament narratives were as important to Jesus as formal messianic prophecies. He was drawn into these stories as easily as into the parables, so as to identify himself with certain Old Testament figures or to hear himself addressed in the dramatic words of certain narratives. This seems to have happened with respect to the accounts of Israel's desert wanderings (i.e., in the three temptations) and possibly also with respect to Nebuchadnezzar's dream and Abraham's near-sacrifice of his son Isaac. Analogies between his own situation and the situations of such traditional figures were very real to him, long before some of them became part of Christian typology.

A possible further example of this phenomenon can be seen in connection with the cleansing of lepers and the raising of the dead. Jesus' confrontation with his fellow townpeople in Nazareth (which Luke has used to introduce the Galilean ministry) has only indirectly to do with healing. Jesus speaks of good news for the poor and the coming of a kind of Jubilee year (Luke 4:16–21; cf. Lev. 25:8–55), but his hearers have in mind his healing ministry, and especially the healings he has done in the rival town of Capernaum. He anticipates the words they seem afraid to utter: "Physician, heal yourself!" and "Do here in your own country the things we have heard you did in Capernaum" (Luke 4:23). Luke admits here what he has already implied at the start of his account: that this incident actually did not happen at the very beginning of Jesus' ministry, but well into it (cf. Mark 6:1–6). He had taught in other synagogues and had already acquired a reputation (Luke 4:14–15). He had performed some of his healings, and had probably applied to himself the metaphor of a physician (cf. Mark 2:17).

Jesus answers the self-invoked challenge with the principle that no prophet gains acceptance in his own country (Luke 4:24). He illustrates this principle from two biblical incidents: Elijah and the widow of Zarephath (1 Kings 17:7–24), and Elisha's cure of Naaman the Syrian (2 Kings 5:1–27). The point of the illustrations in Luke's immediate context is that prophets of God sometimes minister to outsiders instead of God's own people. This truth will be amply demonstrated from Jesus' ministry as well. The good news comes to the poor instead of the rich, the weak instead of the strong, sinners instead of the righteous, prostitutes instead of priests, crooked tax-collectors instead of scholars, Gentiles instead of Jews.

But of more immediate interest are the specific examples to which Jesus appeals. Luke merely refers to Elijah's having been sent to "Zarephath of Sidon, to a woman who was a widow," but the full story in 1 Kings 17 includes Elijah's miraculous provision of flour and oil for the impoverished widow (1 Kings 17:7–16) and the raising of her son from the dead (vss. 17–24). The latter miracle convinces her that Elijah is a man of God, and that the the word of the Lord truly comes from his mouth (vs. 24). Luke is more specific about the second incident, in which Elijah's successor, Elisha, makes a leper clean by commanding him to wash in the Jordan river. Luke's interest is in the fact that Naaman the leper was a Syrian even as the widow was a Phoenician from Sidon. Naaman's story, originally told to glorify Israel's river and Israel's God (2 Kings 5:8, 12, 15, 17) ironically becomes in Luke's hand an example of how God can bypass Israel to heal the Gentiles!

What is remarkable is that these two programmatic illustrations involve precisely the raising of someone from the dead and the cleansing of a leper. There is no reason to think they are Luke's own selections, out of all the stories he might have chosen to illustrate the theme of salvation for the outsider. It is more likely that Luke found them in his tradition, whether of this incident or of another, and adapted them to his purpose. The subsidiary theme in this encounter at Nazareth is healing, and it is scarcely accidental that Elijah's and Elisha's miracles correspond to two unique facets of Jesus' own heal-ing ministry—the cleansing of lepers and the raising of the dead. If

Jesus was as sensitive to biblical narrative as to biblical prophecy, a strong possibility exists that he, and not Luke, introduced Elijah and Elisha into this or some other controversy about healing. He may, of course, have introduced them to justify his healing ministry to Gentiles (e.g., the centurion's servant, and the Syro-Phoenician woman's daughter), or he may even have used them, like Luke after him, to dramatize his concern for sinners and outsiders generally (including Gentiles) *without* specific reference to healing.

The alternatives are not mutually exclusive, because we know that Jesus was quite capable of applying stories and parables differently to different situations. But first of all he must have taken these miracles of Elijah and Elisha simply for what they were on the surface: stories respectively of raising a dead boy and cleansing a leper. As such, they would have been either illustrations or prototypes of his own healing works. Either Jesus saw his activities paralleled in the lives of the two Israelite prophets, or he attempted to make their stories his own by reenacting what they had done. It has often been suggested that Jesus acted out certain messianic roles—that of Isaiah's suffering servant, for example. His messianic healings of the blind, the deaf, and the lame can be understood as the acting out of such a role.[2] But here we have something a bit different, the acting out of a *story* role.

The picture is complicated by the fact that Elijah had become in certain contexts a messianic figure.[3] If we confuse the category of narrative with that of messianic expectation, we might be tempted to conclude that since Jesus identified John the Baptist as Elijah, he must have identified himself as Elisha! But Jesus was interested in these stories for their own sake, not as sources for a cast of characters in a messianic drama.

Audience identification here prompts him not only to think of himself in certain ways (for example, as a sower or a son) but also to act in certain ways. The roles are no more fixed than they are in the parables. He can *be* either Elijah or Elisha, in the sense that he sees parallels between his own situation and that of either of theirs, and he can bring their stories to bear, as occasion arises, on different aspects of his ministry.

The stories are a given; Jesus does not invent them. Though they are not parables but part of the history of his people, they function for Jesus in much the same way that parables do. They become guiding images for his ministry. In this sense Elijah and Elisha are prototypes. Yet it is doubtful that their stories alone impelled Jesus to heal lepers and raise the dead in conscious imitation of what they had done. The Gospel narratives suggest instead that Jesus usually performed these miracles in response to the initiatives of others. Then he saw his actions mirrored or dramatized in the lives of the two great prophets.

THE LEPERS

The basic account of the cleansing of a leper is found in Mark 1:40–45. It follows a section summarizing Jesus' early ministry of exorcism in Galilee. After an evening of healing many demoniacs who had come to him for help (Mark 1:32–34), Jesus retreated in the early morning to a deserted place for prayer. There his disciples tracked him down and reminded him that the crowds were still looking for him (Mark 1:35–37). So he moved on to other villages preaching in synagogues throughout Galilee, and driving out demons (Mark 1: 38–39). By 2:1 the brief preaching tour is already completed and Jesus is back at Capernaum where he began. The only specific incident placed within this preaching tour is the encounter with a leper, some-where in Galilee, in Mark 1:40–45. The leper approaches Jesus at an unspecified time and place, bows down to him, and seeks his help. "If you will," he says, "you are able to make me clean? (Mark 1:40).

The effect of such words was to put on Jesus the responsibility for the leper's condition. If he chose to heal, then the leper would be clean; if the leper remained a leper, then Jesus would be at fault! To hear this from the leper may, in its own way, have been just as shocking to Jesus as hearing unclean spirits call him the Son of God.

There is an urgency about the leper's appeal. It implies that, like the demoniac in the Capernaum synagogue, he has some kind of supernatural knowledge about Jesus. At any rate, he lays on Jesus an awesome burden. Jesus' angry reaction in verse 43, and perhaps already in verse 41,[4] may be attributable to this sense of burden and pressure.

Just as in the case of the demoniac, Jesus is drawn irrevocably into the action. He meets the leper's challenge head on. He confronts the leper's uncleanness by deliberately reaching out his hand, touching the leper, and saying, "I will—be clean" (Mark 1:41–42). Mark adds that "immediately the leprosy left him, and he was . . . clean" (vs. 42). The language reminds us of the fever that departed from Peter's mother-in-law in Mark 1:31, and the more graphic picture of the unclean spirit that left the man in the synagogue (Mark 1:26). We have here (and probably in Mark 1:31) a quasi-exorcism. The point is not that Mark seriously means to attribute the leper's state to demonic activity. It is only that the sharpness of the confrontation resembles the way in which Mark customarily describes exorcisms. To a limited extent, the conflict is *demonized* in the telling. Jesus warns the leper not to tell anyone (Mark 1:44), just as he had earlier forbidden the demons to speak (Mark 1:34). It should be kept in mind that Mark presents this incident as the only example of Jesus' activity on a preaching tour in which he was said to be "driving out demons" (Mark 1:39).

The incident, in fact, seems to spoil the brief mission, bringing it to a temporary halt. Jesus told the cured leper to say nothing to anyone, but to present himself to the priest and offer for his cleansing what Moses prescribed, as a testimony to them (Mark 1:44). But the leper went out and at once began to "proclaim the matter freely and to spread the word of it, so that Jesus could no longer enter a town openly, but stayed outside in deserted areas, where people came to him from all around" (Mark 1:45). The preaching tour ends as abruptly as it began. Jesus' proclamation (Mark 1:38–39) has given way to that of the cured leper (Mark 1:45), while Jesus himself retires to desert areas similar to those from which the mission had started (Mark 1:35).

Basically, the story of the leper, like most of the exorcisms, deals with a confrontation between the clean and the unclean. The warning to the leper does not stand by itself but is accompanied by a positive command. He is to present himself to the priest and make the proper offering (Mark 1:44). Instead of proclaiming himself clean, he is to follow the way prescribed in Leviticus 14:2–31 to prove himself ritually clean. This is the momentous testimony of the leper's case to the priests and Israel. It is no accident that Jesus deliberately risks uncleanness by touching the leper with his hand. Instead of the clean becoming unclean by such contact, as the law assumed and feared, the unexpected happens—the unclean becomes clean! By this act the old distinctions between clean and unclean are broken down. All things and all people can be made clean. What Jesus accomplished with respect to food by what he said (Mark 7:19) he accomplishes here with respect to a person by the touch of his hand.

The function of this healing is the same as that of the driving out of the unclean spirits (Mark 5:1–20), and the principle involved is no different from the principle by which Jesus responded to the needs even of "unclean" Gentiles (Mark 7:24–30). Once again, the things that had come to be accepted as normal and inevitable are overturned and seen to be abnormal and distorted. Jesus again makes a story world come true, in this case the long-ago story world of Elisha. Jesus' appeal to such a precedent for the cleansing of lepers, and Luke's appeal to it for a ministry to outsiders and Gentiles, are not so far apart as they may first appear.

Matthew's placement of the story of the leper is quite different from Mark's. It comes immediately after the Sermon on the Mount, as Jesus has just descended from the mountain to be followed once more by crowds of people (Matt. 8:1; cf. 4:25). Matthew's context suggests an emphasis on Jesus' strict adherence to the law even in the act of extending grace to persons in need. The demonic element and the note of anger present in Mark are missing in Matthew's version of the story. Rather the point is that, having performed the cure, Jesus insists that the leper fulfill all that the Levitical law requires in the validation of it. And there is no indication that he failed to do so.

Jesus' first healing after the Sermon on the Mount demonstrates that he had truly come not to destroy the law, but to fulfill it (Matt. 5:17). When Jesus responds in the next incident, to a Gentile's need, Matthew is careful to note both an initial reluctance to come to a Gentile home (Matt. 8:7),[5] and the fact that when he does perform the healing he does so from a distance (Matt. 8:8, 13). Jesus does not enter the house of a Gentile, but in the next story he enters a Jewish home and heals Peter's mother-in-law of a fever (Matt. 8:14–15). The kingdom of God is at work in Jesus' deeds, but not in violation of even the letter of the law. Jesus does not do less than the law requires, but more. By a careful selection of Markan and non-Markan incidents and by his juxtaposition of narrative and teaching material, Matthew makes a point slightly different from Mark's.

Luke stays closer to the Markan pattern, yet has some distinctive features of his own as well. Jesus retires from Capernaum to a deserted area, and then undertakes a preaching mission to the other towns (Luke 4:42–43). The itinerary, as in Mark, is extremely vague. The healing of the leper is said to take place in one of the towns (Luke 5:12), presumably picking up the thought of Luke 4:43. But in between, Luke has Jesus preaching in the synagogues of Judea (Luke 4:44) and calling his disciples (by means of a miraculous catch of fish) at Lake Gennesaret in Galilee (Luke 5:1–11). Luke wants to give the impression that Jesus' ministry was not geographically confined. He reached people from Jerusalem, Judea, Galilee, and even the northern coastal areas of Tyre and Sidon (cf. Luke 5:17, 6:17, 7:17). The point made in Luke 4:25–27 about grace reaching beyond Jesus' home town is reinforced as Luke goes along. He takes full advantage of the indeterminate location of the healing of the leper in its Markan setting. It could well be in Galilee or Judea or anywhere.

In Luke as in Matthew, the Markan elements of anger and the

demonic have disappeared. There is no reason for anger because the words, "Lord, if you will, you can make me clean," have become more a polite and humble request than a challenge. Like Matthew, Luke retains the command to the leper to keep silent about the healing and present himself to the priest. But Luke follows Mark a step further, retaining also the notice of how the news about Jesus spread so widely that he had to seek privacy once again (Luke 5:15-16). Where Luke differs from Mark is that he gives no indication that the leper is directly responsible for spreading the news or in any way disobeying Jesus' command. Matthew simply passed over Mark 1:45 in silence, but Luke adapts it in such a way as almost to disengage it from the healing story that precedes it. Luke says that, in spite of Jesus' concern for secrecy, word got around. Mark states that Jesus told the leper to do one thing and the man immediately went out and did the opposite.

The tendency of the other Evangelists is thus to smooth down the rough edges of Mark's narrative, especially Jesus' anger at the leper and his seeming inability to prevent the man from announcing the cure far and wide. But Mark's account conveys best the radical and violent nature of the confrontation between clean and unclean in Jesus' ministry. The healing speaks for itself and comes through clearly in each Gospel. Jesus' concern for the law is also readily apparent, whether or not the cured leper actually fulfilled his legal obligation. There is, after all, nothing radical in the abolishing of the distinction between clean and unclean unless the distinction is real in the first place. The new state of affairs must be validated in the older categories. Compliance with Levitical regulations provides a necessary testimony that something greater than the law has come.

The only other Gospel account of the cleansing of lepers is found in Luke (Luke 17:11-19). Though *ten* lepers are healed at once, the narrative interest is not in the remarkable mass healing itself, but in the fact that only one of the ten returned to give thanks, and he was a Samaritan. This story belongs with those in which the faith of an outsider is commended: i.e., with the healing of the centurion's servant, and the exorcism story about the Syro-Phoenician woman and

her daughter. As in both of those incidents, Jesus performs the cure
from a distance (Luke 17:12). The lepers cry out, "Jesus, teacher, have
mercy on us," and when Jesus has sent them away, they find that they
are clean (Luke 17:13–14). Jesus does not touch the lepers in this case.
No emphasis is laid on the violent encounter between the clean and
the unclean. Jesus merely says, "Go," and they go. The closest parallel
to the earlier Markan incident is that Jesus sends them specifically to
present themselves to the priests (Luke 17:14)—presumably to their
respective Jewish or Samaritan priests.

For all practical purposes, this is not a leper story but an "outsider" story. The fact that ten lepers, rather than ten demoniacs or ten
lame or blind people, are cured is irrelevant to the story's major
thrust. The healing of the centurion's paralyzed (or fevered, or simply
very sick) servant, the cure of the demon-possessed daughter of the
foreign woman, and the cleansing of the ten lepers are all told for the
same purpose: to praise the faith of an outsider. Because the particular
affliction from which they are delivered is not the main point, these
stories are not typical of the respective categories to which they belong. It is also true, as noted before, that Jesus plays a more passive
role in this kind of healing. To the centurion and the Syro-Phoenician
woman he merely echoes and confirms what they have said or believed, while to the lepers he speaks no actual word of healing but
sends them off to the priests to find what they will find. Once again,
Jesus' healings divide themselves into active and passive types.

Mark 1:40–45, with its sharp conflict between clean and unclean,
is the basic or typical leper story in the New Testament. Luke 17:
11–19 is somewhat peripheral to the genre. The brief Markan incident
was doubtless selected from among many with similar characteristics.
Its indeterminate location tends to confirm this. The appeal in the
early church to God's act (Acts 10:15) and to Jesus in particular
(Mark 7:19) in connection with the issue of clean and unclean suggests
that the overcoming of this distinction in many areas may have played
a greater part in Jesus' ministry than the Gospels explicitly state. If
so, it would help to explain both the exorcism of unclean spirits and

the healing of unclean lepers in a context in which such things are not expected—not even as part of the messianic kingdom.

THE DEAD

Twice in the Synoptics and once in John, Jesus is represented as raising a person from the dead. Anyone who has read the letters of Paul is likely to bring to these incidents certain expectations. What is more natural than that these stories should somehow anticipate the resurrection of Jesus himself or, if not that, then the general resurrection to come? Even without a definite theology of resurrection, the reader is likely to see the raising of a dead person as the supreme act of healing. Surely these narratives deserve a central place in the dramatic structures of the Gospels in which they are formed.

The striking fact is that, although all of these things are true in John, none of them are true in the Synoptics. The raising of Lazarus in John 11 is seen as a symbol of eternal life and of the resurrection at the last day (John 11:23–27; cf. 5:25–29). The very contrasts noted between this miracle and the resurrection of Jesus[6] presuppose that the one is a foil for the other. The raising of Lazarus comes almost at the end of Jesus' public ministry as the last and greatest of a series of signs. None of this is true of the raising of Jairus' daughter (Mark 5:21–43 and parallels) or the widow's son at Nain (Luke 7:11–17). Distinctions must be made between the stories in themselves and the theological uses to which they are put. Two out of three are innocent of at least the theological applications most obvious to us. All three require a closer look.

The point has often been made that the raising of Lazarus must not be historical because if Jesus had actually performed such a spectacular feat, it would not have gone unnoticed, and the Synoptic Gospels would surely have made some mention of it. But Mark, Matthew, and Luke seem to have regarded the raising of the dead as just another kind of healing, and therefore contented themselves with a sampling. One or two healings of lepers, one healing of a deaf person, two or three healings of the blind, a few cures of the lame, and several exorcisms have been chosen out of a larger number. Similarly, it appears, only a few stories of the resuscitation of the dead occur. The logic could be reversed: it might be argued that the Synoptic Gospels deliberately played down this aspect of Jesus' ministry in order to preserve the uniqueness of Jesus' own resurrection. All such arguments are influenced too much by the expectations *we* bring to the text (mostly from our reading of Paul). It is better to let the three stories speak for themselves.

The raising of Jairus' daughter follows immediately after the cure of the Gerasene demoniac. All three Synoptic writers preserve the memory that the story is interrupted by another incident of healing, a brief encounter between Jesus and a woman who was hemorrhaging. We have, therefore, a story within a story. The close connection between the two was so firmly embedded in the tradition that it had to be retained. There is no evidence that the narrative was ever told any other way, and every evidence that this was the way it happened.

As Jesus returned from the far side of the lake of Galilee (presumably to Capernaum) he was met on shore by a crowd. Attention centers on Jairus, a synagogue official (only Mark names him), who pleads with Jesus to lay hands on his daughter, who is near death (Mark 5:23), and heal her. In Luke she is said to be dying (Luke 8:42), while in Matthew's text she has "just died" (Matt. 9:18). The difference in Matthew is attributable to his telescoping of the account. In Mark and Luke, the actual news of the girl's death is delayed until a messenger arrives from her home (Mark 5:35; Luke 8:49).

Jesus' pronouncement at that point that the daughter is not dead but only sleeping must not obscure the fact that all three Gospel writers intend to describe an actual raising of a dead person. The pronouncement is an anticipation of what Jesus is going to do. The same device is used in the story of Lazarus with the explicit indication that death is meant (John 11:11–14). Luke takes the most care to avoid any misunderstanding, but all three accounts definitely assume that Jairus' daughter is dead.

Theologically, the use of the sleep metaphor sets the stage for the act of awaking the girl from death (Mark 5:41) with perhaps a faint intimation of the Jewish and Christian resurrection hope. But in the immediate situation, the reference to sleep has the practical function of helping to keep the full extent of the miracle quiet. Jesus is careful to separate the girl's parents and three of his disciples from the rest of the crowd, so that only they are actual witnesses to the miracle. The others are free to conclude if they wish that the girl was indeed not dead, but only sleeping. Otherwise the strict warning not to let anyone know (Mark 5:43; Luke 8:56) makes little sense, for how could a live daughter be kept a secret? When Jesus is alone with the dead girl, her parents, and his disciples, he grasps her hand saying *"Talitha, koum"* (i.e., "Rise, little girl"—only Mark supplies the Aramaic words), and to her parents' amazement she comes to life.

The encounter with the hemorrhaging woman had taken place earlier on the way from the lake shore to Jairus' house. After briefly sketching her medical history (Mark 5:25), Mark tells us that she deliberately touched Jesus' cloak in the press of the crowd and experienced healing (Mark 5:27–29). Jesus asks who has touched his clothing. The woman makes herself known and tells her story. Jesus then says to her, "Daughter, your faith has saved you; go in peace."

Although actual historical sequence is sufficient reason for the intertwining of these two stories, certain details, especially in Mark, help to explain why they were consistently kept together. Both the dead girl and the hemorrhaging woman are "daughters" (e.g., Mark 5:34, 35), the former obviously and the latter perhaps (like the crippled woman of Luke 13:16) as one of God's people, a daughter of Abraham. And is it a coincidence that this woman has been afflicted with a vaginal flow of blood for twelve years, while, according to Mark, Jairus' daughter is twelve years old? Perhaps so, but Mark seems to have had an interest in such coincidences. The child and the childless are together restored to life and health. The unclean womb, and the grieving father and mother receive mercy at almost the same time.

There is no hint in any of the Gospels that the uncleanness of a dead body is particularly at issue in the raising of Jairus' daughter (though all three agree that Jesus touched the dead girl's hand). The privacy of the miracle and the uncertainty almost to the end as to whether the girl is really dead probably explain why this is so. But the linking of this story with one in which the victim is known to all to be ritually unclean (Lev. 15:25–30) suggests that uncleanness is in some sense the enemy here as well. Death is of course the final uncleanness, but the reason the Gospels give no special place to Jesus' resuscitations of the dead may be the writers' awareness that Jesus confronted death in many forms. Was an actual resurrection, after all, different in kind from an exorcism, or the cure of leprosy or any other sickness? Undeniably, such a thing was a bigger miracle, but the basic conflict was the same here as elsewhere. There was no need for rhetoric or profound theologizing. Mark ends the story on a warm and human note: Jairus' daughter must have something to eat!

Once again we have that peculiar combination of active and passive roles that mark Jesus' healing ministry generally. He heals the hemorrhaging woman without knowing what he has done! He merely senses that power has gone out from him. Instead of making him unclean, her touch makes possible her own cleansing. When the woman tells him what has happened to her, he dismisses her in peace because her faith, rather than his act, has saved her. He simply assents to what God has accomplished.

The raising of Jairus' daughter is quite different. Though he acts in response to an appeal, Jesus knows exactly what he is going to do (Mark 5:26, 39) and carefully directs each step of the procedure, from the separating out of the immediate family and three disciples to the ordering of a meal for the restored young girl. The weaving together of an active and a passive healing story into one account suggests that both types were well established in the tradition. There is no way historically that the healings of Jesus can be reduced to either one type or the other.

The raising of the widow's son is found only in Luke (Luke 7:11–17). As he reaches the gate of the Galilean town of Nain, Jesus meets a funeral procession for the only son of a local widow. The initiative lies wholly with Jesus. With compassion he quiets the mother's tears, stops the procession by touching the stretcher on which the dead man lies, and says, "Young man, I tell you 'Arise!' " The dead youth sits up and begins to speak. Unlike the raising of Jairus' daughter, this healing is said to have created a great stir among the townspeople. There is no element of secrecy. "A great prophet has risen among us," they say, and "God has visited his people" (Luke 7:16).

This incident, along with several of the healings that precede it, forms the backdrop for Jesus' answer to the messengers from John the Baptist in prison (Luke 7:22). Both the miracle itself and the reaction to it are reminiscent of Elijah's raising of the widow's son at Zarephath (1 Kings 17:17-24). Luke draws on the very words of this account when he says of the young man that Jesus gave him back to his mother (Luke 7:15; cf. 1 Kings 17:23). In this way, Luke shows his awareness of the parallel between Jesus' ministry and that of Elijah not only as a ministry to outsiders (Luke 4:26) but as involving the raising of the dead to life. Such a miracle gives the impression that Jesus is indeed a prophet (Luke 7:16; cf. vs. 39), Elijah himself perhaps (Luke 9:8, 19), or the "coming one" (Luke 7:20) after the manner of Elijah (Mal. 3:1, 4:5). Despite the risk of misunderstanding involved in such conclusions (Luke 9:18-22), Luke sees them as pointing in the right direction: in Jesus, God *has* visited his people (Luke 19:37-40,44; cf. 1:68). Luke thus hints at a messianic significance to this miracle. At its root, however, lies simply Jesus' imaginative self-identification with Elijah in the presence of an immediate human tragedy.

A progression can be seen in the three examples of Jesus' raising of the dead. Jairus' daughter is on her death bed. The widow's son at Nain is being carried away for burial. Lazarus is already in his tomb, wrapped in graveclothes. Yet reduced to its simplest terms, the Johannine story of the raising of Lazarus exhibits some of the same features found in the two Synoptic stories, especially the raising of Jairus' daughter. Jesus receives an appeal for help from the relatives of someone about to die (John 11:3; cf. Mark 5:23). He uses the metaphor of

sleep, but it soon becomes clear that the sick person has actually died
(John 11:11–14; cf. Mark 5:35,39). He goes to the home of the de-
ceased to help (John 11:15; cf. Mark 5:24), and proceeds to direct the
course of events from beginning to end. He encourages the relatives
to believe that all will be well (John 11:40; cf. Mark 5:36). He specifically commands the dead person to come alive (John 11:43; cf. Mark
5:41 and Luke 7:14), and when the miracle is accomplished, he sees
to it that someone cares for the person's immediate needs (John 11:44;
cf. Mark 5:43 and Luke 7:15).

Although John has woven into the story profound theological
teaching about eternal life and the resurrection at the last day, the
story in itself is not so different from the two shorter ones found in
the Synoptics. It is, of course, possible to argue that the fact that
Lazarus is already in the tomb and "dead four days" (11:39) represents a heightening of the miraculous. The same could be said of the
raising of the widow's son in relation to that of Jairus' daughter.
Certainly, John is fascinated with Jesus' delay in coming to Bethany
(John 11:6) and the consequent accusation that Jesus could have
prevented Lazarus' death (John 11:21,32,37). But along with this are
other elements that suggest a very primitive account. Whereas in the
two Synoptic incidents he told the bereaved not to cry (Mark 5:39,
Luke 7:13), in the case of Lazarus he himself gives way to tears (John
11:35), and not only to tears but to anger.

As Jesus came to the tomb of Lazarus, John says that Jesus "shook
with anger" (John 11:33, cf. vs. 38). We cannot help but be reminded
of the anger with which Jesus confronted the leper in Mark 1:40–45.
Here again in John, Jesus confronts uncleanness. Lazarus has been
dead four days; his body already smells of uncleanness and decay
(John 11:39). On all sides, Jesus has been told in effect that he is
responsible for this death (John 11:21,32,37), even as the leper had
burdened him with the responsibility for his pitiful condition ("Lord,
if you will, you can make me clean"). Once more Jesus is drawn into
a confrontation with the powers of uncleanness and death, and the
confrontation is not an easy or pleasant one, even though Jesus sees

beyond it the "glory of God" with which the story is to end (John 11:4,40). In its way, this confrontation in John is not unlike the one it foreshadows, Jesus' own death, with its twin aspects of suffering and glorification (cf. John 12:27–28,31–32).

It is possible that the almost demonic elements that surface in John's narrative of the raising of Lazarus have been played down somewhat in the simple human interest stories of Jairus' daughter and the widow's son at Nain. To regard the raising of Lazarus as secondary because it has been made to serve a more overt theological purpose, or because the miracle involved is greater, is an oversimplication. A story that has undergone extensive development in some respects may be quite primitive in others. Nor is there reason to doubt the historicity of the three accounts of the raising of the dead solely because they are more miraculous than Jesus' other healings. At any rate, it is doubtful that the Synoptic Gospel writers regarded them as greater evidence of Jesus' power than the cleansing of lepers or the healing of the blind, the deaf, or the lame.

Together, Jesus' acts of healings indicate that he responded spontaneously to extreme human need on a variety of fronts. To a limited extent, he interpreted his healings in the context of messianic expectations, or of historical precedent in Israel's past (Elijah and Elisha). But more characteristically he saw them as acted-out stories, or rather as the acting out of one all-encompassing story, the binding of the strong man and the release of his captives. Our acceptance of them as historical depends largely on our acceptance of *that* story as a true characterization of Jesus' ministry.

11.

FORGIVENESS:
A WORLD UPENDED

The world to which Jesus came was a world not so different from our own. It was a world in which people found themselves victims not only of disease, evil spirits, physical deformity and death, but of religious and social systems and political and economic forces over which they had no control. The Enemy who held them captive was both outside and within. External pressures left them little room to do the will of God, and what opportunities they had were often poisoned (as the Jewish revolt demonstrated) by their own greed and selfishness. Jesus' ministry must accordingly be understood as a ministry of the forgiveness of sins.

THE PARALYTIC

The close association of healing with forgiveness can be seen in the account of the healing of the paralytic at Capernaum. Like the other stories of the healing of the lame, this incident involves a controversy, but this controversy, unlike the others that had to do with the Sabbath, concerned the authority to forgive sins. A paralytic was brought on a stretcher to Jesus' house in Capernaum for healing. According to Mark and Luke he was let down through the roof because the crowds blocked the door. Jesus responded to the faith of the paralytic and his friends, but instead of healing him with a word or a touch simply told him "Your sins are forgiven" (Mark 2:5).

In some circumstances, such words would be only a pious platitude. There was, after all, no obvious way to tell whether the man's sins had actually been forgiven or not. Jesus' word of assurance could be neither verified or falsified. Talk is cheap, and under some conditions Jesus' opponents might well have been content to ignore what he said. But the scribes took Jesus' pronouncement seriously and, among themselves at least, challenged his right to make it: "He blasphemes. Who can forgive sin except one—God?" (Mark 2:7). Their assumption was that the man's sins were *not* forgiven and therefore Jesus was a charlatan and a blasphemer.

Jesus rebuked their unspoken charge by equating "Your sins are forgiven" with "Rise, pick up your stretcher, and walk." If talk is cheap, then which is easier to say? Surely the one is no harder than the other. But the difference lies in what happens next. As soon as someone says to a paralytic, "Rise and walk," he has put his word on the line. The person will either rise and walk, or else remain as he was. There is no hiding from the consequences of such a pronouncement. Without hesitation, Jesus took the next step. "Rise," he told the paralytic, "pick up your stretcher and go home" (Mark 2:11). He did this to let the hearers know "that the Son of man has authority on earth to forgive sins" (Mark 2:10). The linking of forgiveness with healing in verses 10–11 reinforces the explicit connection made already in verse 9. When the paralytic got up and took his stretcher away, he provided visible evidence of Jesus' authority to pronounce his sins forgiven.

The act of healing and the act of forgiveness have in common the element of liberation or deliverance. The narrative makes very clear the predicament from which Jesus' word of healing delivered the man. His body is paralyzed, so that he has to be carried wherever he wants to go. The predicament from which Jesus' word of forgiveness sets him free is not so clear. The particular sins for which he needs forgiveness are not specified. More surprising than this, his forgiveness is not made to depend on any act or attitude of repentance on his part. The most that can be said is that Jesus declares him forgiven in response to the faith of those who bring him, and presumably his own faith as well. But as far as we know, this faith, like that of the centurion, the Syro-Phoenician woman, and the woman with the menstrual flow of blood, is exercised in the hope of physical healing, not in connection with repentance and not to gain deliverance from sin.

Essentially, the paralytic is given something he has not asked for, but as the story unfolds this gift is seen to contain just what he needs. Jesus knew the man's needs better than the man himself. The focus of the narrative, however, is not on the deeper needs that Jesus meets, but on the obvious physical needs that brought the paralytic and his friends to Jesus in the first place. When the story ends, we know only that he can now walk and that the onlookers are amazed. We are not told what it means to him to be forgiven, or what changes forgiveness will make in his life. This healing story points beyond healing to forgiveness. But it leaves us with more questions than answers as to exactly what forgiveness entails.

NOT THE RIGHTEOUS BUT SINNERS

The next story in all three Synoptics has two parts: the call of Levi, the tax collector, at his customs booth by the lake of Galilee, and a dinner Jesus shares with many "tax collectors and sinners" in Levi's house. Mark indicates that all of them were following Jesus (Mark 2:15). The account of Levi's call is therefore not regarded as unique, but as setting a pattern for Jesus' relationship with a whole class of people. Just as in several of the disputes over the Sabbath, the "scribes of the Pharisees" challenge Jesus' behavior: Why does he eat with tax collectors and sinners?

Although no healing has been performed, Jesus replies with a metaphor of healing: Doctors are not for those who are well, but for those who are sick. By the same token, says Jesus, "I have not come to call righteous people, but sinners" (Mark 2:17). The narrative has made it clear that *sinners* is being used more as a sociological than an ethical term. The pairing of tax collectors and sinners three times within Mark 2:15–16 suggests that the intent is not to explore the precise nature of the sinners' sinfulness, but simply to provide an inclusive term for a number of disreputable occupations or classes of people. Tax collectors are singled out explicitly because the programmatic call in the accompanying narrative was in fact the call of a tax collector, Levi. The combination "tax collectors and sinners" serves as Mark's transition to the concluding pronouncement that Jesus has come to call "sinners." The point is simply that Levi gathered a group of people like himself, "tax collectors and [other] sinners" (cf. Matt. 11:19; Luke 7:34, 15:1). Different combinations, such as "tax collectors and prostitutes" (Matt. 21:31f.), "a heathen and a tax collector" (Matt. 18:17; cf. 5:46f.) also occur.

Sinner by itself becomes in certain passages a sociological group designation for tax collectors (Luke 18:13, 19:7), prostitutes (Luke 7:37, 39), Gentiles (Mark 14:41; cf. Gal. 2:15), or any similar group of outsiders whose lives are considered unacceptable to God (cf. Luke 6:32–34).

The thrust of Mark 2:17, therefore, is that Jesus did not come for the benefit of the religious people who set the moral standards for the Jewish community, but precisely to these outsiders. They were labeled "sinners" not because of specific sins they had committed individually, but simply because of who or what they were. Tax collectors as a group had made their peace with the Roman forces of occupation and found a way to make a profit at the same time. Prostitutes as a group had violated sexual purity and in the process made a living off Roman soldiers and others who had no respect for the Jewish laws. Gentiles as a group were by definition unclean. Soldiers in particular, perhaps, were the most obvious reminder of the humiliating presence of pagan authority in Israel (cf. Luke 3:14). And Samaritans were a race that had an age-old hostility with the Jews. Galileans as a group had a reputation for carelessness about the law. Even the beloved and much-romanticized shepherds may have been at least suspect because of their carelessness in distinguishing between clean and unclean animals. In varying degrees, the religious authorities and scribes regarded all who had not undertaken a rigorous discipline similar to their own as a "multitude that does not know the law" and therefore as "accursed" (John 7:49). Though women and children and the poor were not necessarily placed in the same category, Jesus recognized that they, like the others, were powerless in such a culture, and so directed his special love toward them as well.

When Jesus says, "I have not come to call the righteous but sinners," he is setting a genuine priority for his ministry. He does not carry along the hidden assumption that there are in actuality no truly righteous people and that therefore he is sent to everyone indiscriminately, asking only that people begin by acknowledging to him their sinfulness. To the contrary, Jesus here assumes that there are righteous people just as there are "sinners," and that his mission is to one group in preference to the other. He takes for granted the group distinctions the religious establishment imposed and sets his priorities *within* that framework. Ignoring the "good" people, he deliberately goes out of his way to spend time with "tax collectors and sinners," not to introduce them to prayer, fasting, and the ways of piety, but to do the things *they* like to do: eating and drinking and celebrating together. A strange physician this, with many of the same symptoms as his patients! His hearers might well have responded with a proverb handed down in a different context: "Physician, heal yourself" (Luke 4:23).

It is important to notice that Jesus is *not* said to have directed his attention to the righteous first, and then, when they refused his call, to sinners. Nor is it likely that he first brought the message of the kingdom to all indiscriminately, and that Mark 2:17 is a verdict given in retrospect and based on the fact that the sinners and not the righteous were the ones who accepted him. Something along these lines is what we might have expected if the early Christian experience of the Gentile mission were being imposed on the Gospel tradition after the fact. Although the principle, "To the Jew first, and also to the Gentile" finds its appropriate starting point already in Jesus' ministry (e.g., Matt. 10:5,6; 15:24), there is no analogous principle of going "to the righteous first, and also to the sinners." The fact that Jesus focused his ministry *from the start* on sinners and outcasts is as well established as the fact that he focused it on Jews. If he was sent "only to the house of Israel," he was sent specifically to the "lost sheep" within Israel.

At the end of the Lukan story about Jesus and the tax collector, Zaccheus, Jesus declares that the Son of man has come to seek and to save that which was lost (Luke 19:10). Christian theology has so accustomed itself to thinking of the whole human race as being "lost" that such statements are read simply as expressions of Jesus' (or Luke's) universalism. The fact that Jesus is favoring one group over another is obscured. But if that is what he is doing, the question must be asked, "Why?"

Admittedly, Jesus has logic on his side. If he is a healer, it stands to reason that he will concentrate on those who are sick. If he is an exorcist, he will go to those who are possessed. If he comes to bring forgiveness, why should he not spend his time with sinners? These are, after all, metaphors of normalcy. Our problem as modern readers is that because we know the end from the beginning, we think of the scribes and Pharisees (i.e., the "righteous") as *worse* sinners than the prostitutes and tax collectors. Therefore we would have expected Jesus to direct his ministry to all groups without distinction and to let "righteous" and "sinner" be defined on the basis of the varying responses to his call. To show favoritism at the very outset seems to us to overlook the group whose need, though unrecognized, was greater than that of any other.

A possible explanation for Jesus' behavior is that it presupposes something that has gone on before—specifically, the ministry of John the Baptist. What if the principle, "to the righteous first, and also to the sinners" does have some validity, but Jesus represents, as it were, stage two of this agenda? If that is true, then when we read of Jesus' deliberate choice to go to the sinners, we are walking in on a scenario that has partly run its course.

Matthew and Luke differ in their designations of John's audience. Matthew has him addressing "Pharisees and Sadducees," while Luke 3:7 directs the same speech to the "multitudes" who came to receive his baptism (Luke 3:10). Then within this undefined group, Luke singles out "tax collectors" (vs. 12) and "soldiers" (vs. 14). Luke's Gospel reinforces this focus later with a statement that "all the people who heard, and the tax collectors, justified God by being baptized with John's baptism, but the Pharisees and scholars of the law rejected God's will for themselves in not being baptized by him" (Luke 7:29). As in chapter 3, the emphasis is on the fact that the sinners were the ones who received John's baptism, but the concluding verdict on the Pharisees and scholars of the law presupposes that they too had at least the opportunity to do the same. Thus according to Luke, John the Baptist directed his message to all in Israel without distinction, but those who produced "fruit worthy of repentance" by submitting to his baptism and asking "What shall we do?" were precisely such groups as the tax collectors and the soldiers (Luke 3:10,12,14).

Matthew, also, returns at a later point in his Gospel to the matter of John the Baptist's audience. Jesus tells "the chief priests and elders of the people" (Matt. 21:23) that "the tax collectors and the prostitutes are entering the kingdom of God instead of you." The reason, he says, is that "John came to you in the way of righteousness and you did not believe him, but the tax collectors and the prostitutes believed him" (Matt. 21:31f.). The point is that John the Baptist came first to the religious establishment (Matt. 3:7), and then, when this group rejected him, to the outsiders. Here he found a favorable response. Jesus' priorities can thus be explained on the basis of what has happened before. He built on the experience of John the Baptist by concentrating his efforts on groups that had responded favorably to John's message: the prostitutes, the tax collectors, and all such "sinners."

Matthew follows Jesus' reflection on the varying responses to John's ministry with two parables that share a common structure. The first has to do with a landlord and his wicked tenants (Matt. 21:33–46); the second, with a royal wedding feast (Matt. 22:1–14). The first story is found in all three Synoptics, and in the Gospel of Thomas;[1] the second is found only in Matthew, but bears strong resemblance to stories about invitations to a wedding feast in Luke 14:15–24 and Logion 64 of the Gospel of Thomas. Both Thomas and Matthew have placed the two stories together, but Matthew is unique in the parallelism he sets up between the two.[2] The action in each parable unfolds in three stages:

Matthew 21:33–46	*Matthew* 22:1–14
1. The landlord *"sent his servants* to the farmers to collect his fruits" (vs. 34).	1. The king *"sent his servants* to call the invited guests to the wedding . . ." (vs. 3).
2. *"Again he sent other servants* more than the first . . ." (vs. 36).	2. *"Again he sent other servants. . ."* (vs. 4).
3. "So finally he sent to them his son . . ." (vs. 37).	3. "Then he said to his servants . . . 'Go to the street corners and call anyone you find to the wedding . . .' " (vss. 8–9).

The similarities are mostly limited to stages one and two. At stage three the stories go their separate ways because the messages the respective servants delivered were different from the start. In Matthew 21:33–46, the messengers were sent to collect from tenant-farmers the fruit of their labor, which they owed the landlord, whereas the messengers in Matthew 22:1–14 were sent with the happier task of summoning invited guests to a wedding celebration.

In a striking way, these two messages correspond to the major themes in the preaching of John the Baptist and Jesus respectively. John demanded from his hearers that they "produce fruit that is worthy of repentance" because "every tree that does not produce good fruit is cut down and thrown into the fire" (Matt. 3:8,10). Jesus continued the same imagery,[3] and in his own way the same demand, but he introduced a new dimension. Jesus came not only to demand repentance and the bearing of "good fruit" but to call sinners such as Levi the tax collector to a joyous celebration (Mark 2:15–17). The usual signs of repentance (e.g., prayer and fasting) were inappropriate because the bridegroom was present; a wedding celebration was under way! (Mark 2:18–19). Whereas John had come in self-denial and austerity, Jesus had come "eating and drinking" and was called "a glutton and a drunkard, a friend of tax collectors and sinners" (Matt. 11:18–19; Luke 7:33–34).

Yet the placement of the two parables side by side in Matthew's Gospel, with the similarity in their three-stage development, suggests that both are intended in some way as comments on Jesus' ministry. They view his ministry from two perspectives: first as a continuation of John's call for repentance, and second as a call for rejoicing and celebration. Within each parable, Jesus' ministry corresponds to the third stage of the unfolding drama. In the story of the wicked tenants, at the third stage the landlord "sends to them his son" (or "beloved son"). In the story of the royal wedding feast, the third stage is the one in which the king sends out his servants "to the roads and crossroads" to invite to the wedding "everyone they find, both bad and good."

If Jesus found in these stories a point of self-identification, it is natural to suppose that he found it in these features. He would have seen an intimation of his own fate in the fate of the son in the first parable, and an image of his own immediate task in the command to the servants in the second parable to fill up the banquet hall indiscriminately. In each case he would have seen his ministry as coming at the end of a process or series of some kind. Other messengers had preceded him, and because he was the last his message carried an unprecedented urgency.

It is important here, as elsewhere, to distinguish this approach from an allegorical understanding of these stories. The question is "Where did Jesus find *himself* in the parables?" This does not require making a precise identification, for example, of the first two groups of servants in these two stories (e.g., as the early and later prophets, or as the prophets and John the Baptist). The Matthean context suggests that John the Baptist is in view as Jesus' immediate predecessor, and other passages can be cited as evidence that Jesus saw parallels between the ministry of the prophets and his own ministry (Matt. 23:37-39; Luke 13:31-35). Yet the two parables in themselves point only to an awareness in general that something has gone on before.

Those who see in these stories the church's allegorical depiction, after the fact, of the history of salvation are faced with the difficulty of explaining the presence, and absence, of certain details. For example, why is there nothing in the first parable to correspond to the resurrection of Jesus, and why, in the second, does the strange detail of the destruction of the city of those who reject the wedding invitations (Matt. 22:7) *precede* the sweeping extension of invitations to the outsiders? If, as is widely assumed, the destruction refers specifically to the fall of Jerusalem in A.D. 70, and the call of the outsiders refers to the church's mission to the Gentiles, the sequence is hard to explain. In the first parable, the ambition of the tenant farmers to seize the inheritance of the landlord's son has no plausible function as allegory. Despite their highly unusual features—the sudden ugly turn of events in the course of such a routine matter as the collection of rent (Matt. 21:35f.) and of such a joyous matter as the preparations for a wedding (Matt. 22:6), along with the sure judgments that follow (Matt. 21:41, 22:7)—these stories are parables, not allegories. As such they engage Jesus' attention and confirm to him his own task and destiny. In particular, they reinforce to him and his hearers the sense of urgency conveyed more directly in the announcement that the kingdom of God is at hand. Jesus is the last messenger before the end. Building on previous responses, he extends God's forgiveness to outsiders and the disenfranchised, and in so doing faces the possibility of antagonism and death.

Taken together, the two parables have an effect similar to the short parable in Mark 2:18-20, in which the call to celebrate the wedding because the bridegroom has arrived is combined with an intimation that the bridegroom is suddenly to be taken away. Whether the bridegroom's death points to Jesus' passion or Jerusalem's destruction,[4] the combination of this catastrophic element with an emphasis on the sacred joy of the present moment provides a context for understanding Jesus' intention "not to call the righteous, but sinners" (Mark 2:17).

Such examples show how Jesus' parables help illumine his behavior toward sinners both historically, against the immediate background of John the Baptist's ministry, and theologically, as a corollary of his own relationship to God. The latter is expressed most poignantly in three parables in Luke 15 about repentance. Whereas Mark 2:17 states that Jesus came "not to call the righteous, but sinners," the parallel passage in Luke 5:32 adds the words, "to repentance." In some contexts, this addition would suggest that sinners must undertake some kind of penitential discipline in order to deserve the forgiveness being extended to them. We have only to recall John the Baptist's demand that his hearers "produce fruit worthy of repentance." But the context suggests something different. Repentance as Luke uses it in 5:32 later takes on flesh and blood in the parables of the lost sheep, the lost coin, and the lost son. The setting of these parables is much the same as the setting of the dispute in chapter 5 over feasting with Levi and his friends: the Pharisees were complaining about Jesus because he was "receiving sinners and eating with them" (Luke 15:2).

THE LOST SHEEP

The story of the shepherd who left his ninety-nine sheep to go looking for one he had lost (Luke 15:4–7) is a parable of normalcy. The very first words of the story, "What man among you?" (vs. 4) immediately invite the hearer to share the perspective of the shepherd who loses one of his sheep. The implied answer is "*Of course* you would leave the ninety-nine to go after the stray." This would have been standard procedure in any such real-life emergency. When the lost was found, it would also have been natural in real life for the shepherd to invite others to share his joy (vs. 6). So it is, says Jesus, "in heaven," in other words, with God. The hearer is invited to share

God's perspective on the story, to learn how God *feels* about sinners.[5] He is more joyful "over one sinner who repents than over ninety-nine righteous persons who do not need to repent" (vs. 7). We are reminded of the emphasis in the parables of the treasure and the pearl on God's reckless love for even one who needs him, or, in the parables of the net and of the wedding feast, for all indiscriminately.

If we think of Jesus as the first audience of this parable, then it is he first of all who is being invited to share God's perspective on the situation of his day by putting himself in the place of the shepherd. This identification becomes explicit in Jesus' mind, at least in Johannine tradition, with the pronouncement, "I am the Good Shepherd" (John 10:11,14). And so a transition is accomplished from the imagery of the Old Testament, in which God is the shepherd of his people (cf., e.g., Ps. 23; Ezek. 34) to a distinctly new and Christian application in which Jesus is the shepherd. What is noteworthy in our reading of the parable is that the identification Jesus is invited to make, and presumably does make, is no different from the identification the Pharisaic hearers, or the Christian readers, are invited to make. Like the friends and neighbors of the happy shepherd in the story, they are invited to share the shepherd's perspective on what has happened. They, like Jesus, are being asked to share God's perspective, to know how God feels about sinners, and to act accordingly.

THE LOST COIN

The second in the series of three parables (Luke 15:8–10) almost duplicates the first. In this case, the hearer identifies with a woman who has saved ten drachmas and loses one. She lights a lamp and combs the house until she finds it. Then she invites her women friends and neighbors to share her joy. The introduction is much the same as in the first story: "Or what woman . . . will not . . . search carefully until she finds it?"

As in the case of the mustard seed and the leaven in Matthew, we have here twin parables that build respectively on the imagery of a man engaged in a traditionally male occupation (in this case, shepherding) and a woman engaged in a traditionally female occupation (caring for a home and managing family finances). The hearer is asked to share in her feelings of anxiety and joy, and in the application is told, "Thus . . . there is joy before the angels of God over one sinner who repents" (Luke 15:10). In this case there is no reflection on nine (or ninety-nine) righteous persons who need no repentance. The remainder of the woman's ten drachmas do not play quite the same role in this story that the ninety-nine sheep play in the other.

The absence of any reference to the "righteous" suggests that the purpose of these stories is not to identify those who do not need to repent, but rather to demonstrate how God feels about sinners. There is joy, says Jesus, "before the angels of God" when a sinner repents. The hearer is invited to understand and share in that joy by sharing the perspective of the housewife in the brief parable.

Jesus' point of identification in this second story is with the housewife as surely as it is in the first story with the shepherd. The fact that there is no explicit designation in any tradition, of Jesus as the "Good Housewife" corresponding to the designation of him as the "Good Shepherd" in John 10 does not make Jesus' self-identification with the woman in this story any less plausible.[6] As indicated earlier, Jesus' explicit self-identification with a door, a loaf of bread, a vine, or a seed of grain bespeaks a remarkable flexibility in his use of imagery with reference to himself. Although there is no way of telling whether his image of God or of himself as a woman or a housewife ever became explicit,[7] the woman is clearly the point at which Jesus and his hearers, as well as today's reader are drawn into the action. To share her perspective on her problem is to share God's perspective on sinners. They belong to him and he wants them back.

THE LOST SON

The third parable (Luke 15:11–32) differs from the other two in several respects. First of all, as a story it is much more fully developed than the others, being introduced not by a rhetorical question ("What man among you?" or "What woman?") but by a straightforward narrative opening: "A certain man had two sons." (vs. 11).[8] Its three main characters take on flesh and blood in a way that the shepherd and the housewife never do.

Second, this parable gets more directly at the issue of repentance. Each of the first two stories ends with an application to "one sinner who repents" (vss. 7,10), but repentance is represented in each instance simply as being found. The sheep does not return to the shepherd. The shepherd has to go out actively seeking the one stray sheep. Even more obviously, the housewife's drachma is the *object* of a search. It can do nothing to help itself be found! But the lost son is a human being who, coming to himself (vs. 17), decides freely to return to his father's house. His repentance is a conscious and deliberate human act. To the extent that he represents the "sinners" of verse 2, he represents them not only as the objects of God's love but as manifesting an active response to that love. The father, accordingly, becomes a more passive figure than the shepherd in the first parable or the homemaker in the second. He does not follow his younger son to distant countries, or scour land and sea to bring him back. He simply waits. Life goes on, presumably, much as before, but when the prodigal comes home his father welcomes him with joyful celebration and deep expressions of love.

The third difference is that the generalized "friends and neighbors" who are asked to share in the joy of the shepherd and of the housewife, respectively (vss. 6,9) have a particular flesh-and-blood counterpart in the last story: the older brother. Instead of a brief concluding invitation to rejoice, the third parable introduces a whole new subplot (vss. 25–32). The older brother's story is more than a dramatic foil for the story of the prodigal's return. If it were only that, its place at the end of the narrative would have made it a mere anticlimax. Nor is it an appendix to the story proper, imported from a different parable. The best explanation for its place of prominence at the end of the story is that it serves as the equivalent of the "Rejoice with me" at the end of the first two stories in Luke's sequence (vss. 6,9). Just as the indefinite "friends and neighbors" are invited to share

the perspective of the shepherd and of the housewife about their good
fortune, so the older brother is invited to share his father's perspective
about the return of the younger son.

The hearer's point of identification in the first story is with the
shepherd, but the dramatic vehicle within the story itself for that
identification is the "friends and neighbors." What is said to them is
said to the parable's hearers and readers. The point of audience identification in the second story is with the housewife who found her coin,
but the story's dramatic vehicle for the identification is the group of
village women invited to share her moment of joy. In a similar way,
the hearer's most likely point of identification in the third story is with
the waiting father, but within the story the one being asked to see
things from the father's point of view is the older brother. He, therefore, is the point at which the hearer is drawn into the story. Only as
one enters into his world and experience can one decide to rejoice or
not to rejoice with the father over the younger son's return.

What is true of any hearer is true of Jesus as well. Just as Jesus'
self-identification in the first story is with the shepherd, and in the
second with the housewife, so in the third story it is with the father
—ultimately. But he can share the perspective of the waiting father
only by first putting himself in the place of the aggrieved older son.
It is, ironically, through the eyes of one who believes he has been
wronged that Jesus must see the full extent of God's love for sinners.
The older brother has justice on his side, but in the framework of the
older brother's just claims, Jesus learns—and teaches—a lesson of
mercy.

The older brother has often been taken to represent in some way
the Pharisees who grumble at Jesus' compassion for sinners (Luke
15:2). In a parabolic context one is reminded of the parable in Matthew about vineyard workers who labored all day in the hot sun, and
grumbled because a group of latecomers received the same wages as
they (Matt. 20:1–16). But the parable of the lost son betrays no sign
of anti-Pharisaic or anti-Jewish polemic. Closer to the mark is the
suggestion that the older brother is somehow equivalent to the "nine-

ty-nine righteous . . . who need no repentance" in the parable of the lost sheep (Luke 15:7). There is no evidence that the case he makes for himself (Luke 15:29–30) is hypocritical or inaccurate. The father's words of reassurance to him—"Child, you are always with me, and all that I have is yours" (Luke 15:31)—must be given their full force. They are no mere concession to a momentary complaint, but the father's—and the storyteller's—appreciative verdict on a good and useful life. Once again the voice at Jesus' baptism comes to mind: "You are my beloved Son, in whom I am well pleased." Or, in a quite different tradition, the words of Jesus' great farewell prayer in the fourth Gospel: "And all that is mine is yours, and what is yours is mine" (John 17:10).

It is possible to argue, without resorting to allegorical interpretation, that these parallels are no coincidence. Like most other hearers, Jesus would have found himself drawn into the story of the lost son precisely through the figure of the older brother, and so called upon to share in the father's joy and compassion. But for Jesus, unlike other hearers, the self-identification was part of a larger pattern. Here as elsewhere he found his sonship confirmed, while at the same time he learned obedience to his Father's will regarding tax collectors and other prodigals. Yet the older brother in the story, even though his cause is just and his case convincing, is more a negative than a positive example for Jesus. He cannot bring himself to accept the returning sinner as a brother and friend—at least when the story ends he has not yet done so. His decision and his fate are left open-ended. The reader is challenged to follow Jesus into the world of the story and make his or her own decision about accepting and loving sinners. The decision the older brother fails to make is the decision Jesus has already made at the beginning of Luke's narrative context: he "welcomes sinners and eats with them" (Luke 15:2).

The Gospel record of Jesus' behavior toward sinners and the needy reveals how he heard and acted on parables such as these. Like the shepherd and housewife in the first two stories, Jesus assumed an active responsibility for the lost. This is demonstrated in his proclamation of the kingdom of God, in his deliberate choice to spend his time with tax collectors and prostitutes and call them to that kingdom, and in his active healings and exorcisms (e.g., the Gerasene demoniac, the deaf-mute, the blind man, and Jairus' daughter).

But like the waiting father in the third story, Jesus found himself on certain occasions in a more passive role, simply watching something redemptive happen or responding to an intiative from someone in need. This was the case, for example, in his encounters with the Syro-Phoenician woman, the centurion whose child was sick, and the hemorrhaging woman who touched his robe. There is no one style of ministry that characterizes every incident of healing or forgiveness. Jesus' role is sometimes active, sometimes more passive, and frequently both active and passive. Whether he is like a merchant actively looking for good pearls or a man who stumbles across an unexpected treasure in his field, his work is God's work. Once drawn into the world of God the Storyteller, his mission is to do what God would do, what God in fact *will* do and *is* doing in the "real" world.

If Jesus' role of extending forgiveness to sinners is either active or passive, so too is the role of those who are forgiven. Just as healing can be viewed either passively (i.e., as simply being healed), or actively (i.e., as exercising a determined faith in order to lay hold of the kingdom's power), so forgiveness can be viewed in some instances simply as being found and in others as having to be expressed in definite outward acts of love, restitution, or righteousness. The lost sheep and the lost coin are merely passive objects of caring and search, but the lost son consciously changes his mind and decides to return home. The tax collectors share meals with Jesus and his disciples without any of the usual signs of repentance or sorrow. Yet John the Baptist had spoken of "fruit worthy of repentance," and had required of his hearers specific actions: water baptism, honest dealings with regard to money, and the sharing of excess wealth with the poor.

Jesus continued this tradition. Even when his emphasis is on forgiveness as a call to joyful celebration, the Gospels suggest that the positive "fruits of repentance" are not far from his mind. Matthew's parable of the wedding feast, after describing the calling of good and bad alike, ends with a sobering glimpse of the man without a wedding garment and his sad fate (Matt. 22:11–14). The reckless love that sells all it has to buy a field or that gathers all kinds of fish indiscriminately into its net is also a love that at some point sits down and carefully sorts out the good from the bad (Matt. 13:47–50). A tax collector who is touched by Jesus' salvation and joyfully welcomes him as a guest also volunteers to give half of his possessions to the poor and make a fourfold restitution for anything he has kept wrongfully (Luke 19:1–10). It is within this context of active repentance that Jesus says he has come "to seek and to save that which was lost" (Luke 19:10).

THE SINFUL WOMAN

The active faith of a repentant sinner is nowhere better seen than in Luke 7:36–50. Jesus is eating in the home of a Pharisee named Simon when a woman rushes in unexpectedly, weeps and covers his feet with her tears and kisses, dries his feet with her hair and anoints them with expensive perfume from an alabaster bottle. It is clear to the Pharisee, and to Luke, that the woman is a "sinner" (Luke 7:37, 39), i.e., in this context, a prostitute. When Simon wonders to himself how Jesus can be a prophet if he does not realize "what kind of a woman this is who is touching him" (vs. 39), Jesus answers his unspoken objection with a parable (vss. 40–43). The scenario is somewhat reminiscent of the healing of the man with the shriveled hand in Matthew 12:9–14 or the man with swollen limbs in Luke 14:1–6.

Jesus and his opponents are confronted with a situation about which they have a dispute, and Jesus uses a parable to justify his response to the situation (e.g., healing on the Sabbath). Here the Sabbath is not in question, nor is the woman in need of healing. Jesus, in fact, is seen in an unaccustomed role. He does not minister to the woman, or perform any act of kindness on her behalf, at least not initially. Instead, *she* ministers to *him!* For once Jesus is the passive recipient of love rather than its giver. The reckless love of God demands as its appropriate response a corresponding kind of love from those it touches. This is the love the woman gives to Jesus, in the only way she knows.

The parable Jesus tells the Pharisee has to do with two debtors whose obligations were cancelled. One had owed the money-lender five hundred denarii; the other, fifty. "Which of them," Jesus asks, "will love him more?" Simon's answer is the natural one: "I suppose the one who had the larger debt cancelled." Jesus has drawn the Pharisee into the story not as an imaginary participant, but to evoke a judgment as an external observer. The question is not rhetorical, as in Matthew 12:11 or Luke 14:5, but real. The Pharisee's response, like David's answer to Nathan's parable, is self-condemning. By contrasting the Pharisee's behavior with that of the woman, Jesus makes one specific application of the story: the woman is like the debtor who had the larger debt cancelled. It is neither necessary nor legitimate to infer that Simon the Pharisee is therefore like the debtor who had the smaller debt cancelled. His conduct is mentioned only in order to throw into sharper relief the conduct of the sinful woman. Only her sins are said to be forgiven (Luke 7:47–48); the reference to those who love little because they have been forgiven little is a generalization made for the sake of the contrast, and is not brought to bear on Simon in particular.

The hearer's standpoint in relation to the parable of the debtors is an external one, much like that of Simon. The story, with its accompanying question, evokes a judgment: love is the normal response to forgiveness; the greater the forgiveness, the greater the love. Presumably the story evoked such a judgment from Jesus, and, like similar stories, helped shape his decision to invite sinners instead of good people to his kingdom. He sees this decision confirmed in the sinful woman's impetuous outburst of love. From her actions he perceives that her sins are forgiven (Luke 7:47), and on the basis of this perception he pronounces them forgiven (vs. 48).

Though the reaction is one of wonder at his power to forgive sins, Jesus' role is first of all the role of a spectator. The prostitute's spontaneous love is the evidence that God has forgiven her—when, and under what circumstances we do not know. Her actions show that she attributed her deliverance in some way to Jesus, but whatever previous acquaintance they had had is outside the story. The irony of the Pharisee's earlier remark now comes into focus: "If this man were a prophet, he would know what kind of a woman this is who is touching him, that she is a sinner" (Luke 7:39). According to Luke a prophet is just what Jesus is (Luke 7:16), and he knows precisely what kind of a woman this is: a *forgiven* sinner! As in other instances in which Jesus' role is a relatively passive one, he sends her away in peace with the words, "Your faith has saved you" (Luke 7:50). As is often noted, Jesus here acts sovereignly in the place of God, but it should also be observed that his action simply ratifies what God has already done. The woman's anointing is like a parable acted out before his eyes. In her love for him he sees God's love for her and for all sinners reflected. It is a love that cares nothing for propriety or social restrictions, a love that will turn a world upside down in order to express itself. It is a love that does not wait for a more opportune time but seizes the moment without hesitation or regret.

Kindred, though not identical, examples can be seen in some of the parables. The prodigal son in the distant land, reduced to eating the food of pigs, is a more rational, even calculating, figure than the sinful woman, but the move he decides to make is a similarly bold and reckless one. He rehearses to himself exactly what he will do—"I will arise and go to my father, and say to him 'Father, I have sinned against heaven and in your sight. I am no longer worthy to be called your son. Make me as one of your hired servants'"(Luke 15:18f.)— and then he proceeds to do it. Swallowing his pride, he renounces any rights he may have had as a son and throws himself on his father's mercy. In a sense his move is a tactic—the only way out of an otherwise hopeless predicament. But regardless of his motives, his father welcomes him, not as a servant but as a son. He has gambled and won. Like the sinful woman, he has seized the moment, responding to a crisis with desperate—and appropriate—action.

The prodigal's motives may be somewhat mixed, but those of the unjust steward in the next Lukan parable are unscrupulous. He too moves boldly and dramatically, but without shame or moral reservation. Confronted with the imminent loss of his job, he conceives a plan of winning the friendship of those who owe money to his employer by cancelling part of their debts while there is still time (Luke 16:1–7). Luke hastens to record Jesus' own judgment on the story: "And the Lord praised the unjust steward because he had acted wisely" (Luke 16:8). Jesus does not approve the steward's ethics but rather, his activism. Facing a crisis, the steward had assessed the alternatives and without looking back, acted quickly and decisively in his own interests. Those who would respond to God's forgiveness can do no less.

The incident of the sinful woman, the parable of the lost son, and especially the parable of the unjust steward invite hearers to approve of things they would normally not approve of: a woman who "gets carried away" by her emotions, a spendthrift who rehearses a bit too precisely his words of repentance, and an outright cheat who curries the favor of clients at his employer's expense! The same is true in the parable of the merciful Samaritan (Luke 10:29–37). The hearer is forced to admit that the only one in the story who behaved like a neighbor toward the wounded man beside the road was a hated foreigner.

We are not so much called on to identify with the Samaritan, or the unjust steward, or the prodigal son, as to appreciate why, and in what way, their actions were appropriate in their respective situations. The story of the unjust steward leaves us on the outside as spectators looking in, while the story of the lost son engages us personally only toward the end, when the father invites us, like the older brother, to join in the celebration. The story of the merciful Samaritan involves us from the beginning, not, however, in the person of the Samaritan, but in the person of the man beaten and left for dead on the Jerusalem-Jericho road.[9] The story is told in answer to the question, "Who is my neighbor?" (Luke 10:29). The robbery victim is the person in the story who learns the answer to that question. The story teaches him not that he must be a neighbor to the Samaritan, but that the Samaritan has been a neighbor to him (Luke 10:36). He is placed in the position of needing and receiving mercy from another, not dispensing it. The concluding word of advice, "Go and do likewise" (vs. 37), is not intended as a summary of the story's teaching, but as a further implication of it, resuming the discussion of the love command in verses 25-28. The parable proper is both preceded and followed by commands to give love, yet in itself it focuses on the experience of receiving love.[10]

Jesus' experience in real life at the hands of the sinful woman was similar. Like the robbery victim in the parable, he learned who his neighbor was—not the Pharisee but the prostitute. He learned to approve what his culture despised. The woman's actions demonstrated to him that God had touched her, and in obedience to God he declared her sins forgiven.

It may be that Jesus' own experience as well as the precedent of John the Baptist contributed to his preference for sinners over the righteous. It is important to remember that Jesus' attitudes as reflected in the Gospel tradition are not static but changing. Some changes can even be glimpsed in process. As Jesus' ministry begins, he has already opted for the sinners instead of the righteous. He has not, however, made a similar choice to go to the Gentiles instead of the Jews. Rather, he specifically forbids his disciples to go to Samaritans or Gentiles, limiting his mission and theirs to "the lost sheep of the house of Israel" (Matt. 10:5). Yet his experience with the Gentile woman from Phoenicia leads him to approve her faith and heal her daughter. His encounter with the Roman centurion draws from him the surprised comment "Truly I say to you, I have found no one in Israel with faith like that!" (Matt. 8:10; cf. Luke 7:10). The one leper out of ten who returns to give him thanks for healing is a Samaritan. Whether in incidents like these or in parables like that of the merciful Samaritan, Jesus sees in the outsider the evidence that God is at work. The fourth Gospel even depicts Jesus as visiting a Samaritan village —on his way to Galilee, to be sure—and asking a kindness from a Samaritan woman. In the symbolic richness of the Johannine narrative the drink of water he asks from the woman points to the "gift of God" (John 4:10), the Spirit Jesus will give her and her village.

To attempt to pinpoint a specific time at which Jesus changed his stated policy of excluding Samaritans and Gentiles from the sphere of his activity is neither possible nor necessary. Perhaps he never did so, at least not formally or deliberately. Because of possible tendencies of the early church to read its own Gentile mission back into the career of Jesus, it would be difficult to prove that he did so. But few if any scholars would doubt the authenticity of such a parable as that of the Samaritan, or that on occasion Jesus heartily endorsed the faith and love he found in unexpected places. When "sinners"—or Samaritans, or Gentiles—seized the initiative in certain situations, Jesus pointedly reinforced their words and actions as authentic signs of the kingdom of God. In them, God was making a breakthrough. "From the days of John the Baptist until now," Jesus said, "the kingdom of heaven comes with violence, and the violent are seizing it for their own" (Matt. 11:12). The earliest interpretation of this much-debated saying in Luke 16:16 identifies the violent coming of the kingdom with its proclamation by John and Jesus, and the violent seizing of it as "everyone entering it by force." Both versions see a correspondence between God's act and the appropriate human response.

The *violence* of the kingdom of heaven is the power that drives out demons, heals the sick, purifies the unclean, and raises the dead. It is the power that binds the strong man, breaks into his house, and robs him of his captives. It is the love that turns a world upside down to reclaim the poor and the powerless. It is an unpredictable and scandalous love that bypasses the friends of God and risks everything to save his enemies. All human standards are reversed; the bottom is on top; the last are first, and the first last (Matt. 19:30, 20:16). It is not the priests and the Pharisees, but prostitutes, tax collectors, and foreigners who are pressing into the kingdom of God (Matt. 21:31). In the words of Mary before Jesus was born: "He has brought down rulers from their thrones but has lifted up the humble. He has filled the hungry with good things but has sent the rich away empty" (Luke

1:52–53). The recklessness of God displayed in Jesus' ministry demands a corresponding recklessness from those it touches.

If God's forgiveness turns a world upside down, discipleship as defined by Jesus is the art of living in God's topsy-turvy world. What the world accepts as normal is seen to be ugly and distorted, whereas what the world considers intolerable is what Jesus approves and commands. Radical grace implies radical demand. God gives all, and he demands all. He gives himself to those he loves, totally and without qualification, and, in turn, he asks that they give themselves to him and others totally and without qualification. Yet it is not "in return." There is no *quid pro quo*. God does not forgive on the condition that those forgiven become disciples, nor does he later ask that they become disciples in exchange for the mercy they have received. The gift of forgiveness and the demand of discipleship coexist as opposite sides of the same coin. They are separate, yet they are one. This is the mystery of discipleship, which the Gospels articulate over and over again, but which they never solve.

The mystery is maintained even in such a parable as Matthew 18:21–35, in which the unconditional character of God's forgiveness seems, on the surface, to be compromised. A king calls his vassals to account and discovers one who owes an enormous debt of ten thousand talents (two-and-a-half million to over sixteen million dollars, depending on the kind of currency involved). The debtor asks for more time to pay, so that his property will not be confiscated and he and his whole family sold into slavery. Instead of granting an extension, the king simply cancels the debt! Hardly a parable of normalcy! The next development is that the same vassal in turn is owed a hundred denarii—the equivalent of a workman's wages for about three months. He is unwilling to write off the debt, and has the debtor thrown into prison until payment is made in full. The king hears of this, and angrily revokes the cancellation of the vassal's debt and "consigns him to the jailers until he pays back all that he owes" (Matt. 18:34). The contrast between the two attitudes, especially between ten thousand talents and a paltry hundred denarii is ludicrous, and gives the story a comic touch that makes its deadly serious application all the more powerful: "This is also what my heavenly Father will do to you unless each of you forgives his brother from the heart" (Matt. 18:35).[11]

Does this imply that forgiveness can be revoked or that it is conditional on the subsequent behavior of the one forgiven? "Forgive us our debts," Jesus tells his disciples to pray, "as we forgive our debtors" (Matt. 6:12; cf. vss. 14–15). Yet to make forgiveness conditional on anything but God's impulsive love and his in-breaking kingdom is to fly in the face of too much in the Gospel tradition. The solution to the difficulty is that forgiveness, like healing, transforms. Forgiveness in the parable of the unforgiving sinner is represented by canceling a debt. Most discussions of forgiveness assume that cancellation of debt is actually the *definition* of forgiveness. It is not. It is a *metaphor* for forgiveness. As such it has its own validity as long as it is not allowed to crowd out other metaphors—above all the metaphor of healing.

The old-fashioned English phrase, "the remission of sins," captures something that is lost in the more common expression, "forgiveness of sins." Medically, when a disease is "in remission," its power over the victim has been broken, and when sins are in remission, their power is similarly broken. But the opposite is also true. When people show by their behavior—in this case, the lack of mercy—that sin still dominates them, there has obviously been no remission. Nothing has really changed. The individual has accepted no transforming mercy, and can only expect judgment (cf. James 2:13). But in discipleship, with all that it entails—love of enemies, renunciation, and childlike trust—forgiveness shows itself valid and effective.

12.

DISCIPLESHIP
AS THE LOVE OF ENEMIES

A concise way of relating forgiveness and discipleship in the ministry of Jesus is to say that men and women are called to be "imitators of God." Paul puts it just that way, and with specific reference to the work of Jesus: "Be kind and compassionate to one another, forgiving each other, just as in Christ God forgave you. Be imitators of God, therefore, as dearly loved children, and live a life of love, just as Christ loved us and gave himself up for us as a fragrant offering and sacrifice to God" (Eph. 4:32–5:2NIV). Elsewhere Paul can say, as a pastor to his churches, "Be imitators of me, as I am of Christ" (1 Cor. 11:1 RSV). He can remind the Thessalonians of how they "became imitators of us and of the Lord," or "imitators of God's churches in Judea, which are in Christ Jesus" (1 Thess. 1:6, 2:14).

The varied formulas look like fragments from one broad yet very simple pattern: Jesus imitates God, a disciple of Jesus imitates Jesus, and disciples imitate other disciples. The qualities being imitated are not the qualities usually thought of as exclusively divine—omnipotence, universal sovereignty, infinite wisdom—but another set of qualities associated as often with humanity as with deity. Once again, some memorable lines from the apostle Paul are a good place to begin:

> So you see, at just the right time, while we were still powerless, Christ died for the ungodly. One would scarcely have to die for a righteous person—though possibly for a good person someone might go so far as

to die. But God himself demonstrated such love for us that while we were still sinners, Christ died for us. . . . For if we, God's enemies, were reconciled to him through the death of his Son, how much more, now that we are reconciled, shall we be saved through his life!" (Rom. 5:6–8,10).

Paul's emphasis in this passage is on the love of God—in particular his reconciling love for us, his enemies. The implication that we, as God's imitators, should in turn love our enemies is not spelled out, but later in the same epistle Paul can write "Bless those who persecute you; bless and do not curse" (Rom. 12:14 NIV), and "Do not repay anyone evil for evil. . . . Do not take revenge, my friends, but leave room for God's wrath" (Rom. 12:19a NIV). He then quotes from Proverbs: " 'It is my place to take revenge, I will repay,' says the Lord, 'but if your enemy is hungry, feed him; if he is thirsty, give him something to drink. In doing this you will heap burning coals on his head' " (Rom. 12:20). On this passage he comments, "Do not be overcome by evil, but overcome evil with good" (Rom. 12:21).

In both the fifth and twelfth chapters of Romans, Paul has been powerfully influenced by the teaching of Jesus in the Gospels. The statement that "one scarcely dies for a righteous person," and that "Christ died for us while we were sinners," clearly recalls Mark 2:17: Jesus came "not . . . to call the righteous, but sinners." Although Paul has focused his presentation of God's love and forgiveness very intensely on the single event of the cross, the theme itself is unmistakably the same one that surfaced again and again in the ministry of Jesus. God turns a world upside down, not for the sake of his friends, but for his enemies. He risks everything and gives everything to reclaim those who are lost. The theme that we in our turn are called on to love *our* enemies is equally at home in the Gospel tradition. If the "Sermon on the Mount" in Matthew 5–7 and the "Sermon on the Plain" in Luke 6 could be summarized in just one command, it would have to be "Love your enemies." A brief, and admittedly selective, overview of these two discourses (especially Matthew 5:1–48 and Luke 6:20–36) will bear this out.

MATTHEW

The Sermon on the Mount is the first of five discourses of Jesus in Matthew's Gospel. It begins with a series of beatitudes, pronouncements of blessedness (Matt. 5:1–12). Jesus has just made a tour of Galilee "teaching in their synagogues, preaching the good news of the kingdom, and healing every disease and sickness among the people" (Matt. 4:23 NIV). As he begins the discourse, Jesus has two groups of people in view: his disciples (at least the four in Matt. 4:18–22 who have just been called), and "great multitudes from Galilee, the Decapolis, Jerusalem, Judea, and beyond the Jordan" (Matt. 4:25). Matthew records that when Jesus "saw the crowds he went up on a mountainside and sat down. His disciples came to him, and he began to teach them, saying . . ." (5:1–2 NIV).

The almost simultaneous interest in the crowds and in the disciples is a striking feature that reappears in the second of Matthew's five discourses. There again Jesus is described as being on the move, traversing "all the towns and villages, teaching in their synagogues, preaching the good news of the kingdom, and healing every disease and sickness" (Matt. 9:35 NIV; cf. 4:23). Matthew adds that Jesus, when he saw the crowds, "had compassion on them, because they were harassed and helpless, like sheep without a shepherd. Then he said to his disciples, 'The harvest is plentiful but the workers are few. Ask the Lord of the harvest to send out workers into his harvest field' " (Matt. 9:35–38 NIV). He next recruits and authorizes twelve of these disciples to carry out the "harvest" (chapter 10). The theme of the second Matthean discourse is mission, the responsibility of Jesus' disciples to minister to the helpless crowds.

The situation in Matthew 5 is not so different from this as it might at first appear. When Jesus gives the beatitudes, he is speaking to his disciples, but, initially at least, he is speaking *about* "the lost sheep of the house of Israel" (Matt. 10:5), the poor and the needy he sees represented in the crowds pursuing him from every corner of the land. The purpose of the beatitudes is to direct the disciples' attention to the poor, the mourners, the meek, the hungry, and the thirsty, and to remind them of their own responsibility with respect to these disadvantaged of the earth. What we know of the Gospels and of Jesus' ministry generally leads us to expect that the "poor in spirit" and the others being pronounced blessed in God's sight are those who might be classed as the enemies of God, the sinners and social outcasts to whom Jesus directed the bulk of his efforts—prostitutes, tax collectors, Roman soldiers, Samaritans and other foreigners, lepers, the mentally ill, and the demon-possessed! The beatitudes become a remarkably clear expression of God's unconditional forgiveness of sinners, a kind of translation of one major theme of Jesus' parables into nonparabolic language. But it must be added that in the beatitudes the "sinners" seem to have been idealized almost beyond recognition. We hardly recognize in the poor, the mourners, the meek, and in those who "hunger and thirst for righteousness" the motley crew that offended the Pharisees by gathering around Jesus to eat and drink. The sinners are viewed here through the eyes of a Lover, and by that love transformed into the "righteous."

The same transformation can be seen elsewhere in Matthew's Gospel: Jesus comes "not to call the righteous but sinners" (Matt. 9:13), just as he does in Mark, yet at the end of the age it is the righteous who will "shine like the sun in the kingdom of their Father" (Matt. 13:43 NIV). The transformation is complete; the sinners have become the righteous.[1] Likewise in the beatitudes the tax collectors and prostitutes, the poor and all outsiders have been transformed by an eschatological vision. Their transformation is not merely a hope but a present experience. The promises that they *will* be comforted, *will* inherit the earth, *will* be satisfied, *will* receive mercy, *will* see God and become his children are framed by twin assertions that "theirs *is* the kingdom of heaven" (Matt. 5:3,10).

The transformation is carried out not merely by the eight pronouncements that they are blessed, but by the terms with which they are described. They are no longer sinful or selfish or unattractive or unclean. They are beautiful.[2] Although they are poor and weak in themselves, their plight has its own beauty and goodness. The poor are described as "poor in spirit"—i.e., "those who know they are spiritually poor" (GNB). The hungry and thirsty are longing not simply for food but "for righteousness"—or "to do what God requires," (GNB) or "to see right prevail" (NEB). In Jesus' vision, their predicaments have been turned into their virtues and their sinfulness is out of the picture. God's enemies have been made his friends.

What is true of the first four beatitudes is even more true of the last four. Each series ends with a mention of "righteousness" (Matt. 5: 6,10). If the first group are those who "hunger and thirst to see right prevail," the second are those "persecuted for what is right." Their virtue is an active virtue that does not simply arise out of their poverty or weakness. They show mercy to others, they are pure in heart, they make peace, and like the prophets of old they are persecuted for their good deeds (Matt. 5:12). Jesus' vision of their active righteousness arises in part out of his own experience. They are perhaps exemplified in the sinful woman who anointed him, the Samaritan in the parable who showed mercy to his neighbor, the widow who put her small coin in the temple treasury, the tax collector whose prayer was heard, Zacchaeus who gave half of his goods to the poor, and all those whose faith gained healing for themselves or their loved ones.

In the eight beatitudes, Jesus calls his disciples to share his vision of the sinners and their blessedness—or to use Paul's terminology, their justification. As in several of Jesus' parables, the audience is invited to see things the way God sees them. The implication of this vision for the disciples personally does not emerge until a ninth beatitude, in which the change from third to second person suddenly draws the disciples themselves into the vision: "Blessed are you when you are insulted and persecuted and charged falsely with every evil for my sake. Rejoice and be glad, for your reward is great in heaven; the prophets before you were persecuted in just the same way" (Matt. 5:11–12). All at once the disciples are no longer observers, but participants. No longer are they asked merely to appreciate from a distance

God's transformation of sinners into the righteous, but they are themselves caught up in it. Their situation is not the same as that of the
friends and neighbors in the parables of the lost sheep and the lost
coin, or the older brother in the parable of the lost son. They are not
being asked simply to rejoice with God at the reclaiming of those he
loves. Their involvement in the vision is deeper than that, for suddenly
it is *they* who are being reclaimed. The "blessed are you" of the ninth
beatitude reveals the secret that the entire series has been referring to
them! *They* are the poor in spirit, the mourners, the meek, the hungry
and thirsty for justice, the merciful, the pure in heart, the peacemakers, the persecuted. As surely as Nathan's accusing "You are the
man," the ninth beatitude draws the hearers irrevocably into the
action. "You are the people of God. The story was really about you
all the time!"

Obviously, the story was not *only* about the disciples. The initial
point of reference for Jesus' vision was, as we have seen, the needy
multitudes following him. For the disciples, two things were necessary: first, to see the multitudes the way God and Jesus saw them,
through eyes of love; and second, to put themselves unreservedly in
the place of those who desperately needed—and gladly received—that
transforming love. Their rejoicing is not over "sinners who repent"
or over the forgiveness of others, but over their own restoration, and
the great reward awaiting them in heaven (Matt. 5:12; cf. Luke 10:20).

At the same time, their rejoicing takes place in the very teeth of
persecution. Their identity with the poor in spirit comes into focus
precisely at the point of being "persecuted for righteousness' sake"
(Matt. 5:10f.). God had intervened decisively to overturn the world
by making friends of his enemies, but the process was not yet complete. The kingdom of God was near, even breaking in on Jesus and
his world, but not fully or unmistakably present. There were still
enemies, and as long as there were enemies there would be opposition
and suffering. The work of God had only begun.

The theme of the disciples' identity as God's oppressed, yet beloved, people continues in the verses that follow. The "blessed are

you" of the ninth beatitude anticipates Matthew 5:13 ("You are the salt of the earth?) and Matthew 5:14 ("You are the light of the world"). The center of interest is not on what disciples do, but first of all on who they are. Once again, Jesus draws on metaphor to display his vision. They are salt, and they are light, each somehow in relation to the world or the earth. The first image is used negatively, the second positively. Salt's value for the taste or preservation of food is assumed, but here it is seen as diluted and tasteless, fit only to be thrown out and trampled by men (Matt. 5:13).

Light, on the other hand, appears here as a city shining at night on a hill, or a bright lamp illumining everyone in the house (vss. 14–15). "In the same way," Jesus says "let your light shine before men, that they may see your good deeds and praise your Father in heaven" (Matt. 5:16 NIV).

The two metaphors place before the disciples an alternative: to "be overcome by evil," or to "overcome evil with good" (cf. Paul in Rom. 12:21). Jesus' explicit command to love enemies comes near the end of the Sermon on the Mount's first major section (Matt. 5:44), but the enemies have already made their appearance in the text, in the indefinite insulters, persecutors, and false witnesses of the ninth beatitude, and in the men (i.e., the people of the world) who trample down useless salt, or rejoice in a shining light, as the case may be.

Perhaps the alternative is one Jesus himself confronted. John's Gospel presents him as saying "I am the light of the world" (John 8:12; cf. 9:5, 12:46), while the First Epistle of Peter offers him as a model for all disciples: "To this you were called, because Christ suffered for you, leaving you an example, that you should follow in his steps. . . . When they hurled their insults at him, he did not retaliate; when he suffered, he made no threats. Instead, he entrusted himself to him who judges justly" (1 Peter 2:21, 23 NIV). There is indeed a certain appropriateness in the liberty taken by the 1970 musical *Godspell,* in which the last beatitude is addressed *to Jesus* by his disciples: "Blessed are *you* when you are insulted and persecuted and charged falsely with every evil. . . ." If the beatitudes are an invitation to put ourselves in the place of the reconciled enemies of God, they are no less an invitation to follow Jesus himself, loving those who are still God's enemies and continuing the work of over-coming evil with good.

Matthew 5:17–48 is a reinterpretation of the Old Testament law, centering on a higher righteousness than that of the scribes and Phari-sees (Matt. 5:20). Using six contrasts or "antitheses" (vss. 21–48), Jesus takes his stand over against the scribal and Pharisaic oral tradi-tions: "You have heard that it was said. . . . But I say to you" (vss. 21, 27, 31, 33, 38, 43). What Jesus says in contrast to the oral tradition takes the form of universal sanctions against "everyone who . . ." or "whoever . . ." does certain things (vss. 22, 28, 32), specific prohibi-tions of other things ("Don't take an oath at all," vs. 34; "don't resist the evil person," vs. 39), and finally the positive command: "Love your enemies and pray for your persecutors; only so can you be children of your heavenly Father" (vss. 44f. NEB).

Love is the fulfilling of the law, just as it is in Jesus' summary of the twofold love command on which all the law and the prophets depend (Matt. 22:37–40). But instead of love for God and neighbor, the antitheses of Matthew's Sermon on the Mount culminate in the command to love *enemies!* Love of neighbors (with *hatred* of enemies as its corollary) belongs rather to the scribal teaching that Jesus rejects! The Gospel writers accept the principle of loving God and neighbor *if* "neighbor" is broadly enough and radically enough defined.

The Lukan account of the command to love God and neighbor (Luke 10:25–28) immediately precedes the parable of the merciful Samaritan, with its implicit redefinition of the neighbor as the enemy (Luke 10:29–37). There is no need to set love of neighbor and love of enemy against each other as inconsistent or contradictory expressions, any more than there is a need to place the Johannine "love for one another" (i.e., for fellow disciples) in sharp contrast to either or both.

But Jesus' most typical expression, the one that arises most natu-rally out of his own experience, appears to be love of enemies. Though not all of the six antitheses in Matthew express this theme directly, it is the thread that holds them together. The command is explicit, or nearly so, in the first (dealing with murder), the fifth (dealing with nonresistance), and of course the sixth and last antithesis.

The first antithesis begins by redefining murder as anger. Jesus goes a step beyond the Ten Commandments. It is not enough simply to avoid killing. In the community of disciples, one must not even become angry with a brother or sister (Matt. 5:22). But that is only the negative side. The mere avoidance of anger is not enough. Positively, one must take steps to bring about reconciliation. The brother or sister must be treated as a brother or sister, not as an enemy. Otherwise our sacrificial offerings are useless, and our worship meaningless. Matthew conveys Jesus' point by appending to the antithesis proper a brief glimpse of a hypothetical situation: "So if you bring your gift to the altar and then remember that your brother has something against you, leave your gift right there in front of the altar; go and first be reconciled to your brother, and then come back and offer up your gift" (Matt. 5:23–24). But even this does not end the matter.

A second postscript, this one parabolic in form, extends the imperative of reconciliation even to enemies: "Come to an agreement with your adversary quickly, while you are with him on the road; otherwise your adversary will deliver you up to the judge, and the judge will turn you over to the officer, and you will be sent to prison. Truly, I say to you, you will in no way get out of there until you have paid the last penny" (Matt. 5:25–26). This is not itself a full-blown parable, but is rather Jesus' application of a story not actually found in the text. Jesus puts his hearers in the place of one of the story's characters, and gives them an appropriate exhortation in terms the story has provided. Far from treating our brother as an enemy, we must treat our enemy as a brother! Whether the juxtaposition of the antithesis proper (Matt. 5:21–22) with its two postscripts (vss. 23–24, 25–26) is the work of Jesus or Matthew, the purpose it serves is quite clearly Jesus' own purpose: the reinterpretation of the Old Testament law in the direction of a radical and unqualified love for our enemies.

In the second, third, and fourth antitheses, Jesus focuses on other concerns (adultery, divorce, and the taking of oaths). Yet even here the relation of the disciple to the enemy is at least on the periphery of his vision. In redefining adultery as lust (Matt. 5:27-30) Jesus mentions not only being led into sin by one's eye (i.e., looking at a woman in order to lust after her), but also by one's right hand, which seems intended to reinforce the previous section by alluding to physical violence against an enemy. The third antithesis (Matt. 5:31-32) envisions a shaky marriage in which the wife has become the "enemy." Jesus forbids divorce out of consideration for her. Divorce is wrong because it leads others (i.e., the wife and her new partner) into the sin of adultery. The fourth warns against taking unfair advantage of an opponent in a dispute by a deceptive use of oaths (cf. Matt. 23:16-22).

The enemy comes explicitly into view in the last two antitheses as the higher righteousness is more and more clearly defined. Jesus' disciples are not to resist an evil aggressor, or retaliate when someone takes advantage of them. Even when physically assaulted, they are to turn the other cheek, and when something is requested or demanded of them, they are to give what is asked—and more (Matt. 5:38-42).

The last antithesis (Matt. 5:43-48) not only summarizes and makes explicit much that has gone before, but also brings to light the purpose of it all. "Love your enemies. . . . so that you may become children of your Father in heaven" (Matt. 5:45). The language is reminiscent of Jesus' blessing on the peacemakers who "shall be called the children of God" (Matt. 5:9).

The theme is the familiar one of becoming followers or imitators of God. Jesus' disciples are to love their enemies because God did so first. Surprisingly, Jesus illustrates this not by pointing to the inbreaking kingdom of God and the mercy being extended to sinners in his own ministry, but with reference to the natural order. God "lets his sun rise on good and bad people alike, and pours rains on the just and the unjust" (Matt. 5:45). A possible reason for this is that Jesus (or

Matthew) is describing God's generous acts only briefly and for illustrative purposes. He does not want the illustration to dominate or displace the main point of the immediate context, i.e., the responsibility of the disciples to love their enemies as well as their friends.

The proclamation of the kingdom and of God's love for sinners was the theme of Matthew 5:1–16, but in verses 17–48 Jesus is giving an exhortation to his disciples based on that good news. When he concludes the section with the command to "Be perfect as your Father in heaven is perfect" (Matt. 5:48), he is not urging an abstract or mystical imitation of God's many attributes and virtues. He has one virtue in mind: God's boundless and extravagant love for sinners, announced in the Beatitudes and displayed throughout Jesus' ministry. The perfection demanded of Jesus' disciples is that same mad perfection of loving our enemies.

The rest of the Sermon on the Mount turns to other important themes such as prayer and the disciplines of piety, trust, and dependence on God, and the discernment of false prophets. There is no sustained emphasis on love of enemies as there was in chapter 5. Nevertheless, the theme surfaces at several points. As a postscript to the Lord's Prayer (Matt. 6:9–13), Matthew appends Jesus' comment relating to the petition for forgiveness: "For if you forgive people their offenses your heavenly Father will also forgive you; but if you do not forgive people, then your Father will not forgive your offenses" (Matt. 6:14–15). Despite Matthew's interest elsewhere in reconciliation within the Christian community (e.g., 5:23–24; 18:15–20), in this passage the application is to human beings generally. In fact, the latter relationship is brought within the sphere of the former, just as in the first antithesis (Matt. 5:21–26). Jesus' disciples are to treat people in general (including an enemy) as they would treat a brother or sister in the community. Again in Matthew 7:12 Jesus returns to the subject of "the law and the prophets" (cf. Matt. 5:17–20), and summarizes the biblical message in what Christians have come to call the "Golden Rule": "In everything, treat people in the way that you want them to treat you." The point is exactly the same as in chapter 5. The Scriptures find their fulfillment in love for all people, including our actual or potential enemies. When a disciple accepts and begins to share the vision of sinners articulated in the Beatitudes, such love becomes both a possibility and a demand.

LUKE

The basic material in Luke on love of enemies (Luke 6:27–36) is shorter and more condensed than in Matthew, focusing for the moment on one command to the exclusion of all others. Luke's beatitudes (Luke 6:20–23) differ in several ways from those found in Matthew. There are four of them instead of nine, and they cannot be separated from the series of four corresponding woes that immediately follows (Luke 6:24–26). There is a rough, but not exact, parallel between Luke's beatitudes and the first four in Matthew. Luke has no equivalent for Matthew's second group of four. Luke, moreover, uses the second person rather than the third person from the start, instead of bringing it in at the end of the series as a rhetorical device to draw the disciples into the action. "Blessed are *you* poor," Jesus says to his disciples, "for *yours* is the kingdom of God." The identification of the disciples with the poor and needy multitude, which in Matthew is accomplished suddenly in the ninth beatitude, is in Luke assumed at the outset, and dominates the entire sequence. The disciples, it would seem, *are* the poor, the hungry, those who weep, and those who are hated. But it is equally apparent, paradoxically, as Jesus continues that they also are the rich, the satisfied, those who laugh, and those the world praises. The beatitudes and the woes confront the disciples with a choice: Which group do they want to be?

The alternative of blessing or curse is a well-known form in biblical literature. But nowhere is the reversal of the world's values quite as stark as here. Surely it is better to be rich than poor, to have enough to eat than to go hungry, to laugh than to cry, to be well-spoken of than hated, and, one is tempted to add, to be righteous than a sinner. Jesus registers a resounding "no" against all such logic. His woes fall on the world's blessed, and his blessings on those who are miserable.

He invites his disciples to choose blessing. The form of the last beatitude ("Blessed are you when people hate you . . .") suggests a similar understanding of the first three ("Blessed are you when you are poor. . . . Blessed are you when you are hungry. . . . Blessed are you when you weep . . ."). To choose blessing is to choose poverty, hunger, tears, and persecution.

These conditions are not idealized or spiritualized to the same extent as in Matthew. For Luke, the poor are not "poor in spirit" or "humble people" but actually poor. The hungry are not hungering for justice but for food! They are pronounced blessed in their predicament, but their predicament is not made into a virtue. Their blessedness lies solely in the coming reversal of their fortunes.

What is promised in each instance corresponds to what the rich and powerful possess now. The rich already have their consolation, but the future (i.e., the kingdom of God) belongs to the poor. In the kingdom, the hungry will have plenty to eat, those who weep now will laugh, and those who are dishonored on earth will be honored in heaven. Knowing this, they can be glad and dance for joy even in the face of hatred and expulsion from the synagogue. Their enemies, on the other hand, will be hungry, and will mourn and weep. Honored among all people, they can expect from God only judgment and woe. To choose the lot of the rich and well satisfied is to choose a curse and not a blessing. We must not forget the troubling line from Proverbs quoted by Paul: in doing good to our enemy we "heap burning coals upon his head" (Prov. 25:21f.; Rom. 12:20 RSV). There are limits to mercy for those who neither show nor look for mercy. The kingdom of God as revealed in Jesus' words and actions means forgiveness for sinners now, without limit and without conditions. But when it comes in its fullness it means two things: mercy to those it has already touched and judgment on those who have trampled it underfoot. When Jesus contemplates the end of the age, there is no evidence that he sees it differently from John the Baptist or any other Jewish prophet or apocalyptic visionary.

The section on love of enemies that immediately follows the

Lukan beatitudes (Luke 6:27–36) addresses itself to those who have made the right decision: "But I say to you that hear..." (vs. 27). The word "but" serves to brush aside the woes and turn our attention once more to the beatitudes, especially the last one. "Blessed are you," Jesus had said, "when people hate you, when they exclude you and insult you and blot out your name as something evil, all for the sake of the Son of man" (vs. 22). Now, after the series of woes, Jesus picks up from there: "Love your enemies; do good to those who hate you; bless those who curse you; pray for those who mistreat you" (vss. 27–28). The next eight verses pursue single-mindedly the theme of loving enemies:

> If someone strikes you on one cheek, turn to him the other also. If someone takes your cloak, do not stop him from taking your tunic. Give to everyone who asks you, and if anyone takes what is yours, do not demand it back. Treat others as you want them to treat you. If you love those who love you, what credit is that to you. Even sinners love those who love them. And if you do good to those who are good to you, what credit is that to you? Even sinners do that much. And if you lend to those from whom you expect to be repaid, what credit is that to you? Even sinners lend to sinners, expecting repayment in full. But love your enemies, do good to them, and lend to them without expecting anything in return. Then your reward will be great, and you will be children of the Most High, for he is kind to the ungrateful and the wicked. Be merciful, just as your Father is merciful" (Luke 6:29–36).

The passage requires little comment. Most of it parallels Matt. 5:38–48, the last two of the Matthean antitheses, but without the antithetical framework ("It has been said... but I say to you"). Luke repeats the specific imperative, "Love your enemies" in such a way as to frame the whole (Luke 6:27,35), while placing almost at the center the one saying that in Matthew is found elsewhere, the so-called "Golden Rule" (vs. 31; cf. Matt. 7:12). The significant remark in Matthew that this saying "is the law and the prophets" (Matt. 7:12) cannot be found in Luke. Neither Luke 6:31 in particular nor the passage in general is presented as a summary or fulfillment of Old

Testament law or Scripture. Jesus is not reinterpreting Scripture, but bringing a new revelation of his own. Yet despite differing methods of constructing this key sermon of Jesus, Matthew and Luke agree in making the love of enemies the pivot on which Jesus' ethic turns.

Luke's contrast between the behavior required of disciples and the behavior of sinners (Luke 6:32, 33, 34) is also noteworthy. "Sinners" here corresponds to Matthew's terms "tax collector" and "heathen" (Matt. 5:46f.). The reference is obviously to the same group to whom Jesus directed his ministry, only viewed this time as they really exist day by day in the world, not idealized or transformed by God's love or by the eschatological vision of Jesus or the Gospel writer. Luke sees them exemplified precisely in the enemies that curse and mistreat the disciples. To love only those who love us and hate our enemies, Jesus says, is to behave as the enemies behave and thus to play into their hands. In Pauline terms it is to let oneself be overcome by evil instead of overcoming evil with good (cf. Rom. 12:21). On the lips of Jesus, these words serve at the same time as a subtle rebuke to the righteous of his day, who sharply distinguished themselves from sinners yet also loved only those who loved them (Matt. 5:43), and performed good works only to gain immediate tangible rewards. The question "What credit is that to you?" (Luke 6:33, 34) functions appropriately as a challenge to either the commitment of his disciples or the hypocrisy of the priests and the Pharisees.

Luke continues in much the same way as Matthew. The goal and basis of Jesus' exhortation to the disciples emerges in Jesus' promise that "your reward will be great, and you will be children of the Most High, for he is kind to the ungrateful and the wicked" (vs. 35). Then, as a summation: "Be merciful, even as your Father is merciful" (Luke 6:36RSV). The two Gospel writers agree in grounding the love of enemies in the imitation of God. For the reader today who has access to both Gospels, Luke's "Be merciful" specifies and clarifies Matthew's "Be perfect." But the Lukan interpretation is implicit in Matthew's context as well, and is demanded by all that the Gospels tell us of Jesus' words and actions.

It is well known that in John's Gospel Jesus commanded his disciples to "love one another" (John 13:34f., 15:12,17) and that the church concluded from this that Christians were to love their fellow Christians, their brothers and sisters in the community of faith. It is equally clear that in the Synoptics, Jesus is represented as calling his attention to the two great commands of Scripture, love of God and love of neighbor (Mark 12:28–34a). Without denying that these emphases were present in Jesus' teaching, it must be recognized that love of enemies is more central to his message than either of them. Luke has brought this out most clearly by his juxtaposition of the "two great commands" with the story of the merciful Samaritan. The effect of the arrangement is to widen the definition of neighbor to include the enemy explicitly. This widening is everywhere presupposed in the Synoptic tradition.

13.

DISCIPLESHIP
AS RENUNCIATION

The responsibilities of discipleship as Jesus expressed them involve more than simply the love of enemies. In fact the latter is a subheading of a more basic category: renunciation. To treat one's enemies in the way Jesus commanded is to renounce vengeance. The Old Testament restricted the practice of vengeance or retaliation. Jesus eliminated it altogether. Renunciation can be defined as voluntarily giving up what we believe we are entitled to, whether it be redress of grievances, a home, a family, possessions, or life itself. Jesus' call to discipleship touches all these areas. Our attention thus far has been directed to one area in particular, the renunciation of retributive justice. This theme is clearly based on Jesus' announcement of radical forgiveness and illustrates well the principle that discipleship means doing what God has done. But Jesus demands renunciation in the other, perhaps more basic and obvious, areas as well.

A useful starting-point in assessing Jesus' demand for renunciation is his story about a man who prepared a great dinner party and invited many guests (Luke 14:15–24). This Lukan parable is often regarded simply as a less colorful version of Matthew's parable of the royal wedding banquet (Matt. 22:1–14). In both stories the invited guests decline and new guests are found. But in Luke the would-be host is not a king but only "a certain man," and the banquet has nothing to do with a wedding celebration. The stock figures of the king and the king's son, and the stock imagery of the wedding and bridegroom are missing. It is as difficult to argue that Luke has deliberately impoverished Matthew's rather splendid account, as it is to maintain that all the splendor—king and prince and nuptials—is merely Matthew's invention. The stock figures are part and parcel of Jesus' own world of imagery. Yet if Luke had found them in his sources it is hard to see why he would not have retained them. We are most likely dealing with two separate stories, similar in general structure but different in detail and purpose—what we might expect if Jesus himself had told the same basic story more than once under varying circumstances.

The most striking difference between the two stories lies not in the presence or absence of particular details, but in the distinct uses to which the stories are put. As it stands, Luke 14:15–24 is a parable about discipleship, while Matthew 22:1–14 is a parable about forgiveness and the call to salvation.

That is why they are dealt with in two different chapters. Matthew's elaborate series of two groups of servants (Matt. 22:3,4), followed by judgment on the rejectors and their city (vs. 7), and a general call to any who were outside in the streets (vss. 8,9), gives way in Luke to a simpler scheme. There is only one servant throughout (Luke 14:17,21,22,23); he issues one call to the invited guests (vs. 17) and the one call is rejected (vss. 18–20).

But Luke elaborates at two points where Matthew is simple. First, he creates a series of his own by enumerating three sample excuses by which the invited guests refuse their invitations to the banquet: "I have bought a field, and I must go out and see it" (Luke 14:18), "I have bought five yoke of oxen and I have to try them out" (vs. 19), and "I have married a wife" (vs. 20). Second, he mentions two general round-ups of outsiders instead of just one (vss. 21,23). The effect of the first of these changes is to focus attention on things that stand in the way of true discipleship—home, property, and family. The effect of the second is not to distinguish two stages in Jesus' mission to sinners or in the church's mission to Gentiles in Luke's day, but simply to make the point that the house must be full, so that none of the originally invited guests will have a place at the banquet. Together, these distinctives emphasize the seriousness of saying "no" to the invitation, no matter what the reason.

Just as Matthew's placement of the parable of the wedding feast reinforces the meaning that arises out of the story itself, so Luke's placement of the parable of the dinner party reinforces that parable's stress on discipleship. This can be seen both in the preceding and following sections (Luke 14:7–14, 25–33). Jesus is seated at table in the house of one of the leaders of the Pharisees on the same occasion on which he healed a man with swollen limbs (Luke 14:1–6). He offers some rather revolutionary advice to guests and host alike (vss. 7–11, 12–14). Allowing his imagination free rein, Jesus surveys the scene before him and asks, "What if everything were just the opposite? What if guests took the last places when they arrived at a wedding feast? What if hosts invited the poor and the handicapped to their parties instead of friends and relatives?" His imaginative vision transforms a normal dinner party into a very strange affair indeed.

The designation of Jesus' brief rules of table etiquette in Luke 14:7–14 as a "parable" (vs. 7) is surprising until we realize that it describes exactly what Jesus is doing. He has turned a real life situation into a parable, not by *telling* a parable (at least not until verse 16) but by inviting his hearers to imagine with him what their festivities would be like in the upside-down world of the kingdom of God:

"When you are invited by someone to a wedding . . ." (vs. 7).

"When you prepare a meal or a banquet . . ." (vs. 12).

His pronouncements take the form of conventional maxims about social behavior. But their content stamps them as parables, for they reflect Jesus' parabolic vision. The points of audience identification are explicit: the guests are to think of themselves as guests in the imagined situation; the host is to think of himself as a host. But they are guests and host in a world gone "mad," where only the poor and blind and lame are invited to banquets, and the humble are the guests of honor at weddings. Jesus' hearers are able to enter into his world of imagination only to a limited extent, and only in the safe conventional categories of familiar apocalyptic teaching: "Blessed is anyone who eats bread in the kingdom of God!" (Luke 14:15).

The "table talk" of Luke 14:7–14 thus sets the stage for the fully developed parable of the banquet by placing the latter in the context of God's reckless love. Once again, radical grace and radical discipleship are seen to be two sides of the same coin. In Luke 14:15–24, attention shifts to discipleship and the things that hinder it: land, possessions, and a wife (vss. 18–20). The lesson of the parable is unfolded in the explicit teaching on discipleship that follows in Luke 14:25–33. The scene has shifted from the Pharisee's house, and Jesus is addressing a crowd that has joined him on his way: "If anyone comes to me and does not hate his father and mother and wife and children and brothers and sisters, yes and even his very life, he cannot be my disciple" (vs. 26). As so often in Jesus' teaching, the straightforward statement is buttressed with metaphor and parable. The renunciation of family culminates in the renunciation of life itself. Jesus reinforces the latter with the vivid metaphor of condemned criminals carrying their crosses to the place of execution: "Whoever does not carry his cross and come after me cannot be my disciple" (vs. 27). Jesus and his followers alike are to live as those condemned to die.

The refrain, "he cannot be my disciple" (Luke 14:26,27) occurs for a third time in verse 33, after twin parables about a tower builder (vss. 28–30) and a king faced with war (vss. 31–32). The hearers' point of identification is unmistakable in each case. "Who of *you*," Jesus asks, "when planning to build a tower, does not first sit down and count the cost . . ." (vs. 28). Some of his hearers had doubtless built towers in their vineyards. Identification with a king contemplating war required a little more imagination. Yet the reference point is no less clear: "*Or what king* . . . will not sit down first and decide if he is strong enough . . ." (vs. 31). The conclusion is: "So none of you, unless he gives up all his possessions, can be my disciple" (vs. 33).

A long tradition of associating Christian discipleship with the phrase, "counting the cost," makes these stories seem more natural and easy illustrations of discipleship than they actually are. Taken by themselves, without the context of verses 25–27 and without the concluding word about giving up all possessions, these stories, especially the second, take on a life of their own. The tower builder and the king are not renouncing their possessions but conserving them, and assessing their strength carefully. If their resources are not adequate, the conclusion seems to be, "Give it up. Don't get involved. It's not worth the gamble"—hardly the attitude of the "violent" who take the kingdom of God by force!

It is possible that one or both of these stories had other applications besides the one given here. They have in common the feature of someone taking positive steps ahead of time to get ready for some crisis or major undertaking. The tower builder and the king both "sit down first" (Luke 14:28,31) to calculate the chances of success in their respective ventures. If we think back on Jesus' ministry as a whole, the most plausible application that comes to mind is to the necessity of repentance in view of the inbreaking kingdom of God. "Repent," Jesus had said, "for the kingdom of heaven is at hand" (Matt. 4:17). The imminent crisis required preparation and alertness from all who heard the warning.

The idea of getting ready in advance also appears in a third story, found in the Gospel of Thomas 98: "The kingdom of the Father is like a man who wanted to kill a powerful man. He drew a sword within his house [and] ran it through the wall, so that he might know whether his hand would be strong [enough]. Then he killed the powerful man." There is no way of knowing whether this story goes back to Jesus, but if it does, it may well have been a companion to the canonical parables of the tower builder and the king contemplating war.

Of the three, the parable of the tower builder is most easily adaptable to the theme of discipleship. Starting a tower that one is unable to finish is rather like putting one's hand to the plow and then looking back (Luke 9:62, clearly a metaphor about discipleship). Starting a

fight with a powerful man or going to war unprepared have obvious
points of similarity to these situations, yet breathe a different atmosphere—one of conflict and violence. They betray a kinship with
another Lukan parable that has a quite different application.

Luke's version of the Markan metaphor of the "binding of the
strong man" is apparently independent of Mark: "When the strong
man, fully equipped, guards his own courtyard, his possessions are at
peace; but when someone stronger than he breaks in and defeats him,
he carries away all the weapons the strong man was counting on and
divides up the loot" (Luke 11:21; contrast Mark 3:27). This parable
brings us back to the world of Jesus' initial proclamation of the
kingdom of God. We hear in it the noise of battle, the clash of two
kingdoms, two households, two strong men. Is it possible that the
parable of the king contemplating war had its origin in the same
dualistic setting? Here too a strong man confronts someone stronger
(ten thousand troops against twenty thousand!), and the apparent
word of advice to him is "Sue for peace before it is too late!" (Luke
14:32). In the Thomas parable, a man practices at home with his
sword before going out to kill a "powerful man."

The legacy of centuries of allegorical interpretation makes it natural to assume that the strong man is always Satan and the stronger
is always Jesus. But the imagery is flexible. The question must first be
asked, "With whom will the hearer identify?"—or, if the hearer's
vantage point is a purely external one, "What judgment about the
situation is the hearer to make?" In Luke 11:21 the hearer's point of
identification is with the strong man destined to be attacked and
robbed by someone stronger. So too in Luke 14:31–32 the hearer is
asked to put himself or herself in the place of a king faced with odds
he cannot overcome. The best recourse is to seek terms of peace. But
in both Mark's and Matthew's version of the strong man story, the
hearer's identification is with the indefinite *anyone* who plans an
assault on the strong man's house and finds that the strong man first
must be bound. And in the Gospel of Thomas the main character is
similarly the man who carefully plans an attack with his sword.

Jesus' proclamation of the kingdom of God, his authority over the unclean spirits, and his acts of healing and forgiveness make it clear that his own identification was with the victor. Though there is ample evidence elsewhere that he foresaw the "defeat" that took place in his own death (and in metaphorical terms at that), the counsel to give up the struggle and come to terms with the Enemy can hardly be reconciled with his behavior as described anywhere in the Gospel tradition! Rather, it was his first hearers—those to whom he said "Repent, for the kingdom of heaven is at hand"—who would have seen themselves in the role of the strong man in trouble, or the king confronted with hopeless odds. To them the "enemy" was the stronger king and his inbreaking kingdom. Their only hope was to sue for peace.

Using a different metaphor, Jesus told them, "While you and your adversary are still on your way to the magistrate, do your best to settle with him out of court; otherwise he will drag you to the judge, and the judge will hand you over to the police, and the police will put you in prison. You will not get out of there, I tell you, until you have paid the last penny" (Luke 12:57–59). Like the unjust steward, who made his own kind of surrender to his master's debtors (Luke 16:4–7), they are to anticipate the disaster ahead and take firm action to escape. Though Matthew, as we have seen, applied the little parable about settling out of court to the responsibility of Jesus' disciples to love their enemies (Matt. 5:25), its original use was clearly as a general warning of judgment addressed to Jesus' contemporaries.

In much the same way, Luke has taken a story about two kings at war that was probably first told in the context of the inbreaking kingdom of God and Jesus' call to repentance, and has applied it to the Christian disciple's responsibility to put aside family and material possessions. In itself the moral of the story is, "You don't have a chance. Surrender now before it is too late, and get the best terms of peace you possibly can!" But in its Lukan setting, it says, "Discipleship is like a war that demands all your resources. Muster everything you have in Jesus' service, that you may truly be his disciple. Renounce all claim to your possessions, for they are his." Ironically,

Luke himself preserves echoes of the earlier use of the story in his account of Jesus weeping over Jerusalem. "If only you knew," Jesus cries out to the city "the terms of peace; but as it is, they are hidden from your eyes" (Luke 19:42).

The case is somewhat different with the parable of the tower builder. The application in this case to discipleship is very natural, and this may well be the setting in which Jesus first used the story. An unfinished tower in one's vineyard is, after all, a stark reminder of failure to carry out a commitment—no less stark, surely, than a field left half plowed (again cf. Luke 9:62). But where is the emphasis of the story? On being sure that the job gets done, or on being sure not to try to build a tower when one doesn't have the resources? The analogy with Luke 9:62 suggests the former, while the analogy with the parable of the two kings favors the latter alternative.

The distinction between wise and foolish building is a familiar one in Jesus' storytelling (cf. Matt. 7:24–27; Luke 6:47–49), but in one Lukan parable in particular a building project is specifically discouraged. The rich man in Luke 12:16–20 who tore down his barns and built bigger ones where he could store his grain and settle in for many years of ease is called a fool, and is told: "This very night your life will be taken; then who will get these things you have hoarded?" (Luke 12:20). In this case, the man had the resources with which to build, but his buildings did him no good, because for him the end had come. The thrust of the story is distinctly eschatological. For Jesus' contemporaries as well, the end is near, and they must act accordingly. They must repent. But the terminology is not explicitly that of repentance, or surrender to God, but of having the right attitude toward material possessions (cf. vss. 15, 21–34).

This parable, with its context, furnishes a possible clue to the shift in the application of some of Jesus' stories from a repentance setting to a discipleship setting. As early as the ministry of John the Baptist, repentance involves certain basic, perhaps minimal, obligations with regard to material possessions. Soldiers are to be content with their wages. Soldiers and tax collectors alike are to renounce dishonesty and extortion. All who have food and clothing beyond their immediate needs are to share with those who have none (Luke 3:10–14). The repentance of Zacchaeus, the tax collector, calls from him the promise that "I will give half of my possessions to the poor, and if I have cheated anyone of anything, I will restore it four times over" (Luke 19:8). Such passages suggest that whatever else it is, discipleship in the Gospels is an extension of repentance. Therefore, Jesus' calling of a whole generation to repentance and a small group of associates to discipleship will inevitably have some features in common. It is by no means surprising that stories and metaphors he used in the one connection appear in the other as well, whether with the same or a different application.

This seems to have happened to both the parable of the rich fool and the parable of the tower builder. The close structural similarity between the latter and its companion piece about the king faced with war (i.e., sitting down first, and taking steps in advance to prevent disaster) virtually guaranteed that the companion piece as well would be adapted to the discipleship setting. In both stories, Luke represents Jesus as saying, "The kingdom of God requires of you everything you have; you must renounce all claim to your possessions, your home and family, your very life if you want to be a disciple." It might appear that the operative image behind Jesus' demand is that of holy war, because possessions, home, and life itself are precisely what a soldier renounces when he goes off to battle. But if this is the case, there is no particular emphasis on it in the immediate context. The parable about building seems to have brought the parable about war along with it into their present context, not the other way around. If discipleship is like war, it is also like building a tower or plowing a field. Like all such enterprises it requires persistence and a firm commitment. Because it also involves personal sacrifice, suffering, and death, the war metaphor is undeniably apt, yet relatively undeveloped in the Gospel tradition.

Another image, introduced briefly and right at the beginning of Jesus' ministry, is that of fishing. "Follow me," he tells Simon and

Andrew, "and I will make you fishers of human beings" (Mark 1:17 and Matt. 4:19; cf. Luke 5:10). This strange metaphor recalls the parable of the net with its overtones of judgment (Matt. 13:47–50), as well as the warlike picture in the prophecy of Habakkuk of the dread Chaldean, for whom God "has made human beings like the fish of the sea . . ." to "bring them all up with hooks, or catch them in his net, or drag them away in his seine . . ." (Hab. 1:15).[1] In the very act of making a word play on the occupation of the fisherman at the lake, Jesus calls them from that occupation to become his followers. Simon and Andrew left their nets, their very livelihood, to follow Jesus, and James and John left their father, Zebedee (Mark 1:18,20). Renunciation of material possessions and family are, right from the beginning, conspicuous in the call to discipleship. The specifics of what discipleship entails for Jesus are summed up simply and radically as the renunciation of home, and life. Home can be understood as subsuming family and material possessions under a single heading. Life can refer either to actual loss of life (i.e., martyrdom) or to risking one's life in the course of sharing Jesus' ministry.

The context under discussion in Luke 14 touches on all these aspects. To be a disciple, one must "hate his father and mother and wife and children and brothers and sisters, yes and even his very life" (Luke 14:26). In the parable of the supper the hindrances to discipleship are, respectively, a field, a yoke of oxen, and a wife (Luke 14: 18–20). Near the end of his ministry, Jesus tells Peter, "There is no one who has left home or wife or brothers or parents or children for the sake of the kingdom of God who will not receive them back many times over in this age, and in the age to come eternal life" (Luke 18:29). The things of home are to be "hated" in the one instance and "left" in the other. Mark has no parallel to the first enumeration, but his own, longer version of the second bears comparison with Luke: "There is no one who has left home or brothers or sisters or mother or father or children or fields, for my sake and for the sake of the gospel, who will not receive back a hundred times over, now in this age, homes and brothers and sisters and mothers and children and fields, with hardships, and in the age to come eternal life" (Mark 10:30).

Quite clearly, Luke has smoothed out the awkwardness of Mark's list. He has polished Mark's grammar, removed the abrupt reference to hardships and the redundancy of "now in this age," and avoided Mark's repetition of the whole list in enumerating what the disciple will receive back as recompense: homes in place of a home, brothers and sisters in place of brothers and sisters, mothers in place of a mother, etc. That Mark's procedure got him in difficulty is seen in the awkward omission of "fathers" from the second list—a disciple has, after all, only one Father! Mark wants to stress the significance of new relationships within the new community of disciples. The particulars of his text may have raised more questions than they answered, however. Brothers and sisters, yes; perhaps even mothers and children, but what are the new homes and the new fields? Matthew has simplified Mark in much the same way, but with touches of his own. He has formulated the whole saying positively rather than negatively, and he has avoided making promises for "this age" (Matt. 19:29). The rewards will be given in the new creation when Jesus and twelve of his disciples will sit on thrones "judging the twelve tribes of Israel" (Matt. 19:28).

In view of the tendency of the later Gospels to smooth out the difficulties in Mark, it is all the more noticeable that Luke introduces a difficulty of his own with his mention of leaving one's *wife* for the sake of the kingdom of God (Luke 18:29). That this detail is not accidental is shown by its presence in Luke's earlier list as well: a man must hate his father, mother, *wife*, children, brothers, sisters, and his own life in order to be a follower of Jesus (Luke 14:26). If Luke were original, it is easy to see why Matthew and Mark would have omitted "wife" from their lists. Hating one's wife or leaving one's wife would have been strong—and strange—counsel for a disciple of Jesus to accept. And for Mark to have assimilated "wife" into his pattern of "homes in place of a home," "brothers and sisters in place of brothers and sisters," would have been intolerable! Yet Luke's motives in introducing such ideas on his own initiative are also far from clear. Divorce for the sake of Christ is a theme that appears in later legends about Jesus and the apostles, but in the context of an un-Jewish (and unbiblical) rejection of sexuality.[2]

Neither Luke's Gospel nor the book of Acts shows evidence of fostering such views. But if these harsh words are not taken quite so literally, they begin to make sense, whether in Luke's text or in Jesus' actual speech. The mention of the wife in Luke 14:26 is often explained by a reference back to the last of three excuses in the preceding parable of the dinner party ("I have married a wife and I cannot come," 14:20), but this does not remove the difficulty. It merely illustrates how the responsibilities of marriage can stand in the way of radical discipleship. More to the point is the possibility that just as *hating* one's relatives does not refer to an emotional dislike, but simply to loving Jesus more (Matt. 10:37), so *leaving* a wife may refer to a decision not to marry rather than to the break-up of an existing marriage.

The radical way of putting things is, of course, thoroughly characteristic of Jesus' teaching. Marriage in the New Testament is never something evil. It is simply one of the normal activities of this life that will stop when the kingdom of God arrives in its fullness. In answer to a question of the Sadducees, Jesus states that when the dead are raised, men will not marry and women will not be given in marriage (Mark 12:25; cf. Matt. 22:30). As in the time of Noah, the routine of life's activities—"eating and drinking, marrying and giving in marriage"—will continue right up to the time of the sudden catastrophe, in this case the coming of the Son of man (Matt. 24:38f.; cf. Luke 17:27–30). The implication is that at that moment all these things will stop. To try to rescue the things in one's home, or to turn back to protect one's field (Luke 17:31) is to court disaster. When Luke's account goes on to mention "two in one bed" and "two grinding together" (Luke 17:34–35), it suggests once more that marriage and the partnership it involves comes to an end at the final day of the Son of man (cf. vss. 22,24).[3]

The demands of that day represent a kind of intensification of the demands of discipleship. One must not turn back (vs. 31), and "whoever seeks to preserve his life will lose it, while whoever loses it will save it" (vs. 33). To be a disciple is to anticipate in whatever ways possible the conditions of that last day of crisis and of the kingdom of God itself.

With regard to marriage, Luke's version of Jesus' reply to the Sadducees provides a possible illustration of this principle. "The children of this age marry and are given in marriage, but those considered worthy to attain to that age and to the resurrection from the dead neither marry nor are given in marriage, nor can they die any more, for they are like the angels, and, being children of the resurrection, are children of God" (Luke 20:34–36). There is an ambiguity here that is not present in the parallel passages of Mark and Matthew. Do the children of God forego marriage only in the age to come, or already in this life? The reference to immortality and to being like angels indicates the former. Yet the strong contrast between the children of this age who marry, and the children of God or children of the resurrection who do not, suggests the appropriateness of celibacy as an option for the follower of Jesus even now.

Again it is Luke that is distinctive. But the question must be asked whether the pressing of celibacy as an option is a Lukan contribution or whether it goes back to Jesus. Although Luke seems to have given it special emphasis, the likelihood is that it originates with Jesus. For Jesus to speak of voluntary celibacy as hatred or even as a kind of divorce typifies the strong language that the Gospel tradition leads us to expect from him. Apart from Luke, the clearest evidence of such a teaching is Matthew 19:12, in which Jesus mentions three types of eunuchs: those who were born that way, those who were made eunuchs by being castrated, and those who "made themselves eunuchs for the kingdom of heaven." Then he adds, "Whoever is able to accept this, let him accept it." Clearly the first two types of eunuch are being listed for the sake of the third. "Eunuchs for the kingdom of heaven" is Jesus' characteristically startling metaphor for celibacy as an option for his disciples. Because this verse is found only in Matthew, as part of an appendix to the Markan-Matthean passage forbidding divorce, it is usually discussed in connection with Matthew's distinctive interests, not as an authentic word of Jesus. Yet when it is seen to coincide in meaning with some distinctively Lukan sayings, the possibility arises that Luke and Matthew may owe their distinctiveness to Jesus himself!

Perhaps the strongest indirect evidence that Jesus' call to discipleship included the option of celibacy is found in the divorce passage to which the Matthean saying about eunuchs is attached (i.e., Mark 10:2–12, Matt. 19:3–9). Jesus assumes a role otherwise unfamiliar to him in the Gospel tradition, the role of legislator. He makes a legal pronouncement on a question that is put to him, without appreciably changing the terms in which the question is asked. The Pharisees want to know if it is lawful for a man to divorce his wife and Jesus replies that it is not. Jesus' more typical response to such questions is to challenge the questioner's assumptions, or to introduce a principle that renders the usual alternative irrelevant. The Sabbath is made for human beings, and not human beings for the Sabbath! The question of whose wife a woman will be in the resurrection is pointless because in the resurrection there will be no marriage! But here Jesus meets the question head on, and in the questioner's own terms. Why? Another puzzling aspect of this exchange is that it takes place in a context, not of ethical teaching or debate over the law, but of teaching about discipleship and its implications (cf. Mark 9:33–50, 10:13–45).

In Mark, the question about divorce is raised in two stages: first by the Pharisees (Mark 10:2–9), and then by Jesus' disciples (Mark 10:10–12). The discussion with the Pharisees proceeds exegetically. Jesus responds to the question of whether it is lawful for a husband to divorce his wife with a question of his own: "What did Moses command you?" (Mark 10:3). When reference is made to the provision in Deuteronomy 24:1 for a certificate of dismissal, Jesus appeals instead to a principle as old as the creation. God "created them male and female; because of this a man shall leave his father and mother and the two shall become one flesh" (Mark 10:7f., citing Gen. 2:24). Reinforcing the last words of the quotation, Jesus concludes "So as a result they are no longer two, but one flesh; thus what God has joined together, let no human being separate" (Mark 10:8f.). Only the last clause speaks directly to the Pharisees' question, but the way has been carefully prepared by the strong insistence on the oneness of male and female in the marriage relationship.

Stage two of the discussion finds Jesus alone with his disciples "in the house" (Mark 10:10; cf. 9:28). Their question is vague. Mark says merely that they asked him about this (i.e., about the answer he had just given to the Pharisees). It is therefore to his disciples that Jesus makes the quasi-legal pronouncement that has drawn to itself so much controversy: "Whoever divorces his wife and marries another commits adultery against her; and if she marries another man after she has divorced her husband, she commits adultery" (Mark 10:11f.). This is the concrete application of the broad principles expressed in verses 6–9, but what began as a debate with Jesus' scholarly opponents ends as a warning to his disciples. *They* must not violate the principle, old as creation, that marriage makes a man and a woman one flesh. They must not divorce their wives even for the sake of the kingdom of God! Above all, they must not fall victim to the supreme irony by divorcing their wives for such lofty motives and then turning around and marrying someone else! Those who do must be called by their right name —not disciples, but adulterers! The vehemence of Jesus' language is called forth not by the debate with Pharisees over the law, but by contemplating the possible abuse of his own principle of renunciation as applied to marriage.

Matthew's postscript (Matt. 19:10–12) addresses the question of celibacy directly and makes these Markan concerns explicit. Matthew ignores Mark's two stages so that the formal prohibition of divorce and remarriage, no less than the exegesis of Genesis 2:24, is addressed to the Pharisees, who first raised the question. But then Matthew brings the disciples on the scene with the comment that it is therefore better for the sake of the kingdom of heaven not to marry. In other words, Matthew preserves the memory of Mark's two stages even though they are not the same two stages. Moreover, Matthew preserves the memory that the second stage addresses, not divorce as such, but divorce for the sake of the kingdom. The orientation of the two accounts can be shown as follows:

		Mark	Matthew
1.	Jesus and the Pharisees: the interpretation of Genesis 2:24	10:2–9	19:3–9
2.	Jesus and the Disciples	10:10–12	19:10–12

Whereas stage two in Mark addresses the disciples' question negatively—absolutely no divorce, even for the sake of the kingdom—stage two in Matthew addresses it positively—celibacy for the sake of the kingdom *is* an option, though only for some. Each of the Synoptic Gospels in its own way thus bears explicit or implicit witness to Jesus' affirmation of celibacy in connection with the call to discipleship. It seems to have been precisely this affirmation that made it necessary for him to affirm, in the strongest terms possible, the indissolubility of marriage.

Clearly, discipleship is the theme in the sections that follow in Mark, Matthew, and Luke. The positive side of discipleship finds expression in the living metaphor of the child (Mark 10:13–16). But Jesus is not finished with the theme of renunciation. He is leading up to the great summary of this theme in Mark 10:28–31, but first comes the incident that touches off the summary by eliciting Peter's word of defense: "Behold, we have left all and followed you" (Mark 10:28). According to Mark a man asks Jesus "Good teacher, what must I do to inherit eternal life?" (Mark 10:17). In reply, Jesus focuses on the designation *good,* pointing him to God, who alone deserves to be called good, and to several of the Ten Commandments. The God-centered quality of Jesus' answer surfaces again in his appended remarks to his disciples. Salvation is humanly impossible, but with God "all things are possible" (Mark 10:27). To call God alone "good" is to recognize him as the Source of all kindness and mercy.[4] Even when one has obeyed all the commandments, one thing is still necessary: to become God's imitator, to be merciful as he is merciful, or good as he is good, but with the understanding that our mercy, our *goodness,* is derivative and not our own. Concretely, what is necessary is to renounce material possessions, to sell what we have and give to the poor. It is to follow Jesus (Mark 10:21).

At this point we learn that the man (a young man in Matthew; a ruler in Luke) is rich. His sorrowful departure provides the occasion for Jesus' reflections on wealth as an obstacle to discipleship. It is easier, Jesus says, for a camel to go through the eye of a needle than for someone rich to enter the kingdom of God (Mark 10:25). The kingdom is the kingdom of the poor. To inherit it, one must not simply give to the poor, but in giving must become poor. What is implicit in the Beatitudes is made explicit here. The secret is out. The disciples themselves are the poor to whom the kingdom belongs, the hungry who shall be filled, the meek who shall inherit the earth. To them in particular God is "good." His mercy endures forever. In Jesus, who became poor before them, God's goodness is displayed. In the renunciation of wealth they become his followers.

The grotesquely exaggerated image of a camel trying to get through the eye of a needle stamps on the memory of disciple and teacher alike the impossibility of anyone, the rich in particular, entering the kingdom of God. That the principle extends beyond the rich is shown in Mark by Jesus' unqualified exclamation "How hard it is, my children, to enter the kingdom of God!" (Mark 10:24); and in all three Synoptics by the sweeping question "Who then can be saved? "As the context makes clear the kingdom of God cannot be entered unless God gives it and it is received in poverty, as a little child (cf. Mark 10:15, Luke 18:17). Specifically, this means following Jesus. It means leaving home and breaking old ties with family and material possessions. "Foxes have holes," Jesus says elsewhere, "and birds of the air have nests, but the Son of man has nowhere to lay his head. . . . No one who puts his hand to the plow and looks back is fit for the kingdom of God" (Luke 9:58,62). There is no time to set one's house in order, no time even to bury a close relative (Luke 9:59–61). The urgency of the hour demands that God's reckless and self-renouncing love reproduce itself in those who receive it!

The ultimate renunciation is, of course, the renunciation of life itself. This can be seen first of all in those metaphors that speak of bodily mutilation. If one's hand or foot causes a person to sin, it should be cut off. If one's eye becomes an occasion for sin, it should be plucked out. It is better to enter life crippled or blind, Jesus says, than to be consigned to hell with one's body intact (cf. Mark 9:43–48 and Matt. 18:8f., 5:29f.). To carry out such grim commands literally would obviously not guarantee salvation. Rather, Jesus' point is to weigh certain alternatives against each other. Which counts more, one small part of a person's body, or the whole body—the person's very life? Clearly the part must be sacrificed for the whole, if it comes to that. But in Jesus' use of metaphor, the eye or the limb represents the heart, the very core of a person's existence. He indicates elsewhere that the root of sin is in the heart, not in the bodily members (Matt. 5:28; Matt. 12:34 and Luke 6:45; and Mark 7:21 and Matt. 15:19).

To speak of one's eye or hand or foot causing one to sin is to use a figure of speech known in rhetoric as synecdoche (i.e., the part representing the whole). The real alternative is not between an eye or a limb and one's whole body, but between one's whole existence in this world and one's participation in eternal life, or the kingdom of God. Two or three specific, violent metaphors have here replaced a more general but equally violent one. Plucking out an eye or cutting off a hand in order to save one's life is simply a vivid and grotesque way of saying that one must *die* in order to live.

This principle of life through death comes to direct expression elsewhere, most notably in the context of the first clear intimation that Jesus himself must die (Mark 8:34–37; Matt. 16:24–26; Luke 9: 23–25). Those who would be Jesus' disciples must take up their crosses and follow in his train like criminals condemned to die by crucifixion (cf. also Matt. 10:38; Luke 14:27). It is striking that the cross is mentioned as the instrument of execution in connection with disciples *before* it is mentioned in connection with Jesus. At the heart of Jesus' stern demand is an irony: those who try to keep their lives safe will die, while those who lose their lives for Jesus will live (cf. also Matt. 10:39, Luke 17:33). Life here, as in the Old Testament, refers without distinction to physical life and eternal life. John's Gospel makes the same point while distinguishing between the two. "Whoever loves his life loses it, and whoever hates his life in this world will keep it for eternal life" (John 12:25). Hating one's own life is simply the logical extension of hating one's parents or wife or children (cf. Luke 14:26). It means living for the sake of Jesus, putting him and the kingdom of God ahead of everything else.

In Jesus' world of metaphor, the seed of grain that falls to the ground, dies, and then springs up to bear fruit, is Jesus himself, but the parable is not exhausted in his individual experience. He draws everyone to himself, and the seed of grain portrays the experience of his followers as well. They too must die in order to bear fruit (John 12:24–26,32). Jesus himself is the model for renunciation, most clearly, of course, in his death on the cross—the renunciation of life in order to gain life—but at every other point as well. *He* has left home and has nowhere even to sleep (Matt. 8:20; Luke 9:58). *He* has renounced family in favor of a new circle of friends who do the will of God (Mark 3:33–35 and parallels). Looking back on Jesus' life, Paul can say, "Though he was rich, for us he became poor, so that we, through his poverty, might become rich" (2 Cor. 8:9; cf. Phil. 2:7–8). In renunciation, as in the love of enemies, the imitation of God becomes a reality, both for Jesus and for his disciples. They practice renunciation because God himself did so first—when out of love he gave up his only Son that sinners might live.

14.

PRAYER
AND TRUST

If the supreme metaphor of renunciation is death, then the corresponding positive metaphor of discipleship is life. A disciple is one who *lives*. This new life can be a future hope. To "enter into life" (Mark 9:43, 45), or to "inherit eternal life" (Mark 10:17 and parallels) is the same as entering or inheriting the kingdom of God at the last day. Prior to that, one may enjoy all sorts of new relationships with fellow disciples in the community of faith (Mark 10:29f). But even prior to these horizontal relationships is the more basic vertical relationship to God as Father. The metaphor is that of becoming a child. The positive way of saying that one must die in order to live, is to say that one must be born again.

BECOMING A CHILD

Jesus, on at least two occasions, uses children as flesh-and-blood metaphors for discipleship or trust in God. To settle a dispute among his disciples, he brings a small child among them and compares or identifies himself with such a child: "Whoever receives one such child in my name receives me, and whoever receives me receives not me but the one who sent me" (Mark 9:37; cf. Matt. 18:5, Luke 9:48). Here the principle of self-identification with a parabolic figure again comes to the surface. The child is the only character in this acted-out para-

ble. In fact, the child *is* the parable. The disciples are left to make up
the story for themselves, and decide in exactly what respect Jesus
intends to identify himself with this child. Jesus' statement here
closely parallels such nonparabolic sayings as Matthew 10:40: "Whoever receives you receives me, and whoever receives me receives the
one who sent me" (cf. Luke 10:16; John 13:20).

Just as the disciples are Jesus' agents or representatives in this
formula of commissioning, so the child is Jesus' agent or representa-
tive in the present passage. The child is Jesus' surrogate, and thus a
surrogate for the disciples as well. In his own way, each Gospel writer
makes the comparison between the child and the disciples explicit.
Mark prefaces the presentation of the child with the principle that "if
anyone wants to be first, he will be last of all and servant of all" (Mark
9:35). Matthew has a more elaborate saying, possibly from a different
context: "Truly, I say to you, unless you turn and become as children,
you shall by no means enter the kingdom of heaven. So then whoever
humbles himself as this child is the greatest in the kingdom of heaven"
(Matt 18:3–4). Luke places a similar pronouncement at the end of the
passage: "For the one who is least among all of you is great" (Luke
9:48). Form and placement may vary but the child in each case
exemplifies the humility that should characterize the disciples.

On another occasion, children are brought to Jesus to receive his
touch and his blessing. When the disciples object, Jesus says "Let the
children come to me, and do not forbid them, for of such is the
kingdom of God" (Mark 10:14; Matt. 19:14; Luke 18:16). In Mark
and Luke he adds "Truly, I say to you, whoever does not receive the
kingdom of God as a child will by no means enter it" (Mark 10:15;
Luke 18:17). This is the Markan and Lukan equivalent of Matthew's
"Truly I say to you" formulation in the earlier passage (Matt. 18:3).
John's Gospel uses still another version: "Truly, truly I say to you,
unless a person is born again, he cannot see the kingdom of God
. . . Truly, truly I say to you, unless a person is born of water and
Spirit, he cannot enter the kingdom of God" (John 3:3,5). These
pronouncements all have in common the "truly" formula (single or

doubled), the use of a negative conditional or relative clause ("unless
. . ." or "whoever does not . . ."), and a reference to entering or seeing
the kingdom of God. They all suggest a common tradition. The most
radical formulation is that of John's Gospel, in which Nicodemus
captures the grotesqueness of the metaphor with his question, "How
can a person be born when he is old? Can he enter his mother's womb
a second time and be born?" (John 3:4). The "large and startling
figures" of the Synoptic Jesus meet us unexpectedly here in the fourth
Gospel as well.

The child metaphor thus occurs basically in two kinds of sayings: agency or commissioning sayings in which "this child" or "one
such child" appears unexpectedly as the parabolic equivalent of
"you" (i.e., you disciples), and sayings that emphasize in solemn
and straightforward terms ("truly I say to you . . .") the urgent
necessity of becoming a child or of receiving the kingdom as a child
would receive it. In the first, the disciples are invited to see themselves in the figure of the child standing among them, much as they
are invited into the world of Jesus' parables. In the second, the application is made and the metaphor becomes an exhortation: they
must *turn* (Matt. 18:3) and become like children, or they will not
enter the kingdom of God.

Aside from the definite intimations of humility and servanthood
each of the Gospel writers supplies (i.e., Mark 9:35; Matt. 18:4; Luke
9:48), the precise implications of childlikeness in these passages are
left to the reader's imagination. The quality that most naturally comes
to mind is a certain simplicity or innocence, an almost naive trust in
God's goodness and power.

Quite apart from the metaphor of the child, is this kind of trust
a part of discipleship as Jesus defines it? The answer is seen most
clearly in connection with Jesus' teaching on prayer, and especially
in connection with his own prayer life. It has been amply demonstrated from the baptism and the temptation onward that what Jesus
heard from his Father or experienced in his Father's world was determinative for what he said and did. But this religious experience must

be set in its appropriate context, an inevitable context for any devout first century Jew, the context of prayer.

The Gospels make no mention of Jesus' observance of the stated hours of prayer three times a day, perhaps because it is assumed. But they frequently mention the habit of praying for extended periods of time and in deserted places. Early in his Gospel, Mark describes what he apparently regards as an example of Jesus' customary practice: "And very early, while it was still dark, he got up and went out, and headed for a deserted place, and there he prayed" (Mark 1:35). Solitary prayer seems to have been Jesus' way of escaping the demands laid on him by the crowds as a result of his healing ministry (e.g., Mark 1:37; Luke 4:42). Luke in particular picks up on this characteristic activity of Jesus, citing instance after instance of it in his Gospel. After the healing of the leper, with the popularity among the crowds that it precipitated, Luke mentions that Jesus customarily "withdrew to deserted places and prayed" (Luke 5:16). Before choosing the Twelve, Jesus "spent a whole night praying to God" (Luke 6:12). It was "while he was praying privately, and his disciples were with him." (Luke 9:18), that he elicited from Peter the acknowledgment that he was "the Christ of God." At the transfiguration, Jesus went up the mountain "to pray," and it was "while he was praying" that his appearance changed (Luke 9:28–29).

THE LORD'S PRAYER IN LUKE

By this time his disciples had had ample opportunity to watch him at prayer and wonder why he had not yet initiated them into his prayer life. Pharisees said to Jesus on one occasion "John's disciples fast frequently and offer prayers, as do the disciples of the Pharisees, but your disciples eat and drink" (Luke 5:33). On another occasion, according to Luke, Jesus "was in a certain place praying" in his customary way—privately and yet in the presence of his disciples. When he had finished, one of the disciples said "Lord, teach us to pray, just as John taught his disciples" (Luke 11:1NIV). This request becomes Luke's setting for his form of the Lord's Prayer, as well as

for some specific teaching on prayer and the answering of prayer
(Luke 11:2–13). Such a setting for the Lord's Prayer is entirely plausible, but whether it came early or late in Jesus' ministry is not certain.
Whenever it came, it probably marked a decisive change in the disciples' lifestyle and their relationship to Jesus. Up to this point they had
apparently been known more as lovers of the good life than as men
of prayer. Now they would share in Jesus' solitude and learn something of his intimacy with the Father and his struggles against Satan.

Luke has placed this incident within his "Travel Narrative", from
Luke 9:51 to 19:44, with Jesus on his way to Jerusalem. That journey
becomes the framework for much of Luke's distinctive tradition as
well as for some material Luke has in common with Mark or Matthew. Since the journey, like Matthew's Sermon on the Mount, has
become in all likelihood a magnet attracting material from every stage
of Jesus' ministry, the fact that the Lord's Prayer has been placed here
does not necessarily mean that it was given near the end of the
ministry or on the road to Jerusalem, although there are some indications that it may have been. The disciples' question obviously presupposes a considerable period during which they and Jesus did *not* pray
together. Luke 5:33 confirms this. The tradition that Jesus and his
disciples were more given to parties than to prayer and fasting is not
likely to have been invented by Christians after Jesus' death! Luke
may have been especially careful to stress that Jesus prayed intensely
and alone in order to counter any impression that during his ministry
Jesus and his disciples had not been particularly known as a praying
community. Such an impression is more likely to have arisen if Jesus
gave his disciples the Lord's Prayer near the end of his ministry than
if it was part of his teaching all along.

To this day pilgrims to Jerusalem are surprised to find the medieval Pater Noster church, traditionally associated with the giving of
this prayer, on the Mount of Olives just outside Jerusalem, rather than
somewhere in Galilee.[1] The location suggests that at some point the
Lord's Prayer was thought to have been given during (or just before)
Passion week. Luke summarizes Jesus' activity during Passion week

as teaching in the temple during the day and spending his nights on the Mount of Olives (Luke 21:37–38). After the institution of the Lord's Supper, Jesus is seen going out "as was his custom" to the Mount of Olives, accompanied by his disciples (Luke 22:39). It was here that he told them to "pray not to get into temptation" (Luke 22:40,46). Here, too, he himself prayed, "Father, if you choose, remove this cup from me. But let your will be done and not mine" (Luke 22:42).

Obviously the Mount of Olives was associated with Jesus' prayer life from very early times. This fact by itself may account for the late tradition associating the Lord's Prayer with the Mount of Olives. Also, a harmonistic reading of Luke and John together could have led medieval readers to identify the "certain village" of the Mary and Martha incident (Luke 10:38–42) with Bethany, less than two miles from Jerusalem (John 11:1,18; 12:1). If so, it would have been natural to locate the "certain place" of Luke 11:1 somewhere on the Mount of Olives. Such an assumption would of course play havoc with the Lukan Travel Narrative, for as late as Luke 17:11 Jesus is still "passing through Samaria and Galilee." Only in Luke 19:1 does Jesus reach Jericho, and not until Luke 19:29 does he "draw near to Bethphage and Bethany toward the so-called 'Mount of Olives.' " But Luke's freedom in arranging his material allows for the possibility that the late tradition may be correct. If Luke has indeed used the Travel Narrative as a framework for incorporating material from many different times and places, then he may have chosen vague terms like a "certain village" (Luke 10:38) or a "certain place" (Luke 11:1; cf. 22:40) as deliberate adaptations of narratives that originally had more specific geographical associations, i.e., Bethany and the Mount of Olives, respectively. It is impossible to be certain, but there is every likelihood that Jesus taught his disciples the Lord's Prayer rather late in his ministry, and even that he did not do so until the last week of his life. In any event, the petition he told them to make on the night of his arrest ("not to get into temptation," Luke 22:40,46) sounds very much like an allusion to that prayer.

If it is true that Jesus did not teach his disciples a prayer until near the end of his ministry, then the English term, "the Lord's Prayer," has a certain legitimacy. The *Pater Noster* is Jesus' prayer before it is the disciples' prayer. It is not only the prayer he taught; it is the prayer he prayed. Instead of "Our Father who is in heaven," as in Matthew, the address in Luke is simply "Father." Joachim Jeremias has demonstrated that the Aramaic "Abba" on the lips of Jesus in prayer gave voice to Jesus' unique consciousness of God as his Father and of himself as Son.[2] This Aramaic form does not occur in the Lord's Prayer, but is found once in the Gospel tradition, in the Markan account of Jesus' prayer in Gethsemane, on the slope of the Mount of Olives: "Abba—Father—all things are possible for you. Remove this cup from me—yet what matters is not what I want, but what you want" (Mark 14:36). "Father" appears to be Mark's translation for the benefit of his Greek-speaking readers.[3] Paul uses "Abba" twice, each time with "Father" as the translation, in connection with the derivative sonship of Christians. "Abba" is the cry of those impelled by the "Spirit of sonship" (Rom. 8:15) or the "Spirit of his Son" (Gal. 4:6). It is a term of intimacy, the first stammering word a small child uses to address his or her father.[4] The Aramaic word seems to have been preserved in the Greek-speaking churches because of the memory that this was Jesus' own way of addressing God. If Jesus saw himself in the image of the child, as his use of this image suggests, it is not surprising that he consciously addressed God as his Father in this childlike way.

In particular, the Lukan form of the Lord's Prayer makes good sense as a prayer of Jesus. The simple Lukan address, "Father" is echoed not only in the "Abba-Father" of Mark 14:36, but in the parallel in Luke 22:42 ("Father . . . remove this cup from me"), the prayers from the cross in Luke 23:34 ("Father, forgive them . . .") and Luke 23:46 ("Father, into your hands I commit my spirit . . ."), as well as several prayers in the Gospel of John.

Especially noteworthy is John 12:27f., a Johannine equivalent of the Gethsemane account. "What shall I say?" Jesus asks. He tries

"Father, save me from this hour" (John 12:27), but immediately rejects it as an unsuitable prayer: "No, this is why I came to this hour." The prayer he then chooses as the right one—"Father, glorify your name"—sounds as if Jesus is beginning to recite something close to the Lukan form of the Lord's Prayer: "Father, hallowed be your name. . . ." If so, he does not finish, because a voice from heaven responds in the distinctively Johannine language of glorification (John 12:28–30).

The address, together with the first petition of the Lord's Prayer, may have originally been intended as a capsulization of the entire prayer. In any event, the hallowing or glorification of God's name is indirectly a theme in Jesus' last prayer in John's Gospel: "And now glorify me, Father, with the glory I had with you before the world existed" (John 17:5). This petition repeats the one with which the prayer began: "Father, the time has come. Glorify your Son, that your Son may glorify you" (John 17:1NIV). Jesus had glorified God by making his name known in the world (vss. 4,6), and now God's name would be made known in the glorification of the Son—i.e., in Jesus' passion and in the consequent gift of eternal life. The hallowing of God's name centers on Jesus himself and on his disciples. Concerning them, Jesus prays: "Holy Father, keep them in your name, this group that you gave me . . . I have kept them in your name . . ." (John 17:11f.). "Consecrate [i.e. hallow] them in the truth; your word is truth . . . and for their sakes I consecrate myself, that they too might be consecrated in truth" (John 17:18f.). At the end of the prayer, Jesus summarizes: "And I have made known to them your name, and I will make it known, that the love with which you loved me may be in them, and I in them" (John 17:26). The Johannine interpretation of "hallowed be your name" suggests that the petition has in view the completion of Jesus' own work and the spiritual formation of his disciples.

"May your kingdom come" requires little comment. The kingdom of God is the heart of Jesus' message. What is more appropriate than that the proclaimer of the kingdom should himself turn to God again and again to invoke its coming? "Your will be done, as in heaven so on earth" is not found in the Lukan form of the prayer, but does occur in Matthew's slightly longer version (Matt. 6:10) and in the second-century Didache (8:2). It may have been added as an explanation of what the hallowing of God's name and the coming of his kingdom were understood to mean concretely. But Jesus' prayer in Gethsemane (Mark 14:36 and parallels) indicates that this petition belonged to Jesus' vocabulary of prayer.

It is quite possible that the specific prayer Jesus taught his disciples may have drawn to itself other petitions Jesus was known to have used on a variety of occasions. The phrase, "as in heaven, so on earth" is reminiscent of Jesus' prayer of thanksgiving on the return of his disciples from a mission: "I thank you, Father, Lord of heaven and earth . . ." (Matt. 11:25; Luke 10:21). Sayings of Jesus (especially about prayer) may also have contributed to Matthew's formulation: e.g., "Truly, I say to you, whatever you bind on earth will be bound in heaven and whatever you loose on earth will be loosed in heaven. . . . If two of you agree on earth about anything they ask, it will be done for them by my Father in heaven" (Matt. 18:18–19 RSV).

The plurals in the last half of the Lord's Prayer make it clear that in its present form the prayer is designed for Jesus' disciples. Jesus' own prayers as we find them in the Gospel tradition are always singular. He prays as an individual and not as part of a community. As has often been noted, he speaks to his disciples about God as "your Father" and as "my Father," but never as "our Father."[5] The Matthean address, "Our Father who is in heaven," must therefore represent an adaptation of Jesus' private prayer to the disciples' needs and situation. The same is true of the recurring "we," "us," and "our" in the last half of the prayer. But this purely formal observation by no means excludes the possibility that Jesus privately prayed, "give *me* today my bread for tomorrow." "Do not bring *me* to temptation," or "Deliver *me* from the Evil One." The conflict with Satan and the demons that characterizes his ministry from its beginning makes the last two of these altogether fitting as petitions of Jesus. When he tells his disciples in Gethsemane to pray "not to get into temptation," he is presumably inviting them to share in what is his petition as well ("Watch with me" is his command, according to Matt. 26:38,40). The request for "tomorrow's bread today" probably reflects Jesus' personal daily dependence on the care and faithfulness of his Father, as shown for example in the temptation narrative, not, as many have thought, some bold and grand hastening of the future messianic banquet.[6]

The one stumbling block to the view that this was first of all Jesus' own prayer is the forgiveness petition. Christians are taught that Jesus is sinless. He forgives sin; he does not seek forgiveness. But if he was baptized by John "for the forgiveness of sins," it is not so strange that he should also *pray* for forgiveness. This is possible because he identified himself fully and radically with his people in all their sinfulness. In the baptism he anticipated the cross. If by a kind of transference he truly "bore" the sins of many, it is not surprising that he would at times petition God for forgiveness.[7] In every known form of the Lord's Prayer, the forgiveness petition is made to depend in some way on the petitioner's responsibility to forgive others (cf. Matt. 6:14–15; 18:21–35). This triangle of forgiveness seems to have planted itself deeply in Jesus' consciousness, and may in fact have been the basis of his urgent sense of obligation to extend the forgiveness of God to those who needed it most (cf., e.g., Mark 2:5, 10, 17; also Luke 23:34).

Thus the *Lord's Prayer* is just that, though it is of course the *disciples' prayer* as well. In both Luke and Matthew it becomes an important focus for Jesus' teaching on the subject of prayer and trust.

The Lord's Prayer is immediately followed by two brief parables (Luke 11:5–8 and 11:13) that frame the straightforward assurances of answered prayer in verses 9–10. Each of these is introduced with a rhetorical question: *"Who of you . . . ?"* (vs. 5) and "Which of you fathers . . . ?" (vs. 11). Like so many of Jesus' parables and metaphors, these are imaginary situations in which the hearer is explicitly asked to put himself or herself in the place of one character in particular. They are also parables of normalcy. The implied answer to the rhetorical question in each case is, "No one, of course!" In these stories, Jesus is emphasizing normalcy by means of a comic description of something abnormal. They are imaginary or "what if" stories, each leading to an absurdity. The first centers on a friend-to-friend relationship, the second on a father-son relationship.

THE FRIENDS AT MIDNIGHT

The theme of Luke 11:5–8 is friendship. The word *friend* occurs four times in the four verses. The emergency with which the story begins is itself occasioned by the unexpected arrival of a friend (vs. 6). The host, caught unprepared, goes in turn to the house of another friend to borrow three loaves of bread (vs. 5). But the chain of friendship is broken with the man inside the house. He is a comic figure because his actions grossly contradict the initial assumption that he is a friend. The hearer's reaction to his behavior is "Some friend! Friends don't behave like that!" Yet this is the character with whom the hearer is asked to identify! The sense of unreality is heightened by the ludicrous way in which this man is described. One can almost hear Jesus reciting the man's lines in the mocking, dull accents of a sluggard trotting out one lame excuse after another ("Don't bother me. The door is already locked, and my children are with me in bed. I can't get up . . .").

The next verse brings us back to reality. Such a scene would never happen. Who would be so selfish as to begrudge a friend three loaves of bread for a day or two in an emergency? The rhetorical question with which the story began has already made the answer clear. Any friend would grant such a request without hesitation; that is what makes him a friend. The last verse of the story adds a qualification based on a shrewd assessment of human nature, but one which does not change the main point. Even if the friendship by itself were *not* a strong enough motivation, the man inside the house would still get up "because of his shamelessness."[8] This could mean because he himself would be ashamed not to, or it could refer to the impudence of the borrower, who in effect has put him on the spot. The householder's reputation for hospitality is at stake and he can hardly say no.

The Greek for shamelessness or impudence *(anaideia)* has led to the widespread assumption that the point of the story is *persistence* in prayer. But the emphasis does not lie here at all. The word is simply part of the imaginary situation. The question of why a person would get up in the night to respond to a friend's need is a secondary question. The point is that, one way or another, he or she *will* get up, and that we can count on God to do the same. The man at the door is not particularly persistent. He merely makes a simple impromptu request. Nor do the promises that follow in Luke 11:9–10 depend on persistence. On the contrary, they suggest that persistence is unnecessary because God stands ready to give what is asked.

A possible reason for the impression that persistence is the theme of this story is the existence of another parable in which it *is* the theme, Luke 18:1–8. Jesus tells his disciples a story about an unjust judge and an oppressed widow "to the effect that they must continually pray and not give up" (Luke 18:1). The judge, who "neither fears God nor cares about human beings," nevertheless finally agrees to see that justice is done on the woman's behalf because she keeps bothering him. He takes up her cause to get rid of her, so that she won't eventually wear him out (Luke 18:5). Jesus invites the hearers not so much to put themselves in the place of this judge as to attend to his words and draw a conclusion. If even an ungodly judge is moved by such persistence, how much more will God "vindicate his elect, who cry out to him day and night while he patiently waits? I tell you, he will vindicate them quickly, but when the Son of man comes will he find on earth that kind of faithfulness?" (Luke 18:7–9). That persistence is unmistakably the point is shown by the last words of the story, by the Lukan formula with which the story is introduced ("pray and not give up," vs. 1), and by the strongly eschatological character of the Lukan context (i.e., Luke 17:20–37: "When will the kingdom of God come?").

The parable of the friends at midnight is quite different. The unjust judge is a credible character in a credible story, while the crotchety householder is an absurd caricature in a deliberately absurd fantasy. Those who have already prayed long and hard may need to be reminded that persistence pays off, but in Luke 11:5–13 Jesus' concern is rather with those who need encouragement in order to pray at all.

THE CRUEL FATHER

The rogues' gallery concludes. The absurdity of the crotchety householder is matched by that of the cruel father in Luke 11:11–13 (cf. Matt. 7:9–11). Once again the comic figure is the one with whom Jesus invites the hearers to identify: "Which of you fathers, when your son asks you for a fish will give him a snake instead? Or who, when he asks you for an egg will give him a scorpion?" Ridiculous! To put oneself in the place of a father who would surprise his son with such gifts is all but impossible. By reducing the abnormal to the absurd, Jesus reminds his hearers of what a normal father is like. Even in a "wicked generation," a normal father does the best he can to meet his children's needs and to grant their reasonable requests. "So if you, though evil, know enough to give good gifts to your children," Jesus concludes, "how much more will your Father from heaven give his good Spirit[9] to those who ask him?"

The point is much the same as in the preceding parable. If giving is normal in some relationships even in a twisted world, why can't we count on God to be as normal or as "human" as we are with our friends and with our own children in time of need? In these stories, God is not an enemy with whom we must struggle persistently, but a friend and father who is more ready to answer than we are to ask.

The two parables serve to reinforce the assurances of answered prayer in Luke 11:9–10 (paralleled exactly in Matt 7:7–8). These assurances are unconditional. They appear in two sequences of three: first as imperatives with corresponding promises attached ("Ask, and it will be given," meaning "If you ask, it will be given"), and then as general principles ("For everyone who asks receives . . ."). The petitions are designated first prosaically ("ask") and then in terms reminiscent of the imagery of Jesus' parables ("seek" and "knock"). There is no explicit indication of who is being asked for what, and the answers to the requests are spoken of in impersonal terms ("it will be given to you," "it will be opened to you," or "you will find"). But the impersonal future passive forms here, as elsewhere in the New Testament, represent an indirect way of referring to the action of God. The same is true of other grammatical forms, such as "you will receive" or "you will find" when they function as equivalents. The meaning is, "Ask God and he will give you, seek from God and you will find what he has for you, knock and God will open the door."[10] The second sequence repeats the first, only now as a marvelous generalization rather than a command: in Jesus' vision, all prayers are answered, all searches successful, and all visits find someone at home!

This passage is one of the purest examples of Jesus' absolute and unqualified promise of answered prayer. Other examples are John 15:7 ("Ask whatever you wish, and it will be done for you") and John 16:24 ("Ask and you will receive"). In each of these cases, however, the promise is conditioned by something in the context. In John 15:7, the condition is "*if* you dwell in me and my words dwell in you . . . ." In John 16:24, it is "until now you have asked nothing *in my name* . . . " It is the petitioner's relationship to Jesus that makes the promise valid. More precisely, it is the petitioner's relationship to the *risen* Jesus. Dwelling in Jesus like branches in a vine is possible only when (in Johannine terms) he has gone to the Father and sent from the Father the Spirit of truth. The phrase "in my name" similarly implies Jesus' physical absence. To pray in his name is to pray when he is not around to do the praying, just as to teach or heal in his name is to do so when he is not around to do the teaching or healing. Baptism in Jesus' name takes place only after his passion and resurrection, and the same is apparently true of suffering for his name.[11] In the farewell discourses of John's Gospel, "asking in Jesus' name" apparently means coming to God in prayer on the authority of Jesus as risen Lord and Son of God.

The tradition of Jesus' promises of answered prayer seems to have developed as follows. At the earliest stage, no conditions whatever were attached to the promise (Luke 11:9–10; Matt. 7:7–8). This is still the case in Mark 11:24, in which the only condition is believing that the unconditional promise holds good: "believe that you have it, and it will be yours." In Matthew 21:22, however, the condition is "believing" in a more general sense, i.e., being a believer, or being in right relation to God. In John, as we have seen, the assurances are conditioned either by some statement in the context, or by the phrase "in my name." The tradition developed, as it did because it was assumed that conditions had been implied from the start. Jesus could not have made prayer a means for realizing one's private whims or selfish desires.

But what is the equivalent, in the earlier formulations, of the phrase "in my name" that becomes so conspicuous in the later ones? The most plausible equivalent is the parable, or parables, that Jesus employed as the vehicle for his promises of answered prayer. The developing tradition represents a formalizing of a truth Jesus first expressed in a radical and unqualified way, but in the context of parables or metaphors. The disciples are invited to ask God as a child would ask its father, with the assurance that God would no more withhold from them what is good than they would from their own children. The assurance presupposes that they have become children for the sake of the kingdom of God, or received the kingdom as a child would receive it.

If Jesus first heard the metaphor in this way, its meaning for him would have been much the same. If he asked God for a fish, would he receive a stone? Not if God was to him "Abba," as his recorded prayers indicate. If a friend came to him for bread in the middle of the night, would he turn that friend away? No more would God turn him away, for God was both father and friend (cf. John 5:20, 15:15). For the disciple to come to God simply and gladly as a child would come is to come in the place of Jesus. It is to pray in Jesus' name. The phrase, "in my name," takes the place of such parables as the friends at midnight and the cruel father, and captures the heart of their message. As so often in Jesus' ministry, "in the beginning was the story." Only when Jesus' impending absence is in view does prayer with the authority and privilege of a child of God come to be called prayer "in Jesus' name" (cf. John 16:24).

THE LORD'S PRAYER IN MATTHEW AND LUKE

Some additional comments are necessary on the respective uses of the Lord's Prayer in Luke and Matthew. Instead of suggesting an occasion that prompted Jesus to give the prayer, Matthew has simply incorporated it into Jesus' first major discourse, the Sermon on the Mount. Specifically, it comes within that part of the Sermon in which Jesus comments on the three pillars of Jewish piety: almsgiving (Matt. 6:2–4), prayer (6:5–15), and fasting (6:16–18). The section on prayer is much longer than the other two because Matthew has expanded it with a considerable block of material that has no counterpart in the sections on almsgiving and fasting. A comparison of the three sections (apart from vss. 7–15) shows that they fit into a tight, symmetrical pattern and share a common structure. Jesus is warning against ostentation in all three areas and contrasting the practice required of his disciples with the practice of the "hypocrites" (i.e., the Pharisees). But in Matthew 6:7 he departs from the pattern. Having warned against Jewish prayer abuse in verses 5–6, he now turns his attention to Gentile prayer abuse. If the Pharisees were guilty of ostentation in prayer, the Gentiles were guilty of babbling and unnecessary repetition. They probably invoked the names and attributes of many gods for magical purposes. Against such practices, Jesus reminds his disciples that "Your Father knows the things you need before you ask him" (Matt. 6:8).

Next, the Lord's Prayer is introduced as, among other things, a model of brevity. The fact that the prayer is part of a section that breaks into the stereotyped pattern of reflections on Judaism's "three pillars" may give the impression that it is somehow extraneous to the Sermon on the Mount. This is particularly the case in view of the likelihood that historically the prayer was given much later in Jesus' ministry. But such an impression would be misleading. In fact, the prayer has been skillfully and carefully integrated into its present literary context in Matthew. First, Matthew has anticipated his longer form of the address, "Our Father who is in heaven" with his repeated use of such phrases as "your Father in heaven" (Matt. 5:16), "your Father who is in heaven" (5:45, 6:1; cf. 7:11), "your heavenly Father" (5:48; cf. 6:14,26,32), or simply "your Father" (6:4,6,8; cf. 6:15,18). Jesus in the Sermon on the Mount speaks repeatedly of "your Father in heaven" or the like, and in the middle of it gives his disciples a prayer in which they in turn address God as "our Father who is in heaven." They learn to pray within the context of a specific block of teaching about the Father's love and care for them. Near the end of the Sermon, Matthew attributes to Jesus another phrase that reveals the basis of his father-child relationship: "he who does the will of my Father who is in heaven" (Matt. 7:21 RSV). Jesus' sonship is once again seen to be the foundation and presupposition of our own.

The second way Matthew has integrated the Lord's Prayer into the Sermon on the Mount is by making it a partial key to the structure of the last half of the Sermon. The last three petitions of the prayer (from Matthew 6:19 on) appear to have been developed catechetically. Thus Matthew 6:19–34 may be regarded as an elaboration on the bread petition, Matthew 7:1–12 on the forgiveness petition, and Matthew 7:13–27 on the temptation/deliverance petition. Jesus reflects on the proper attitude of a disciple, first to material things, then to fellow-disciples and fellow human beings, and finally to the ultimate issue of life, the choice between good and evil. The connection with the Lord's Prayer is clearest with respect to Matthew 6:19–34, slightly less direct in Matthew 7:1–12, and rather indirect in Matthew 7:13–27.

In Matthew 6:19–34 Jesus focuses on two wrong attitudes toward material things, greed (vss. 19–24) and anxiety (vss. 25–34). What is required instead is childlike trust in God, who protects and cares for the birds of the sky, and who clothes in splendor the flowers of the field. That the Lord's Prayer is still in view is shown by the close similarity between Matthew 6:8, in the immediate context of the prayer ("Your Father knows what things you need before you ask him"), and Matthew 6:32 ("your heavenly Father knows that you need all these things"). Both statements are accompanied by warnings not to be like the heathen (vs. 8a) or the Gentiles (vs. 32a). The Lord's Prayer as a whole seems to be echoed in Matthew 6:33, with its emphasis on the priority of the things of God (his kingdom and his righteousness) over the material needs of human beings.

The next verse builds implicitly on the bread petition: we pray for "tomorrow's bread today" and must therefore not be anxious about it. When we ask God to meet our needs, we trust in his power and willingness to do so. Clearly, Matthew has interpreted "bread" as real food (along with clothing and shelter). He has not spiritualized it as the word of God (despite the valid principle expressed in Matthew 4:4), or as the Holy Spirit, or as Christ. Nor has he "eschatologized" it as the "bread of the age to come" or as participation in the great "messianic banquet" of Jewish expectation.[12] For him it is the prime expression of the notion that prayer is the key to trusting God for day-by-day material needs, even as childlike trust in "our Father who is in heaven" is the mark of authentic prayer.

As prayer and trust are mutually interrelated, so forgiveness is intertwined with both. Immediately after the prayer, Matthew fastens his attention on the forgiveness petition. Only those who forgive others can expect God to forgive their own offenses (Matt. 6:14–15). Picking up this thread in Matthew 7:1–12, he uses the principle of "Judge not, that you be not judged" (Matt. 7:1–5,12) as a frame for another section on prayer reminiscent of Matthew 6:5–15. Matt. 7:6–11 belong together; verse 6 vividly reinforces the warnings against ostentation in 6:1–18 while Matthew 7:7–11 recalls the emphasis of Matthew 6:5–15 in particular on simplicity and directness in prayer.

Instead of two parables bracketing the direct promise of answered prayer, Matthew uses only the second, the parable of the cruel father. His adaptations serve to integrate the assurances of answered prayer

into the Sermon on the Mount as a whole, relating them especially to
the responsibility of mutual forgiveness. The dualism inherent in
"Lead us not into temptation, but deliver us from the Evil One" is
reflected in the rest of the Sermon on the Mount: the way of destruction and the way of life (Matt. 7:13–14), the warnings against false
prophets (Matt. 7:15–23), and the brief parable of the wise and the
foolish builder (Matt. 7:24–27). Even though the Sermon on the
Mount is probably not the original setting of the Lord's Prayer, the
prayer is not an interpolation in the usual sense of the word. It has
become rather the core that interprets, and is in turn interpreted by,
the teaching material with which Matthew has surrounded it.

In Luke, as we have seen, Jesus' encounter with Mary and Martha
"in a certain village" (Luke 10:38–42) and the giving of the Lord's
Prayer "in a certain place" (Luke 11:1–4) seem to have been brought
into their present context together. At any rate, their close connection
provides independent support for Matthew's apparent emphasis on
prayer as the alternative to anxiety. Martha's shortcoming is that she
is "anxious about many things" (Luke 10:41). Luke elsewhere regards
anxiety as a major threat to the life of a disciple (cf. Luke 8:14; 12:11,
22–32; 21:34), a threat to be overcome by hearing the word of God
(Luke 8:15,21), by the Holy Spirit (Luke 12:12), by seeking the kingdom (Luke 12:31f.), or by prayer (Luke 21:36). Jesus tells Martha that
anxiety must be overcome by reducing the scope of her concern from
many things to "few things, or one" (Luke 10:42).[13]

The few things on which one must concentrate are perhaps represented in the next several verses by the petitions of the Lord's Prayer:
God's name, his kingdom, the forgiveness and protection that he
grants—all that is involved in the coming of the Spirit. The Spirit is,
of course, not mentioned in the prayer itself, but when Jesus comes
to apply the accompanying parables directly to the disciples, he concludes "how much more will your Father from heaven give his good
Spirit to those who ask Him?" (Luke 11:13).

Luke appears to have summarized the Lord's Prayer as a prayer
for the Spirit.[14] He has *spiritualized* the prayer in that he sees all its

petitions pointing to the same reality, whether described positively, as God's name or kingdom or Spirit, or negatively as forgiveness of sins or help against temptation. Even the bread petition can be seen in this light. The three loaves in the parable of the friends at midnight do not represent food or material things in particular, but anything that human beings rightly and properly seek from God. All requests finally come down to one request—for the presence, or Spirit, of God. In Luke, as in Matthew, prayer is the supreme expression of childlike trust and, along with renunciation of oneself and the love of one's enemies, a hallmark of true discipleship.

15.

JESUS
AND HIS FUTURE

At the heart of the Gospel tradition, behind Jesus' proclamation and parables, behind his healings and exorcisms, behind his gift of forgiveness and his call to discipleship, is a person. In every facet of his ministry, Jesus was a credible human being who learned from his experiences and shared what he learned with his disciples. Yet to confront this person and learn from him is to encounter mystery.

THE SON OF MAN

The mystery of Jesus' person comes to expression most conspicuously in his favorite term for himself, "Son of man." Instead of "I" Jesus often refers to himself in an odd, third person manner as "Son of man." In Greek (and in English) the term has been made into a title, probably formed on the analogy of "Son of God," but its Aramaic original, *bar nasha* meant simply *a man* or *a certain person.* It was not a formal title, but an indefinite designation widely used in the telling of stories. And yet *Son of man,* unlike a son or a shepherd or a servant, a door or a vine or a seed of grain, is not a metaphor. It is not a stock figure from the world of Jesus' parables, unless we think of the indefinite "someone" or "a certain man" with which a few of the stories begin. But it is unlikely that these are connected with *Son of man* because the "Son of man" sayings in themselves are not parabolic. The term *Son of man* occurs in the applications of certain parables (e.g., Matt. 13:37; Luke 18:8; Matt. 24:44 and Luke 12:40), but not in the stories proper.

Traditionally, Jesus' "Son of man" sayings have been divided into three groups.

1. Those in which he refers to himself in his present situation on earth: the Son of man "came eating and drinking" (Matt. 11:19; Luke 7:34), "has nowhere to lay his head" (Matt 8:20; Luke 9:58), "is Lord of the Sabbath" (Mark 2:28 and parallels), "has authority on earth to forgive sin" (Mark 2:10 and parallels), and "sows the good seed" (Matt. 13:37); whoever "says a word against the Son of man will be forgiven" (Matt. 12:32; Luke 12:10).

2. Those in which he refers to his passion: the Son of man "must suffer many things and be rejected . . . and be killed, and rise after three days"—or "on the third day" (Mark 8:31 and parallels; cf. Mark 9:31, 10:33 and parallels). All that the prophets wrote about him must be fulfilled (Luke 18:31). He came "not to be served but to serve, and to give his life a ransom for many" (Mark 10:45; Matt. 20:28). As Jonah was three days and nights inside the great fish, so the Son of man will be "three days and nights in the heart of the earth" (Matt 12:40). As Moses lifted up the serpent in the desert on a pole, "so shall the Son of man be lifted up" (John 3:14).

3. Those that predict that the Son of man will come in glory to judge the world and vindicate the people of God: those who are ashamed of Jesus and of his words now will themselves be put to shame by the Son of man "when he comes in the glory of his Father, with the holy angels" (Mark 8:38 and parallels). The high priest, Jesus says, will see the Son of man "seated on the right hand of power and coming in the clouds" (Mark 14:62; Matt. 26:64). His coming will be like a lightning flash, lighting up the sky from one horizon to the other (Luke 17:24; Matt. 24:27). He will be seen coming in the clouds with great power and glory, and then he will send his angels and gather his chosen ones from the four winds, from the end of the earth to where the sky ends" (Mark 13:26–27 and parallels). When he "sits on

the throne of his glory," his disciples will sit with him "on twelve thrones, judging the twelve tribes of Israel" (Matt. 19:28). All this is to take place in the future, but no one knows the exact time of the Son of man's coming (Matt. 24:43–44; Luke 12:39–40).

It is important to notice that the third group of sayings stands somewhat apart from the first two. In the passion sayings and the sayings referring to Jesus' present situation, *Son of man* is simply the equivalent of "I." But why would Jesus speak of himself in this indirect manner? Such language, like his use of the emphatic "I" in certain sayings (e.g., Matt. 12:28), may well have called his hearers' attention to what he was saying, and caused them to raise questions about who he really was (cf., e.g., John 9:36; 12:34). But did he choose the term deliberately with this purpose in mind? Did he in fact choose the term at all, or did it arise naturally and inevitably out of his personal religious experience?

A few scholars have noted a possible background for Jesus' use of "Son of man" in the Old Testament book of Ezekiel.[1] The prophet Ezekiel in his visions is consistently addressed by the Lord God as "son of man," apparently to remind him of his own mortality (over ninety occurrences in all). The relevance of this material for the New Testament use of "Son of man" should not be tied to the question of whether Jesus saw specific parallels between himself and Ezekiel. There is little or no indication in the Gospels that this is the case. Its relevance lies rather in the evidence it furnishes that Jewish visionaries were conscious at times of being addressed in their visions as "son of man." Isolated examples of the same phenomenon can be seen in Daniel 8:17 and Enoch 60:10. When Paul in 2 Corinthians 12:2 describes a visionary experience he refers to himself in the third person as "a man in Christ." It is therefore possible that Jesus' designation of himself as "Son of man" in connection with his present experience and with his anticipation of suffering and death simply represents the carrying over of a term by which he himself was conscious of God addressing him.

In this view, the "I" implicit in the self-designation "Son of man"

is the "I" of the prophet or visionary. Though not itself a metaphor
—Jesus was, after all, quite literally a man!—the term "Son of man"
belongs to the world of Jesus' parables and metaphors, not as a
character in that world but as a term for the one through whose eyes
that world is perceived. Like Ezekiel, Jesus customarily hears God
addressing him as "Son of man"; the instances in which he hears
himself addressed as "Son of God" or "my beloved Son" stand out
precisely because they are exceptional.

Unlike Ezekiel, Jesus seems to have carried this reminder of his
humanity over into his public teaching. Or, more precisely, he carries
it over in a different way than Ezekiel had done. Instead of stating
formally "The Lord God said to me, 'O thou son of man . . . ,' " Jesus
simply uses "Son of man" along with "I" as a self-designation in
handing on the revelation he has received. His emphasis throughout
is on the actual message he has to proclaim, not on the process or the
visionary framework by which he received that message.

The first two groups of "Son of man" sayings appear to represent
conclusions Jesus has reached about himself on the basis of revelation
or experience. He knows that he has been given authority to forgive
sins and authority over the Sabbath. He has no home on earth, and
he has come eating and drinking. He knows, at some point, that he
will be rejected by the rulers and high priests, and be killed, and rise
again from the dead on the third day. The *Son of man* is not a
character in a story with whom Jesus learns to identify. *Son of man*
is rather the "I" who makes the self-identification, whether with a
bridegroom or a servant, a shepherd or a housewife or a beloved Son.

The third group of "Son of man" sayings is different. Here it is
not immediately apparent that "Son of man" is a substitute for "I."
Jesus speaks of the Son of man as of a supernatural being distinct from
himself. Rudolf Bultmann has argued that these sayings are authentic,
but that Jesus was indeed referring not to himself but to a transcen-
dent messianic figure yet to come.[2] It is not hard to see how someone
could draw this conclusion from the third group of sayings. When a
person already on earth speaks of a man, or a son of man who will

come in the clouds (presumably to earth) with his holy angels, will gather his chosen ones from all directions, set up a throne and institute judgment, it strains credulity to think that he means himself! If he is already on earth, how is it that he "comes"?

Only the presumed unity of this third group of sayings with the first two guarantees that in such a pronouncement the Son of man means Jesus. In that case the third group actually presupposes the second: if the Son of man is to come, he must first go (Mark 14:21), i.e., he must die and be raised from the dead. Yet for the most part, groups two and three represent separate traditions. Only in Luke 17:24–26 are they combined: "For as the lightning flashes from one horizon to the other, so will be the Son of man in his day. But first he must suffer many things and be rejected by this generation. And just as it was in the days of Noah, so it will be in the days of the Son of man." Elsewhere, if there is a Son of man passion saying, there is nothing about his future coming, or his day, and vice versa. The evidence suggests that these two types of sayings have different origins in the tradition.

The root of all the sayings about the Son of man's glorious coming appears to have been Daniel 7:13–14 (RSV): "I saw in the night visions, and behold, with the clouds of heaven there came one like a son of man, and he came to the Ancient of Days and was presented before him. And to him was given dominion and glory and a kingdom, that all peoples, nations, and languages should serve him; his dominion is an everlasting dominion . . . and his kingdom one that shall not be destroyed."

The association of this "son of man" with a kingdom is a striking parallel to the thought of Jesus as presented in the Gospels. In Daniel it is all part of a vision, and similarly in the Gospels, the sayings about the coming Son of man sound like descriptions of something Jesus has seen. The language, however, is not the mundane language of the world of Jesus' parables, but the exalted, majestic language of apocalyptic vision. What is displayed in these sayings is nothing less than the end of history as Jesus' contemporaries knew it, and the start of a new world. It is in a new world (Matt. 19:28) that the Son of man will sit on the throne of his glory and the disciples will judge the tribes of Israel. Jesus speaks as if he, like Daniel, has been granted to see into that new world. He has seen what he says the high priest will see, the "Son of man seated on the right hand of power and coming in the clouds" (Mark 14:62). He has seen the gathering of the chosen, the setting up of the Son of man's throne (". . . to him was given dominion and glory and a kingdom . . ."), and the ensuing judgment. In these sayings he invites his disciples to share his vision.

Formally, Rudolf Bultmann's impression is correct. The Son of man whom Jesus sees *is* a figure external to himself—initially. But the same process of identification that draws him imaginatively into the world of his parables is at work here as well. There is little doubt that in the Son of man of Jewish apocalyptic tradition, beginning with Daniel and continuing in the so-called Similitudes of Enoch (e.g., Enoch 46—48, 62—63, 71), and in the apocalypse of 4 Ezra 13, Jesus came to see his own role and destiny. Those who confess *him,* Jesus of Nazareth, are the ones whom the Son of man will confess before the angels of God (Luke 12:8), and at his coming the Son of man, accordingly, will be ashamed of those who are ashamed of *Jesus* (Mark 8:38; Luke 9:26).

When the "Son of man sits on the throne of his glory," it is *Jesus'* disciples who will reign with him (Matt. 19:28), and the Son of man's coming is said to be "in the glory of his Father" (i.e., the one whom *Jesus* calls Father). He who hears himself addressed as "Son of man" thus experiences identification with that other son of man who dominates his vision. Though the translation of Enoch 71:14 is much disputed, it appears that something of the kind is going on there as well. After a series of visions of the "son of man who has righteousness" (cf. Enoch 46:3), Enoch the seer is finally told, "You are the son of man who is born in righteousness," or (according to a different rendering) "You, son of man, who are born in righteousness . . ." (cf. Enoch 60:10). In either case an identification is being made between the visionary and a major figure in his visions. Whether it is all a literary device, or whether it rests on the actual experience of an individual or an apocalyptic community in late Judaism, it furnishes a possible analogy to the experience of Jesus.

The merging of the first two groups of Son of man sayings with the third produces a kind of polarity in Jesus' outlook on the future. On the one hand, he sees rejection and death in store for him, followed by resurrection after two or three days—however he may have understood it. On the other hand, he sees himself carrying out the role of the messianic Son of man, coming to earth "in the clouds" to rule and execute judgment. He comes to earth, presumably, from heaven. The apocalyptic sayings seem to presuppose not only his resurrection but some kind of ascension or exaltation as well. Exaltation is suggested in the Synoptic Gospels only in the reference, in Jesus' word to the high priest, to being "seated on the right hand of power" (Mark 14:62). John's Gospel, however, places its major emphasis on this aspect of the Son of man's activity.

It is as Son of man that Jesus compares himself to a seed of grain that dies and is lifted up from the earth (John 12:23–34). It is as Son of man that he will "ascend to where he was at first" (John 6:62; cf. 20:17). Even apart from the term "Son of man," it is John who emphasizes that before Jesus can *come* to his disciples he must first *go away* (John 14:2–3,12,28; cf. 16:7ff.). A rather highly-developed christology is necessary, it seems, to overcome the polarity in the Synoptic Son of man sayings and place them in a coherent framework. In the Synoptics themselves, as probably in the consciousness of Jesus, the polarity remains. His future is two-pronged. His life is pointed toward the passion and at the same time toward the final realization of the kingdom of God. What does *not* emerge clearly from the Son of man material is the interval between them.

The situation is similar with respect to the Synoptic accounts of the institution of the Lord's Supper. Jesus' references to his body and especially to his "blood of the covenant poured out for many" (Mark 14:24; Matt. 26:28) point unmistakably to the cross, but his accompanying vow of abstinence has as its apparent goal the realization of the kingdom: "Truly I say to you that I will no more drink the fruit of the vine until that day when I drink it anew in the kingdom of God" (Mark 14:25; Matt. 26:29 has "kingdom of my Father").

Luke has the same two points of reference, but weaves them into a more complex pattern. Jesus begins by pronouncing the vow of abstinence twice, first concerning the passover ("I will eat it no more until it is fulfilled in the kingdom of God," Luke 22:16), and then concerning the cup ("I shall not drink the fruit of the vine until the kingdom of God comes," Luke 22:18). Next he breaks the bread, speaks of his body as "given for you," and gives the cup as "the new covenant in my blood, poured out for you" (Luke 22:19–20).

The word "covenant" or "testament," used here in connection with his redemptive death, is echoed a few verses later in connection with a promise of the kingdom: "And I covenant to you, just as my Father covenanted to me, a kingdom, that you may eat and drink at my table in my kingdom, and you shall sit on thrones judging the twelve tribes of Israel" (Luke 22:29–30).

The twin focus is on Jesus' redemptive death and on the coming kingdom. Only the words found in Luke, "Do this in remembrance of me" (Luke 22:19), which Paul elaborates and emphasizes (1 Cor. 11:24–26), suggest an interval or waiting period between them.

THE ABSENT LORD

At this point it is possible to generalize. Looking at the Synoptic Gospels as a whole, the story of Jesus' life may be regarded as ending either in his death and resurrection or in the future coming of the Son of man. From a literary point of view the Gospels may be regarded as having their climax in either the passion story (Mark 14—16) or the immediately-preceding last discourse of Jesus on the Mount of Olives (Mark 13). The latter affords the disciples an apocalyptic glimpse of the course of events down to the end of the age and the coming of the Son of man, without particular reference to Jesus himself. It is in fact assumed that he will be absent, for, as he says, "many will come in my name, saying 'I am he!' and shall deceive many" (Mark 13:6 and parallels). This chapter is obviously the Gospels' longest and most significant reflection on the interval between the passion of the Son of man and his glorious coming. Ironically, however, Jesus plays no direct part in it. The interval is just that—a pause or hiatus in the divine plan, a period of waiting and watching for signs that point to the end but do not determine its exact time. The basis for the certainty of its coming is laid in the passion narrative that follows, particularly in the promise of the kingdom given at the last meal. Jesus' decisive role in bringing about the kingdom's full realization on earth now becomes clear. By his death the promise is sealed, and the disciples' participation in the kingdom of God is guaranteed.

Matthew alone among the Synoptic writers appends to the Olivet Discourse a series of parables, all of which share with the discourse proper the theme of an interval or a period in which Jesus is absent. Programmatic for Matthew is the single parable already appended to the discourse in Mark:

> It is like a man who went away and left his household in charge of his servants, each with his assigned task. To the doorkeeper he gave the task of keeping watch. You then must keep watch, for you do not know when the lord of the household is coming—whether in the evening, or at midnight, or when the rooster crows, or at dawn. In case he comes suddenly, don't let him find you asleep. What I say to you, I say to all: "Stay awake!" (Mark 13:34–37).

The same theme of responsibility and accountability during Jesus' absence finds expression in Matthew's parables of the householder and the thief (Matt. 24:43–44; cf. Luke 12:39–40), the good and the evil servant (Matt. 24:45–51; cf. Luke 12:41–46), the wise and the foolish virgins (Matt. 25:1–13), and the entrusted talents (Matt. 25:14–30); cf. Luke 19:11–27). Matthew caps the series with a parable-like judgment scene different in some ways from the preceding stories, yet like them addressing the question of human responsibility during the time of the Son of man's absence (Matt. 25:31–46).

It is helpful to survey these stories and try to determine their most appropriate points of audience identification. The brief parable of the householder and the thief is particularly reminiscent of the imagery of the strong man whose house is plundered by someone stronger (Luke 11:21–22), the rich fool who built bigger and bigger barns and thought he was secure (Luke 12:16–20), or the king faced with war against odds that were too great (Luke 14:31–32). The hearer's identification is with the householder. One's house must be always well guarded so that the thief cannot break in undetected and rob it (cf. Matt. 6:19–20; Luke 12:33). The original application of the story was probably to the necessity of being ready for the in-breaking kingdom of God. But another identification is also possible. Would not the violent, who seized the kingdom by force and made it their own, have put themselves in the place of the thief breaking into the household by night? Would this not have been Jesus' application as well? If he saw himself as the one binding the strong man (Mark 3:27 and parallels), or as the one who tried out his sword by piercing a wall (Gospel of Thomas 98), then why not also as a thief digging at night through the wall of an unguarded house? Such an image would have been an appropriate expression of his often-told story of the clash of the two households and the two kingdoms.

The parable of the good and the evil servant (Matt. 24:45–51) invites the hearer, right at the outset, to emulate the "faithful and wise servant" (vs. 45). He has the responsibility, in his master's absence, for the well-being of his fellow servants, and he is blessed in fulfilling that responsibility (vss. 46–47). But if he turns out instead to be an evil servant (vs. 48), mistreating his charges and neglecting his duties, his master will return unexpectedly and "cut him to pieces" (vs. 50). The hearer is impelled to ask, "Which kind of servant am I?" If the point of identification in the preceding story was with the householder, in this case it is explicitly with the servant. This would have been no less true for Jesus himself than for his disciples. Surely the alternatives of good and bad servanthood confronted him from the start of his ministry. His self-understanding as shepherd points clearly to his sense of responsibility for the "lost sheep of the house of Israel" (Matt. 9:36; 15:24). As Son of man he had come to seek and save what was lost (Luke 19:10). It is this same sense of responsibility that finds expression here in the self-image of the servant.

If it is possible to speak of an original meaning for this story, that meaning is perhaps best understood as accountability to God, in view of the coming of God's kingdom—both Jesus' own accountability, and the accountability of those who responded to his call. But in the period of Jesus' absence, the point of reference changes. Jesus is now seen as the master instead of the servant, and application is made to the church living between the Son of man's passion and his coming in glory. The same kind of development is traceable here as in the interpretation of the parable of the weeds. Jesus' own self-identification was with the servants who asked about the weeds (Matt. 13:27–28), but in the interpretation the Son of man is identified with the householder who sowed the good seed and answered the servants' questions.[3] There is no reason to believe that the stories themselves have been substantially modified in the telling, but the applications are different. The actors have in some instances been assigned new roles. Jesus the faithful and wise servant has become the absent Lord. His role as servant now falls to the reader, who is moved to ask Jesus' question over again: "Which kind of servant am I?"

The alternative, "wise or foolish?", governs the next story as well (Matt. 25:1–13). The five wise young women were those who took extra oil for their lamps in case of an unforeseen change in the bridegroom's plans. When the bridegroom arrived unexpectedly in the middle of the night after a long delay, they were prepared to meet him even though they, like the five others, had been asleep. The five foolish young women, caught short because they had failed to make the proper preparations, missed the bridegroom's arrival and found themselves excluded from the wedding.

The fact that all ten women slept suggests that the parable was not tailor-made for its concluding admonition, "Stay awake, for you don't know the day or the hour" (vs. 13). Its emphasis on taking prudent steps to forestall trouble is more reminiscent of Luke's tower-builder who first sat down to estimate whether he had enough resources to finish his project, or the king facing war who stopped to ask himself whether his ten thousand soldiers could stand against his enemy's twenty thousand (Luke 14:28–32). Or we might think of the unjust steward, who saved himself from a financial crisis by slyly writing off the debts owed to his master (Luke 16:1–7). Like the women who brought extra oil, he is said to have acted wisely (Luke 16:8). Or we might recall again the man in the saying in the Gospel of Thomas who tested his sword ahead of time (Logion 98).

Such parallels suggest that, as Dodd and Jeremias pointed out a number of years ago, the parable of the ten young women was first a parable of crisis and only later a parable of the absent Lord.[4] It arises out of the crisis precipitated by the presence of Jesus and his proclamation of the kingdom of God. The chief point of audience identification is with the women. It leaves the hearer with the question, "Have I taken the right steps to get ready for the kingdom and the impending judgment?" In John the Baptist's terms, "Have I produced fruit worthy of repentance?"

An intriguing possibility, in fact, though one that must remain speculative, is that this story goes back precisely to John the Baptist who, according to one tradition, applied the metaphor of the bridegroom to the Coming One for whom he was waiting (John 3:29). If his identification was with the "friend of the bridegroom," as this passage indicates, it would not have been strange for him, by the use of parables, to put his hearers in the place of young women waiting to escort the bridegroom to the wedding hall. For them the question would be, "Are you ready for the bridegroom's coming?" It would represent an adaptation of John's repentance proclamation to that late stage in his ministry in which the profile of the Coming One had begun to emerge clearly.

As for Jesus, who would have inherited this story from John, his self-identification with the bridegroom is attested in Mark 2:18–20. Unlike the disciples of John and of the Pharisees, Jesus' disciples cannot fast, because the bridegroom is with them" (Mark 2:19). On the other hand, he never identifies himself with the friend of the bridegroom or with any other member of a wedding party. It is likely, therefore, that the later church's apparent identification of the expected bridegroom with Jesus stands in continuity with Jesus' own understanding of that figure. There is evidence, as we saw earlier, that Jesus at some point anticipated his own death in connection with the bridegroom metaphor. "Days will come," he says, "when the bridegroom will be taken from them . . ." (Mark 2:20). "Days will come," he says much later, "when you will desire to see one of the days of the Son of man, and you will not see it" (Luke 17:22). Assuming that the parable of the young woman was originally a parable of crisis, the figure of the bridegroom was perhaps what made possible and appropriate its adaptation to the period of the Son of man's absence, between his passion and the day of his triumph.

The parable of the talents (Matt. 25:14–30) has, in common with the three preceding stories, the theme of absence. As in Mark's story of the doorkeeper (Mark 13:34–37), a man goes on a journey and entrusts three of his servants with responsibility, in this case the responsibility to invest his money wisely. Two of them do so, returning to their master twice the amount he had left with them. The failure of the third is not that he made a poor investment, but that he made no investment at all! He takes the one talent he has been given (about a thousand dollars), and buries it in the ground for safekeeping (vs. 18). He has risked nothing, and he gains nothing! The master, when he returns, is angry with this worthless servant. Taking away the one talent he had given him, he sends him "into the outer darkness" (vss. 26–30).

This story also has a realistic life setting within the ministry of Jesus. The proper response to the kingdom of God is *not* to play it safe, but to risk everything, like the man who came across a treasure in a field, or the merchant who found the perfect pearl, or the shepherd or the housewife looking for what they had lost. For Jesus it meant risking all for the "lost sheep of Israel," for the tax collectors and prostitutes to whom he was sent. For Jesus and others it meant risking all for the sake of the kingdom of God itself, the supreme good

outweighing wealth and family, even one's very life. In the parable's
present context, the man going on a journey and leaving money with
his servants is assumed to be Jesus in his death and resurrection. The
servants are the readers of the Gospel awaiting his return. Yet the
basic thrust of the story remains unchanged. The crisis continues in
the absence of Son of man. What is still demanded is the kind of faith
that is not afraid to take risks.

The main differences in the Lukan parable of the pounds are: (1)
the man goes on the journey in order to be crowned king; (2) the
amount of money involved is smaller (one *mina* to each servant, i.e.,
about twenty dollars), but the rewards are enormous (the governing
authority over ten cities and five cities, respectively); the principle is
that by proving themselves trustworthy in a "very small matter"
(Luke 19:17) they qualify for a great reward; (3) The story of the
servants is interwoven with a story of judgment on those who had
resisted the new king's claim to the throne (Luke 19:14, 27).

Efforts to find an allegory of Jesus' ascension and return in this
parable are less than convincing. The story in Luke is told because "he
was near Jerusalem, and they thought the kingdom of God was going
to appear at once" (Luke 19:11). In the triumphal entry that follows,
Jesus is hailed as "king" (Luke 19:38), but the conclusion of the
matter is that the city does not know the terms of peace or the "time
of its visitation" (vss. 42, 44). The rejection is not in a "distant
country" (cf. vs. 12) but here and now. Jesus and his disciples stand
at the *end* of their long journey to Jerusalem, and it is not a journey
from which Jesus will *return*.

If this is an allegory, it is surely not Luke's allegory. The parable
is more likely the product of combining a story about a rejected and
vengeful king with a more modest version of Matthew's parable of the
talents. The vengeful king is rather like the vengeful lord of the
vineyard in the story of the wicked tenants (Luke 20:9–19; Mark
12:1–12; Matt. 21:33–46), or the vengeful king (Matt. 22:7) whose
wedding invitations were scorned. The theme of the journey may have
been what drew the two subplots together. Whether the interweaving

of the two threads is the work of Jesus or of later tradition is more
difficult to say. It does not seem to have originated with Luke because
for him it would have created more problems than it would solve.

The last of Matthew's parables of absence (Matt. 25:31–46) is not
strictly a parable at all but an apocalyptic vision of the final judgment.
This is clear from the way in which the scene is introduced: "When
the Son of man comes in his glory, and all his angels with him, then
he will sit on the throne of his glory, and all the Gentiles will be
gathered before him (Matt. 25:31f.; cf. 19:28). Yet the vision has
within it certain parabolic elements. The Son of man separates the
Gentiles "as a shepherd separates sheep from goats," placing the
"sheep" at his right hand and the "goats" at his left (vss. 32f.). Then
the Son of man is abruptly referred to as the "king" who says to those
on his right "Come, you blessed of my Father, inherit the kingdom
prepared for you from the creation of the world" (vs. 34).

An array of characters from Jesus' parables are thus introduced
in quick succession: the shepherd, the king, and (implicitly) the Son.
But the dominant figure is the king. The shepherd is introduced only
for the sake of the division into sheep and goats. The phrase "blessed
of my Father" simply belongs with Jesus' characteristic "Son of man"
language.[5] The Son of man has just been described as sitting on a
throne (vs. 31), and it is as king that he now addresses those on his
right and on his left. The parabolic elements in this scene might be
summed up as a parable about a king in disguise.

The crucial "inasmuch" statements of verses 40 and 45 presuppose the king's absence, as in other parables about an absent master.
Whether he has gone to a distant country or whether he merely rules
from a distance, his subjects are not conscious of having been in close
touch with him. But the absence is an illusion. Actually, he has been
present all along, disguised as the hungry, the poor, the destitute, the
sick, or the prisoner. This parable goes beyond the other Matthean
parables of absence in two ways. First, the image of the household and
the householder has given way to that of the kingdom and the king.
Second, instead of saying the master of the house may return at any

time, Jesus is now saying that the king may be present in any person in need. To touch—or not to touch—the poor is to touch, or not touch, the king himself. The present moment counts. If it is an interval, it is nonetheless an interval that matters. The hearers' action or inaction has eternal consequences.

How would Jesus have heard such a parable? There are two possibilities, not mutually exclusive. His actions toward the poor, the sick, and the oppressed, as well as the Beatitudes that he pronounced over them, suggest that he heard this parable of the king in disguise much as anyone might hear it. He had, from the beginning, proclaimed the kingdom of God, and it would have been natural for him, as for any Jew of his time, to see God as the king. If so, then his own place was with those being called to account. As in the parable of the good and the evil servant, he was confronted with an alternative. Would he minister to the hungry and thirsty, the stranger, the destitute, the sick, and the prisoner, or would he not? The answer is written on almost every page of the Gospels.

But is that all there is to it? Was Jesus no different from other hearers? Matthew obviously saw it differently because he identified the reigning Son of man with the king. Does this identification have a basis in the self-consciousness of Jesus? There are passages in the Gospels that suggest that he was indeed capable of seeing himself in the role of the king. He had entered Jerusalem as a king. He had said that to receive others in his name was to receive him, whether he was speaking of little children (Mark 9:37 and parallels) or of his own disciples sent on a mission (Matt. 10:40; Luke 10:16; John 13:20). "Anyone who gives a cup of cold water to one of these little ones because he is a disciple," Jesus said, "will surely not lose his reward" (Matt. 10:42; cf. Mark 9:41). Agents or emissaries became important precisely because Jesus assumed he would not be around indefinitely. As his passion began, he had reminded his disciples, "You will always have the poor with you, and you can do good to them whenever you choose, but you will not always have me" (Mark 14:7; cf. Matt. 26:11, John 12:8). Whether his surrogates in any particular saying are the poor, or children, or his disciples, his situation is comparable to that of the king in the story.

These "agent-sayings," like the bridegroom saying in Mark 2:20, or like the Son of man sayings taken as a whole, presuppose a period in which Jesus will be absent. Yet like the parable of the king in disguise, they also affirm that in certain other people his presence on earth will continue. Against this background, it is likely that at some point in his ministry Jesus found his self-identification with the disguised king. As soon as the parable took its place within the framework of an apocalyptic Son of man vision, this identification became fixed. Jesus was the Son of man/shepherd/king. The "least" were, according to Matthew, his disciples, whom he had already designated in 10:40–42 as his agents. The Gentiles being divided into sheep and goats were those to whom the disciples would be sent (cf. Matt. 28:18–20), and they would be judged by how they had treated these emissaries of Jesus.[6] The calling of the disciples was therefore not so much to *help* the poor and afflicted as to *be* poor and afflicted (or, in other terms, to become like children) in the pursuit of their mission. In the interval, the time of Jesus' absence, what had once been Jesus' role now became theirs.

The extension of Jesus' person in the persons of his followers can also be expressed by the idea of a "church." Paul's way of saying it was that the church was Jesus' "body" (1 Cor. 12). At his conversion, Paul learned that to persecute Christians was to persecute Jesus himself (Acts 9:5, 22:8, 26:15). In the Gospels, Jesus is represented only once as predicting in so many words the formation of a church *(ekklēsia).* In response to Peter's confession of him as "the Christ, the Son of the living God," Jesus says "Blessed are you, Simon bar Jonah, because flesh and blood have not revealed it to you, but my Father in heaven. And I say to you that you are Peter, and on this rock *(petros)* I will build my church *(ekklēsia)* and the gates of hell shall not stand against it. I will give you the keys of the kingdom of heaven: whatever you bind on earth will be bound in heaven and whatever you loose on earth will be loosed in heaven" (Matt. 16:17–19).

Both the authenticity and the interpretation of this passage, found only in Matthew, are much disputed. The literature that has grown up around it is enormous.[7] But one or two aspects that have not been widely discussed are worthy of note. The image is that of a house. Jesus is the builder, and he proposes to build on a sure foundation. The most striking parallel is the story of the two builders found in both Matthew and Luke, at the end of the Sermon on the Mount (Matt. 7:24–27) or Plain (Luke 6:47–49). This parable, like so many others, leaves hearers with a choice to make. Will they be wise or foolish builders? Will they build on the rock or on the sand? The wise builder is the one who hears Jesus' words and puts them into practice. The foolish builder is the one who hears but does nothing about it. In the promise to Peter about the church, Jesus himself has taken on the role of the wise builder who builds his house on a rock. In the terms of the parable, for Jesus to build on the rock would presumably be to hear the words of God and carry them out (cf. the Scripture cited in Matt. 4:4: "Man shall not live by bread alone, but by every word coming out of the mouth of God"). In the context of his exchange with Simon Peter, he hears Peter's confession as a word from God: "Blessed are you . . . for flesh and blood have not revealed it to you, but my Father in heaven").

Jesus' future is thus summed up in the metaphor of building. He will build his house on his followers and on the revelation granted to them. The interval between his passion and his victorious coming is not empty or undefined. It is filled with the same rich metaphors that dominated Jesus' own ministry: the clash of two houses or two kingdoms, the binding of the strong man and the release of his captives. The church that Jesus will build is a house against which Satan's house, the "gates of hell," will be unable to stand. The work of binding and loosing—binding the strong man and loosing his captives—, the work that dominated Jesus' ministry and filled his vision, will be the work of his disciples during the period of his absence.

Despite the fact that it stands alone in the Gospel tradition, this explicit promise of an on-going community between Jesus' death and the full realization of the kingdom of God is constructed out of elements firmly rooted in Jesus' ministry from the very beginning. These elements suggest that Jesus' vision of the future included not only his own death, resurrection, and glorious coming, but also—at least to a limited degree—a new "house" to be built, a new community of Jesus' followers to whom he promised victory over death and hell. Their victory, as well as their suffering and poverty, was to be an extension of his own, for they would become the heirs of his religious experience and of his theological vision.

NOTES

CHAPTER 1: THE BAPTIZER

1. Cf. Raymond E. Brown, *The Birth of the Messiah* (Garden City, NY: Doubleday, 1977) and J. Gresham Machen, *The Virgin Birth of Christ* (New York: Harper, 1930).
2. This is called the "criterion of dissimilarity." See, e.g., Norman Perrin, *Rediscovering the Teaching of Jesus* (New York: Harper and Row, 1967), pp. 39–43.
3. Evidence for the existence of such groups by the third century is provided in the Jewish-Christian Pseudo-Clementine Recognitions I, 54 (The Ante-Nicene Fathers, VIII, pp. 91f.).
4. Cf. the response to Peter's Pentecost message in Acts 2:37.
5. Again cf. Luke's language in connection with the preaching of Peter (Acts 2:40).
6. The intention of John 1:31 is realized in 2:11: Jesus is "made known to Israel" when his glory is "made known" to his *disciples.* Nathanael the disciple is called a "true Israelite" (John 1:47) and confesses Jesus as "King of Israel" (John 1:49). See my article "Alleged Anti-Semitism in the Fourth Gospel," *Gordon Review,* 11 (1968), pp. 19–20.
7. Cf. Walter Wink, *John the Baptist in the Gospel Tradition* (London: Cambridge University Press, 1968).
8. Or according to some very ancient manuscripts of John 1:34, "The Chosen One of God."
9. Cf., e.g., C. H. Dodd, *Historical Tradition in the Fourth Gospel* (Cambridge: At the University Press, 1963), pp. 273–74.
10. See above, note 3.
11. Cf. Eusebius, Ecclesiastical History 3. 24. 11–13.
12. According to the Synoptic Gospels he baptized in the Jordan, whereas according to the fourth Gospel he seems to have baptized in springs and pools on either side of the Jordan(John 1:28, 3:23).
13. See, e.g., E. Hennecke, *New Testament Apocrypha* (ed. W.

Schneemelcher; Philadelphia: Westminster Press, 1963), 1:363–417.
14. See, e.g., W. H. Brownlee, "John the Baptist in the New Light of Ancient Scrolls," *The Scrolls and the New Testament* (ed. K. Stendahl; New York: Harper, 1957), pp. 33–53.

CHAPTER 2: THE BAPTISM OF JESUS

1. Jerome, Against Pelagius 3, 2. See M. R. James, *The Apocryphal New Testament* (Oxford: At the Clarendon Press, 1955), p. 6.
2. To understand this, it is helpful to consider the notion of "substitution" set forth in the novels of Charles Williams. See especially Mary McDermott Shideler, *The Theology of Romantic Love: A Study in the Writings of Charles Williams* (Grand Rapids: William B. Eerdmans, 1966), pp. 148–68.
3. Cf. R. E. Brown, *The Gospel According to John (i–xii),* vol. 29 in the Anchor Bible (Garden City, NY: Doubleday, 1966), pp. 88f.
4. Cf. Hennecke-Schneemelcher, *New Testament Apocrypha* 1:157f.
5. See, e.g., R. H. Stein, *The Method and Message of Jesus' Teaching* (Philadelphia: Westminster Press, 1978), pp. 42–44; G. G. O'Collins, *What Are They Saying about Jesus?* (New York: Paulist, 1977), pp. 63–74.

CHAPTER 3: IN THE DESERT—AND BEYOND

1. Herman Ridderbos, *The Coming of the Kingdom* (Philadelphia: Presbyterian and Reformed, 1962),p. 62.
2. See, e.g., Ulrich Mauser, *Christ in the Wilderness* (Naperville, IL: Allenson, 1963).
3. Jesus' saying on discipleship, "What good will it do a person to gain the whole world and lose his own soul?" (Mark 8:36 and parallels) sounds curiously like an echo or reflection of just such a temptation.
4. Cf. 1 Kings 19:4–8.
5. The apocryphal Gospel of the Hebrews, in an apparent later reflection of Matthew's account, speaks of Jesus being taken by the Holy Spirit "to the great mountain of Tabor"—in Galilee! Hennecke-Schneemelcher, *New Testament Apocrypha* 1:144.
6. See above, p. 6, n. 2.
7. "Pronouncement story" is the term used by Vincent Taylor in *The Formation of the Gospel Tradition* (London: Macmillan, 1933; 2d ed., 1935), pp. 63–87. It is equivalent to what the German form critics called "paradigm" (Martin Dibelius) or "apophthegm" (Rudolf Bultmann): a

story told as a rhetorical setting for an especially meaningful or well-remembered saying of Jesus.

8. On Jesus' religious experience, see James Dunn, *Jesus and the Spirit* (Philadelphia: Westminster, 1975), pp. 11–92.

CHAPTER 4: THE ANNOUNCEMENT OF A KINGDOM

1. This is an element of truth in Adolf Harnack's classic statement of nineteenth century liberalism, *What Is Christianity?* (New York: G. P. Putnam's Sons, 1901). See, e.g., pp. 19–70.
2. See, e.g., W. G. Kummel, *Promise and Fulfillment* (Naperville, IL: Allenson, 1957), pp. 19–25.
3. See, e.g., G. E. Ladd, *The Presence of the Future* (Grand Rapids: Eerdmans, 1974), pp. 122–48.
4. See above, pp. 45–46.
5. The classic example is C. H. Dodd's *The Parables of the Kingdom* (rev. ed.; New York: Scribner's, 1961), which simultaneously became a milestone in modern research on Jesus and the kingdom of God, and on Jesus' parables. The same close link can be seen in a different way in the more recent work by Norman Perrin, *Jesus and the Language of the Kingdom* (Philadelphia: Fortress, 1976).

CHAPTER 5: IMAGES OF THE KINGDOM

1. Cf. *The Parables of Jesus,* rev. ed. (New York: Scribner's, 1963), p. 101.
2. See, e.g., Dodd, *Parables of the Kingdom,* p. 159; Jeremias, *Parables of Jesus,* p. 230.
3. Cf. the section-headings in part III of Jeremias' *The Parables of Jesus,* "The Message of the Parables of Jesus" (table of contents, pp. 5–6).
4. Dodd, *Parables of the Kingdom,* pp. 1–2.
5. Ibid., p. 1.
6. Cf. Flannery O'Connor's remark about literary symbolism, quoted by L. D. Rubin, Jr., in *The Flannery O'Connor Bulletin* 6 (1977), p. 71: "So many students approach a story as if it were a problem in algebra; find X and when they find X they can dismiss the rest of it."
7. See Perrin, *Jesus and the Language of the Kingdom,* pp. 127–81.
8. E.g., Dodd, *Parables of the Kingdom,* p. 4; Jeremias, *The Parables of Jesus,* pp. 12–18.
9. See especially A. Farrer, *The Glass of Vision* (Westminster: Darre Press, 1948), Lecture III, pp. 35–56.
10. For a review of the use of the term "language event" see Robert Funk,

Language, Hermeneutic, and Word of God (New York: Harper and Row, 1966), pp. 20–71.

11. Perrin, *Jesus and the Language of the Kingdom,* e.g., pp. 29–34. Perrin borrows this terminology from Philip Wheelwright, *Metaphor and Reality* (1962). A steno-symbol has "a one-to-one relationship to what it represents," while a tensive symbol has "a set of meanings that can neither be exhausted nor adequately expressed by any one referent . . ." (Perrin, p. 30).

12. *Language, Hermeneutic, and Word of God,* p. 179.

13. Funk, *Language, Hermeneutic, and Word of God,* p. 137; J. D. Crossan, *In Parables: The Challenge of the Historical Jesus* (New York: Harper and Row, 1973), p. 12. The source is C. S. Lewis, "Bluspels and Flalansferes," *The Importance of Language,* ed. M. Black (Englewood Cliffs, NJ: Prentice-Hall, 1962), pp. 36–50.

14. *In Parables,* p. 13.

15. *In Parables,* p. 32.

16. Amos N. Wilder, *Early Christian Rhetoric:The Language of the Gospel* (New York: Harper and Row, 1964), p.93.

17. See, e.g., Amos 7:1–9, 8:1–3, Ezek. 15:1–8, 17:1–10, Enoch 37—71, and the third major section of the Shepherd of Hermas (the Similitudes, or "Parables which he spoke with me").

18. See above, p. 40, n. 5.

19. Cf. Wilder, *The Language of the Gospel,* p. 68.

20. On the first two of these, see C. H. Dodd, *Historical Tradition in the Fourth Gospel* (Cambridge: University, 1963), pp. 379–82, 386; B. Lindars, *The Gospel of John. New Century Bible* (Greenwood, SC: Attic, 1972), pp. 221, 325; J. A. T. Robinson, *Can We Trust the New Testament?* (Grand Rapids: Eerdmans, 1977), pp. 106–07.

21. Flannery O'Connor, *Mystery and Manners* (New York: Farrar, Straus and Giroux, 1970), p. 34.

22. Cf. A. Farrer, *A Rebirth of Images* (Boston: Beacon, 1963), especially pp. 13–22; also *The Glass of Vision* (n. 9, above).

CHAPTER 6: THE PARABLE COLLECTIONS: A CLOSER LOOK

1. Note the phrase "He who has ears to hear, let him hear" (Mark 4:9, 23) and "Be careful how you hear" (Mark 4:24).

2. Daniel 4:9, 19. See J. D. Crossan, *The Dark Interval. Towards a Theology of Story* (Niles, IL: Argus, 1975), pp. 93–96.

3. The parallel in Luke 17:34f. is slightly different. See below, p. 256, n. 3

4. See *In Parables,* pp. 63–66; and *The Dark Interval,* pp. 105–08.

5. That is, the Samaritan is an ethical model to be followed ("go and do likewise"), while the woman baking bread is not, but simply a figure in a story.

6. Crossan also recognizes the similarity between the hidden treasure and the pearl on the one hand and the lost sheep and lost coin on the other, and assimilates the latter to the former in exactly the manner of Thomas: "In these parables the searcher is usually seen as the human person and the object found is God or the kingdom of God (or of heaven). I would suggest that this is also what Jesus, as distinct from Luke, intended the stories of the Lost Sheep and the Lost Coin to indicate as well" (*The Dark Interval,* p. 99).

7. See below, pp. 211–13, 248.

CHAPTER 7: THE PARABLES AND THE PASSION

1. J. R. R. Tolkien, "On Fairy Stories," *The Tolkien Reader* (New York: Ballantine Books, 1966), pp. 71–73.

2. *The Parables of Jesus,* pp. 17–18.

CHAPTER 8: JESUS AND THE UNCLEAN SPIRITS

1. See the Testament of Solomon as translated in the *Jewish Quarterly Review* 11 (1898), pp. 1–45.

2. Geza Vermes, *Jesus the Jew. A Historian's Reading of the Gospels* (New York: Macmillan, 1973), p. 24.

3. Cf. R. T. France, "Exegesis in Practice: Two Samples," *New Testament Interpretation. Essays on Principles and Practice* (ed. I. H. Marshall; Grand Rapids: Eerdmans, 1977), pp. 256–57.

4. See J. Barr, *Fundamentalism* (London: SCM, 1977), pp. 239–51.

5. See, for example, the symposium, J. W. Montgomery, ed, *Demon Possession* (Minneapolis: Bethany Fellowship, 1976).

CHAPTER 9: THE MESSIANIC HEALINGS

1. Mark 9:14–29; Matthew 9:32–34, 12:22–34; Luke 11:14.

CHAPTER 10: THE UNCLEAN

1. The exceptions are the healings of Peter's mother-in-law (Mark 1:30–31; Matt. 8:14–15) and the royal official's son (John 4:46–54).

2. See Matthew 8:17 and 12:17–21, for example.
3. See Malachi 4:5–6 and John 1:21.
4. In Mark 1:41, according to some manuscripts, Jesus "was angry" rather than compassionate or sympathetic.
5. See above, p. 164.
6. Contrast the description of Jesus' open tomb and the graveclothes in John 20:1, 5–7 with John 11:38, 44.

CHAPTER 11: FORGIVENESS: A WORLD UPENDED

1. Cf. Mark 12:1–12, Luke 20:9–19, Thomas 65.
2. Thomas 64—65 has the two stories in reverse order and lacks the parallel structure of Matthew's account.
3. Cf. Matthew 7:16–20; 12:33–37; Luke 6:43–45.
4. See above, pp. 143–45.
5. Cf. the experience of Hosea the prophet in Hosea 1—3.
6. Cf. Crossan, *The Dark Interval,* pp. 97–98.
7. The Old Testament tradition of wisdom as a woman might conceivably have influenced him in that direction (Luke 7:35/Matt. 11:19, Luke 11:49).
8. Note the same opening in another parable containing much the same cast of characters (Matt. 21:28).
9. Robert Funk, *Language, Hermeneutic, and Word of God,* p. 214.
10. Ibid., p. 210.
11. The contrast between large and small debts is reminiscent of the parable of the two debtors attached to the incident of Jesus and the sinful woman (Luke 7:40–43). But the latter is a parable of normalcy, and Matthew 18:21–35 is not. The amount of money involved is many times greater, and the one forgiven much does *not* (as we might expect) "love much"!

CHAPTER 12: DISCIPLESHIP AS THE LOVE OF ENEMIES

1. A similar transformation can be seen in the use of the phrase "children of the kingdom." In Matthew 8:12 the "children of the kingdom" are those who had once been God's people, but are consigned to the outer darkness. Yet in Matthew 13:38 "children of the kingdom" refers to the good seed in the parable of the weeds. This phrase too has been transferred to sinners and Gentiles.
2. Annie Dillard writes: "People are reasoned, while God is mad. They love only beauty; who knows what God loves?" (*Holy the Firm* [New York: Bantam Books, 1979], p. 79.)

CHAPTER 13: DISCIPLESHIP AS RENUNCIATION

1. See W. L. Lane, *The Gospel According to Mark* (Grand Rapids: William B. Eerdmans, 1974), p. 68 and the literature cited there.
2. See, for example, the Acts of Paul and Thecla in Hennecke-Schneemelcher, *New Testament Apocrypha* (Philadelphia: Westminster, 1964), 2:353–64.
3. Grammatically the "two on one bed" in Luke's Greek text are male, and the "two grinding together" are female! But this appears to be Luke's way of suggesting that each pair is actually male *and* female (i.e. a married couple). To try to convey this idea any other way would have left Luke with the choice of saying either that the woman was taken and the man left, or the other way around, and this of course was not Luke's point.
4. Cf. the use of "good" in Matthew 20:15; also the biblical refrain, "O give thanks to the Lord, for he is good, for his mercy endures forever."

CHAPTER 14: PRAYER AND TRUST

1. See J. Finegan, *The Archeology of the New Testament. The Life of Jesus and the Beginning of the Early Church* (Princeton, NJ: Princeton University Press, 1969), p. 97.
2. *The Prayers of Jesus* (Philadelphia: Fortress Press, 1978), pp. 54–65.
3. For a similar practice on Mark's part, cf. Mark 5:41, 8:34, 15:34.
4. *The Prayers of Jesus,* p. 58.
5. Note, e.g., John 20:17: "I am ascending to my Father and your Father, to my God and your God." The only possible exception is Matthew 17:26–27, in which Jesus and Peter together are used as examples of the "sons" who in principle are exempt from the temple tax.
6. See R. E. Brown, "The Pater Noster as an Eschatological Prayer," *New Testament Essays* (Milwaukee: Bruce, 1965), pp. 217–53.
7. See above, p. 26, n. 2.
8. See A. F. Johnson, "Assurance for Man: The Fallacy of Translating *Anaideia* by 'Persistence' in Luke 11:5–8," *Journal of the Evangelical Theological Society* 22 (1979), pp. 122–31.
9. Or, according to a better-known reading, "the Holy Spirit."
10. Jesus can use the metaphor of knocking in exactly the opposite way, as in Luke 13:25–27.
11. "Believing in his name," on the other hand, is simply a variant expression for "believing in him" whether present or absent, though the shorter expression is by far the commoner one.
12. Jerome (*In Matt.* 6:11) found in the Gospel of the Hebrews the reading

mahar ("future") in the fourth petition of the Lord's Prayer, and on this have been based modern theories of an eschatological prayer for eschatological "bread" (see above, p. 273, n.6).

13. The longer reading "few things, or one" is probably correct in this case.

14. The heretic Marcion (who relied on Luke alone for his Gospel) made this explicit by inserting instead of "Hallowed be thy name" the petition, "Let Thy Holy Spirit come upon us and cleanse us." See Jeremias, *The Prayers of Jesus,* p. 83.

CHAPTER 15: JESUS AND HIS FUTURE

1. See E. M. Sidebottom, *The Christ of the Fourth Gospel* (London: SPCK, 1961), pp. 74–78.

2. Rudolf Bultmann, *Theology of the New Testament* (2 vols.; New York: Scribner's, 1951), 2:9.

3. See above, p. 123.

4. C. H. Dodd, *Parables of the Kingdom,* p. 137; Joachim Jeremias, *Parables of Jesus,* pp. 51–53.

5. Cf. Mark 8:38 and Matthew 16:27, where the Son of man comes "in the glory of his Father."

6. J. R. Michaels, "Apostolic Hardships and Righteous Gentiles: A Study of Matthew 25:31–46," *Journal of Biblical Literature* 84 (1965), pp. 27–37.

7. See R. E. Brown, K. P. Donfried and J. Reumann, eds., *Peter in the New Testament* (Minneapolis: Augsburg, 1973), pp. 83–101.

SCRIPTURE INDEX